FAMIL

Social ch   nd
kin relat

Nickie Charle
Chris Harris

This edition published in Great Britain in 2008 by

The Policy Press
University of Bristol
Fourth Floor
Beacon House
Queen's Road
Bristol BS8 1QU
UK

Tel +44 (0)117 331 4054
Fax +44 (0)117 331 4093
e-mail tpp-info@bristol.ac.uk
www.policypress.org.uk

British Library Cataloguing in Publication Data
A catalogue record for this book is available from the British Library.

Library of Congress Cataloging-in-Publication Data
A catalog record for this book has been requested.

ISBN 978 1 86134 788 6 paperback
ISBN 978 1 86134 789 3 hardcover

Cover design by Robin Hawes.
Front cover: illustration by Karel Lek.
Printed and bound in Great Britain by MPG Books, Bodmin,

This book is dedicated to the memory of

*my parents Freddie Charles (1912–2002) and Mary Charles
(1924–2005), and my dear friend Linda Bretherton (1952–2006) – NC*

*my father Charles M. Aull (1918–2001), my father-in-law
Idris Treharne Davies (1904–2001) and my brother-in-law
W. Huw Davies (1938–2005) – CD*

Angela Harris (1932–1998) – CCH

Contents

List of tables

Preface and acknowledgements

The research reported in this book was inspired by Rosser and Harris's study of the family in Swansea which was conducted in 1960 and published in 1965 as *The family and social change*. It takes the form of a restudy. Rosser and Harris's research was also a restudy insofar as it replicated the methods of Michael Young and Peter Willmott's famous research on Bethnal Green, in the East End of London. Young and Willmott's research, which was carried out in the 1950s, was published in 1957 as *The family in East London* and, as Rosser and Harris's 1965 foreword noted, 'challenged accepted views about the family in urban society'.

Young and Willmott claimed that in Bethnal Green the family had not shrunk to its nuclear core and had not become isolated from wider kin as a result of urbanisation and industrialisation. On the contrary, there were high rates of interaction and exchanges of domestic services between separate households, central to which were the relationships between mothers and their married daughters, these extended families being more widely connected though a dense network of kinship ties. It was obviously important to explore whether these findings were peculiar to Bethnal Green. The 1960 study, therefore, sought to discover whether or not Young and Willmott's findings about the resilience of the extended family would be replicated in Swansea. Swansea was much larger than Bethnal Green in both area and population, with a much lower population density and a different occupational structure and cultural composition. In spite of these differences, the findings of the Swansea study were very similar to those for Bethnal Green and led its authors to ask whether 'we have a regularity of behaviour which is a common feature of urban kinship in Britain'.

British sociologists, however, have never answered that question with an unambiguous affirmative. And far from regarding findings from Swansea as confirming those of the East End of London, their Welshness seems to have had the effect of making them seem, by definition, exceptional and, therefore, unsuitable for this task. We trust that the research reported in this book will fare better. Today Wales is no longer, for most of those resident to the east of Offa's Dyke, 'a faraway country of which we know little'. However, the rapid rate of social and cultural change which is believed to move across Britain from east to west opens the door to the possibility that findings from Wales are not taken seriously and are attributed to 'cultural lag', a terrible epithet to apply to any social phenomenon in a society and discipline which is experiencing extremely rapid social change.

Although in this book we report many differences between the social worlds of Swansea 1960 and Swansea 2002, the most striking among them concern the late ages at which people form procreative households and the historically small proportions living in households comprising parents and immature children. Fewer people are 'doing' family than was the case in 1960, when the average age at first marriage was below 20 and completed 'family size' was around three. However, the character of family life and of the relationships formed by those who do 'do' family in Swansea in 2002 is remarkably similar to that reported by Rosser and Harris for Swansea in 1960 and by Young and Willmott for Bethnal Green in 1957.

Neither the Bethnal Green study nor the first Swansea study confined themselves to the collection and analysis of data on family and kinship, and both were, in their different ways, 'community studies'. Young and Willmott chose a canvas broader than the family and household, but the following two studies had no choice. Any valid comparison concerning family behaviour had to take into account major differences in the structure and culture of the two settlements studied. Rosser and Harris set their 1960 findings, as the title of their book makes plain, firmly in a historical context, so that they had two comparators: Bethnal Green in the 1950s and Swansea at the *beginning* of the 20th century, as evoked in *The family and social change*. The present study also has two comparators, both historical: Swansea at the beginning and in the middle of the 20th century.

We have had two advantages over Rosser and Harris, whose survey analysis was restricted to 65 variables (the number of columns on a Powers Samas punch card), and who had no funding for any substantial amount of semi-structured interviewing to generate qualitative data. For the present study the availability of a computer package (SPSS) for the analysis of statistical data enabled a far more thorough and sophisticated analysis of household composition, residence and contact data than was possible in 1960. Furthermore, ethnographic interviewing was used to explore family life in four localities chosen to represent the socioeconomic and cultural differences characterising contemporary Swansea. It is perhaps appropriate to say here that, when using quotes from our interviewees, all names have been changed to preserve confidentiality although interviewees' sex, age and the area in which they live are indicated in brackets after each quote. In some cases more than one person participated in an interview but the identification relates to the interviewee/s only. Interviewers' comments are italicised in square brackets. Although most of our interviewees lived in one of the four ethnographic areas there are a few who lived nearby but worked in one of the areas. In these cases we have included them in the area where they were interviewed.

Rosser and Harris commented that studying the society in which you live is difficult, and we were aware of this as we conducted the research and wrote the book, particularly as we have all, for considerable periods of time, lived in Swansea and two of us still do. We hope, however, that this insider knowledge has contributed to our 'feel' for the city and the 'urban villages' which constitute it rather than leading us to make unwarranted assumptions about the different parts of Swansea and the people who have their homes there.

This book and the research on which it is based are, therefore, the culmination of many years' work which, although separated by four decades, began at the end of the 1950s. At that time sociology, as an academic discipline, was becoming an established part of many universities and University College of Swansea, a constituent part of the University of Wales, was no exception. The Department of Sociology and Anthropology was established in Swansea at exactly the same time as the research into the family and social change was being carried out by two young researchers, Colin Rosser and Chris Harris, and the first sociology and anthropology students were admitted in 1964. Rosser and Harris were thus founder members of the Department and their research established the Department's reputation in the field of family and community studies. A collective dream of Sociology and Anthropology at Swansea was to revisit this research, and in the late 1990s serious attention began to be paid to exactly how this could be done. It was fortuitous that at this time there was renewed interest both in place-based studies and in the contribution to sociological knowledge that could be made by restudies. Eventually a grant application was completed and submitted to the Economic and Social Research Council (ESRC). The application was successful and in 2000 a researcher was appointed. We had applied for funds for two researchers but, as is often the case, had only been funded for one. Chris Harris, although by then 65 and retired, was persuaded back into harness to act, part time and unpaid, as the second researcher. Without Chris's almost full-time participation in the later stages of the research it would almost certainly have been undoable. It was deeply ironic that, just as the project ended in January 2004, plans were announced that would result in the closure of the Department and the gradual disappearance of sociology and anthropology research and teaching at what is now Swansea University. There is therefore a sense in which the fate both of sociology and anthropology at Swansea and of these two studies separated by almost half a century are inextricably interwoven, with the first study marking the birth of the Department of Sociology and Anthropology at Swansea and the second study marking its demise.

In the course of writing a book and the period of research that precedes it many debts of gratitude are incurred. Collectively we wish to thank all those who contributed so generously of their time, either as survey respondents or as interviewees and, sometimes, as both. We also wish to thank all those individuals and organisations who helped us contact interviewees and who let us 'hang about' in their places of work and participate in events they were organising. Bettina Becker worked as a researcher on the project for three years and conducted the ethnographic studies in the areas which we are calling Fairview and Pen-cwm. Her contribution to the project has been invaluable and her writing up of these two studies provides the basis for some parts of the book. She also carried out some of the interviews in Treforgan. We also thank Stephanie Adams for her interviewing and transcribing skills; she interviewed in Treforgan and transcribed all the tapes meticulously and at fantastic speed. Both Bettina's and Steph's insights into the ethnographic data have assisted us in the analysis we present here. Wendy Ball undertook a preliminary analysis of the network diagrams and conducted a literature search, for which we are very grateful. We also owe a debt of thanks to Beaufort Research for carrying out the survey, to the City and County of Swansea for providing us with Census data corresponding both to our four ethnographic areas and to the boundaries of the then Swansea County Borough, and to the ESRC for funding the research (grant number R000238454). Thanks also to Graham Crow and Ros Edwards for reading and commenting on the book when it was in draft form; we found their observations extremely helpful. Nickie and Charlotte want to thank Chris for his analysis of the survey and Census data and for all the reports he produced during the project; they form the basis of the analysis of the changing occupational structure of Swansea which can be found in Chapter 2 and of the kinship analysis that appears in Chapter 3. Although he did not want to be involved in the actual writing of the book, it would never have seen the light of day without his input and he has read and commented on its various incarnations. Nickie and Charlotte have taken the main responsibility for writing the book and for the analysis of the ethnographic data. Nickie carried out the ethnographic interviewing in Parkfields and Charlotte was responsible for all the number crunching.

We also want to thank our colleagues in the Department of Sociology and Anthropology at Swansea for their support for the project; we hope they will be pleased with the outcome. And although all three of us were members of the Swansea department while the research was being carried out, Nickie moved to the Centre for the Study of Women and Gender in the Sociology Department at the University of Warwick at the beginning of 2005.

Nickie would like to thank her PhD students and co-supervisors at Warwick for bearing with her unavailability during the summer of 2007 and the first few weeks of 2008. Without their forbearance, writing the book would have been much more difficult. She also wants to mention two key members of her personal network, Inka and Topaz, who would not let her forget that fresh air and exercise, twice a day, come rain or shine, were an essential part of writing.

Finally, we wish to thank the late Jo Campling for her belief in this book and for her support in finding a publisher who was interested in publishing it; sadly, she died before the book was completed. We miss her. And thank you to Emily Watt and her team at The Policy Press for being so understanding about the endlessly extending deadlines; we finally made it.

Some parts of some of our chapters draw on papers that we have published elsewhere. Part of Chapter 2 is taken from C. Harris, N. Charles and C. Davies (2006) 'Social change and the family', *Sociological Research Online,* www.socresonline.org.uk/11/2/harris.html; Chapter 3 uses similar material to that which appears in N. Charles, C. Davies and C. Harris (2008) 'The family and social change revisited', in R. Edwards (ed.) *Researching families and communities,* Routledge: London and New York, pp 114–32; Chapter 4 draws on C.A. Davies, N. Charles and C.C. Harris (2006) 'Welsh identity and language in Swansea, 1960–2002', in *Contemporary Wales,* vol 18, pp 28–53; and part of Chapter 8 is based on N. Charles and C. Davies (2005) 'Studying the particular, illuminating the general: community studies and community in Wales', in *The Sociological Review,* vol 53, no 4, pp 672–90.

ONE

Understanding families and social change

This is a book about families and how they have changed since 1960. It is based on the findings of two studies of the family in Swansea (in western industrial South Wales), one carried out in 1960 (Rosser and Harris, 1965), the other in the first few years of the 21st century. It therefore provides a unique perspective on how families in a particular place have been affected by the massive social changes of recent decades. In the 1960 study, Rosser and Harris charted how changes during the period 1900 to 1960 had affected family life, particularly how kin living in separate households related to each other; their focus was on extended families. They characterised the social change occurring between 1900 and 1960 as a move from a cohesive to a mobile society (Rosser and Harris, 1965, 15; Crow, 2002a) and argued that increased occupational and geographical differentiation within kinship networks resulted in a reduction in the 'kin connectedness' of society. Their findings were underpinned by a Durkheimian theoretical framework which understood social change as involving a shift from solidarity based on sameness, including shared occupational status, shared geographical locality and shared norms and values, towards increasing occupational and geographical differentiation, with the attendant risk of a breakdown in solidarity and cohesiveness. In 1960 this breakdown had not occurred, but increasing differentiation had led to a 'modified extended family' which, although under strain, was still able to function as a source of support and identity for its members.

In the 'noughties', in contrast, the relationship between families and social change is understood in different terms, most of which take the 1960s as marking a major social transition. This transition is variously conceptualised as the shift from modernity to post-modernity, reflexive modernity, late modernity or risk society, from industrial to post-industrial society, and from patriarchal to a less patriarchal society. Associated with fundamental structural change are cultural changes involving, *inter alia*, a move from material to post-material values. Concepts such as globalisation, individualisation, detraditionalisation and reflexivity have all been used to try and capture these social changes and to describe the type of society in which we are now living. They have also been influential in research on families. Thus, what is happening to families is often understood in terms of increasing individualisation and detraditionalisation. These concepts are used to explain changes in the social networks within which families exist (and which are partly constituted by kin) and in the moral values underpinning family life. Conceptualisations of social change therefore have implications for how we understand family lives.

It is because of this that in this first chapter we investigate different ways of theorising social change, exploring particularly how changing gender relations and patterns of family formation are seen as a fundamental aspect of social change. In so doing we develop a critique of these conceptualisations which is both theoretical and based on empirical research on families and kinship. In Chapter 2 we explore the structural and cultural changes that have taken place since 1960 and which these theories attempt to explain. These two chapters provide a theoretical and empirical context for our subsequent discussion of continuity and change in family practices. The rest of the book draws on two sets of research findings: those of the original family study by Rosser and Harris and those of the restudy which was carried out between 2001 and 2004. Our findings provide evidence to support a counter-argument to those who posit (often speculatively) that the social change of the last few decades has wrought dramatic transformations in family lives. Undoubtedly significant social change has occurred, which has implications for how people engage in partnering and parenting and for the types of living arrangements in which these family practices take place. But the continuity in family practices which we document in the pages that follow suggests that an alternative conceptual framework is needed to understand the ways in which people 'do' family. This we attempt to develop as the book unfolds.

Understanding social change

Much research on families has drawn on the vision of social change encapsulated in what has come to be known as the individualisation thesis. This thesis has four important components: that people are freed from the constraints of class and gender (that is, agency is freed from structure); that individualisation is institutionalised as 'the most advanced form of societalisation' (Beck, 1992, 131); that social solidarities of family and community are undermined; and that disembedding processes render place insignificant for social interaction (Giddens, 1990, 1991, 1994; Beck, 1992). The decline of family and community is also conceptualised in terms of a loss of social capital where social capital consists of networks, shared norms, values and expectations, and sanctions (Halpern, 2005, 10). And finally, the individualisation thesis argues that externally binding moral codes no longer govern behaviour, thus raising the spectre of a society which is anomic and where the pursuit of individual self-interest is paramount.

These different conceptualisations of social change and how it is affecting social processes within families have been critiqued both theoretically and empirically (see for example Jamieson, 1998; Smart, 2007). In what follows we look first at theoretical critiques and then at those which mobilise empirical data to challenge the explanatory potential of these theories.

Theoretical critiques: the individualisation thesis

Critiques of the individualisation thesis take issue with the way it is constructed on the basis of dualistic thinking, its assumption that the reflexive self is the distinctive feature of contemporary society, and the narrative of change that underlies it. They also point to a lack of clarity in the terminology used by Beck and Giddens, the main protagonists of this thesis, and the gendered subtext of their arguments. Instead of placing all the explanatory weight on an old narrative of the replacement of tradition by modernity, they argue for an alternative view that does not rely on binaries and does not conceptualise temporality as an onward march of unidirectional change.

Narratives of change

Both Beck and Giddens mobilise a narrative of change which relies on a binary conceptual distinction between tradition and modernity. According to the individualisation thesis, processes of individualisation and detraditionalisation are associated with the transition from modernity to reflexive or second modernity (Beck, 1992) or late modernity (Giddens, 1991). This new phase of modernity, rather than undermining the traditions of a pre-modern society, undermines the traditions of modernity itself. This has particular implications for the family because women, as a result of individualisation, are free to engage in wage labour and are no longer dependent on a man for financial support. This leads to the decline of the 'traditional', family which loses 'the monopoly it had for so long' (Beck-Gernsheim, 1998, 67). Beck puts forward a surprisingly Parsonian account of the impact of increasing individualisation, arguing that the requirement of the *labour market* for individual mobility undermines the family. The logic

—

of this 'market model of modernity implies a society *without* families and children. Everyone must be free for the demands of the market in order to guarantee his/her economic existence…. the ultimate market society is a *childless* society' (Beck, 1992, 116). Women's individualisation therefore is seen as allowing reflexive modernisation to complete the process begun by classic modernisation, which is held to imply the eventual disappearance of the family.

This counterposing of tradition and modernity has a long history and was how the classical social theorists attempted to delineate the nature of modern society in the 19th century. The story that unfolds is one of the disappearance of tradition, including the traditional family and traditional communities, particularly in the period of reflexive or late modernity. However, tradition does not necessarily disappear and, if we accept Marilyn Strathern's argument that ideas about tradition and individuality inform how we understand kinship, then tradition is created anew in every generation simply by virtue of children's differentiation from the parental generation (Strathern, 1992). This narrative also defines individualisation processes as peculiar to modern, as opposed to traditional, societies. However, individualism, as Strathern shows, has a long history in English kinship and social understandings of human development (Strathern, 1992). Furthermore it is not useful to try to understand what is distinctive about the self in late modernity by adding to the 19th-century narrative of increasing individualism the notion of its culmination in the reflexive subject (Rose, 1996).

The declining importance of local, 'traditional' communities is also part of this narrative. Beck and Giddens argue that 'traditional', face-to-face communities are being undermined by processes of individualisation and detraditionalisation and that 'traditional' sources of support are no longer available. Both conceptualise this as a process of disembedding. For Beck, *individuals* are disembedded from 'traditional commitments and support relationships', which involves the 'loss of traditional security' such as 'guiding norms' (Beck, 1992, 128). This is similar to Giddens's argument that ontological insecurity characterises late modernity. For Giddens, however, it is *social relations* rather than individuals which are disembedded. Disembedding involves 'the "lifting out" of social relations from local contexts of interaction and their restructuring across indefinite spans of time and place' (Giddens, 1990, 21). The mechanisms that bring about this disembedding are abstract systems which 'separate interaction from the particularities of locales' (Giddens, 1991, 20). In this way they transcend the dependence of inter-human communication on space–time proximity, that is, being together in the same place at the same time. This results in the destruction of community, a destruction which 'has reached its apogee' in the economically developed world.

There are two problems with these formulations, one relating to the idea of detraditionalisation and the other to the notion of disembedding. There is considerable scepticism about the usefulness of detraditionalisation as a descriptor of contemporary social change. Barbara Adam suggests that the contemporary era could equally be conceptualised as one of retraditionalisation 'since the age of uncertainty, contingency and flux seems to bring with it a yearning for the stability of tradition' (Adam, 1996, 139–40). For her, the 'dualism of the detraditionalisation thesis is untenable' (Adam, 1996, 140) and is unable to grasp the ways in which tradition and reflexivity coexist in varying ways in contemporary society. Furthermore, binaries cannot grasp networks and are unable to deal with the loss of the 'other' (cf Strathern, 1992). For Adam, the detraditionalisation thesis (and equally the individualisation thesis) is 'an integral part of the disembedded, disembodied, detemporalised and objective tradition of the Enlightenment' (Adam, 1996, 146).

Similarly, the notion of disembedding is problematic. Giddens's characterisation of late modernity involves the emergence of a society in which, as a result of disembedding, the character of everyday life in 'places' is determined elsewhere. Of itself this characterisation provides no avenue leading to an understanding of what remains of the social life of a locality once disembedding has occurred. It is of no help to be told by Giddens that, although the process of disembedding strips out the backbone of social relations in 'the community', 'local life' and 'practices' do not disappear (Giddens, 1994, 101). In our view, a society in which all social relations and institutions are 'lifted out' of local contexts is inconceivable. Rather, different social institutions will vary according to the degree to which they require to be 'embedded' in matrices of social interaction to function effectively.

The self and reflexivity

An important dimension of life in this new phase of modernity is that individuals have constantly to make choices as to how they are to lead their lives. This requirement, which is inescapable, leads to what has been variously termed a 'do-it-yourself' or 'risk' biography (Beck, 1992; Beck-Gernsheim, 1998), a 'reflexive biography' (Giddens, 1994) or 'reflexive narrative of self' (Giddens, 1992). It has been argued, however, that the emphasis on reflexivity depends on a caricature of subjectivity in 'traditional' societies and that 'reflexivity is ontological to all of humanity, to what it means to be human: irrespective of the strictness of the rules that regulate social life' (Adam, 1996, 139). Instead of relying on the familiar narrative of increasing individualism, attention should be directed to how technologies of the self construct personhood in different cultures and historical periods. Nikolas Rose suggests that rather than one form of subjectivity there are many and that they are influenced by, rather than being disembedded from, place. Furthermore, the self is constructed by regulatory processes which result in the 'folding of authority into the self' (Rose, 1996, 321). In other words, how we understand ourselves, as autonomous, free-acting individuals living in a society which is characterised by risk and uncertainty, is a product of changing modes of governmentality, 'new rationalities of government and new technologies of the conduct of conduct' (Rose, 1996, 320). He argues that 'today as in the past', 'human beings ... inhabit a space of differentiation and choice, of moral dilemmas and ethical contestation' (Rose, 1996, 323). This is not something that is peculiar to late or reflexive modernity.

A major critique of both Beck's and Giddens's notion of reflexivity centres on the disembedded and 'disembodied, rational, masculine subject' at the heart of their conceptual schemas (Adkins, 2004, 148). Lois McNay argues that this is the legacy of Foucault's theorisation of the subject, which does not incorporate the materiality of the body. She points out that the 'recalcitrance of embodied existence' poses problems for a constant refashioning of the self, arguing that Beck and Giddens understand identity in terms of 'symbolic identification' rather than something that involves 'embodied practice'. This leads to a 'tendency to voluntarism' and an 'over-emphasis on the emancipatory expressive possibilities thrown up in late capitalism' (McNay, 1999, 98).

As a corrective to this voluntarism she uses Bourdieu's notion of habitus to explore how important aspects of identities are constructed at a level below consciousness. Habitus is 'a system of durable, transposable dispositions' (McNay, 1999, 99). It involves a practical sense, a feel for the game of a particular field which is pre-reflexive, it is 'a form of knowledge that is learnt by the body but cannot be explicitly articulated' (McNay, 1999, 101). This is important for notions of the reflexive self, as there is 'a layer of embodied experience that is not immediately amenable to self-fashioning. On a pre-reflexive level, the actor is predisposed or oriented to behave in a certain way because of the "active presence" of the whole past embedded in the durable structures of the habitus' (McNay, 1999, 102). This predisposition is not deterministic and there is always the possibility of change, but it does mean that the idea that everything can now be negotiated is questionable and that social practice is often out of reach of conscious control and reflection (Adkins, 2002). Thus, for women, individualisation is a contradictory process which conflicts with embodied aspects of female identity such as 'being there' for others and their responsibility for care work and emotion work within families and intimate relationships. This is not the case for men, something which is recognised by Beck although it is not incorporated into individualisation theory. There are therefore limits on the transformations of identity which derive from 'the deeply entrenched nature of gender identity and also … the way in which gender as a primary symbolic distinction is used to play out other social tensions' (McNay, 1999, 103). McNay's critique of the conception of identity underpinning ideas of reflexivity therefore emphasises the embeddedness of agents, in contrast to the disembedded subjects which march through the pages of Giddens and Beck. And she recognises the fact that gender identity is embodied rather than 'a form of symbolic identification'. Its embodiment makes it less amenable to change than Beck or Giddens assume.

Related to this disembodied, disembedded, reflexive self which is constantly refashioning its own identity is the assumption that all relationships are cancellable. This may be credible for relations between sexual partners or friends, but it cannot be the case for relations between parents – particularly mothers – and children, as Beck and Beck-Gernsheim recognise (Jamieson, 1998). Indeed, Beck argues that individualisation comes up against limits in the form of the wish for children. They are 'wished-for obstacles in the occupational competition, as well as temptations to a conscious decision against economic autonomy and a career', but only for women and only insofar as women remain the main carers. For men there is no contradiction between individualisation and the 'traditional' male role of provider (Beck, 1992, 111). And although relationships in the negotiated family are 'always cancellable' (Beck, 1992, 89) there is an exception to this in relationships between parents and children. 'The child is the source of the last *remaining, irrevocable, unexchangeable primary relationship*. Partners come and go' (Beck, 1992, 118).

And finally, underpinning this conceptualisation of intimate relationships and, by implication, the family, is the idea that the individuals who are coming together in Giddens's 'pure relationship' are unconnected to others and not embedded in a network of social relationships. Once again this assumption is only possible if the conception of the individual implicit in such theories is that of the autonomous individual of liberal thought, a quintessentially masculine conception of the subject. Such a conception ignores both the feminist critique of the masculinity of the Enlightenment individual and alternative conceptions of subjectivity. Such conceptions see autonomy as relational and recognise that a person's connectedness to others is a fundamental aspect of social being (see for example Sevenhuijsen, 1998; Sherwin, 1998). Indeed, Carol Smart has suggested that instead of the individualisation thesis we should develop a new perspective on researching personal life, which she terms the connectedness thesis (Smart, 2007).

Categories

There is a further problem with the categories of these theories insofar as their meaning is not clear. Individualism is a case in point and here the potential for confusion is recognised by Beck and Beck-Gernsheim (2002). They point out that individualisation is not to be confused with liberal notions of individualism, neither does it 'mean individuation – a term used by depth psychologists to describe the process of becoming an autonomous individual.... It is a concept which describes a structural, sociological transformation of social institutions and the relationship of the individual to society' (Beck and Beck-Gernsheim, 2002, 202). It does not imply the self-sufficient individual of neo-liberalism but a 'self-*in*sufficient' individual who is 'increasingly tied to others' (Beck and Beck-Gernsheim, 2002, xxi). This is not convincing, as the reflexive subject of Beck and Giddens is precisely the autonomous individual of liberal thought. This confusion about the meaning of individualisation is therefore at the heart of the individualisation thesis as well as being apparent in much discussion of it and, as Charles and Harris (2007) argue, can be found in recent empirical research on families and intimate life.

Tradition is also left undefined, being 'used, as a kind of blanket term, to refer to beliefs and practices which were allegedly widespread in the past' (Thompson, 1996, 90). It is important to separate out the different aspects of tradition; this reveals that, although some aspects of tradition are declining, others are not and continue to be important for the formation of identity in advanced capitalist societies.[1] Thus John Thompson argues that, although there is a gradual decline in the legitimation and normative aspects of tradition, the hermeneutic and identity aspects retain their significance, and that, 'As sets of assumptions, beliefs and patterns of behaviour handed down from the past, traditions provide some of the symbolic materials for the formation of identity both at the individual and at the collective level' (Thompson, 1996, 93).

Similarly, the traditional family is not satisfactorily defined and the traditional, the bourgeois and the nuclear family are referred to as if they were interchangeable; moreover the 'traditional' family (whatever it is) is replaced by a new, 'negotiated', 'post-familial family' in late or reflexive modernity (Beck, 1992; Beck-Gernsheim, 1998). It is assumed that the reader 'knows' what the traditional family is. Some clues are provided, however, and at several points in the various texts it is asserted that it came into being with industrialisation. This indicates that what is being referred to is a particular form of family which was institutionalised in western Europe in the late 19th century (Therborn, 2004, 301). The confusion, however, remains. Beck and Giddens are not the only ones to be guilty of this terminological and conceptual confusion, but their lack of conceptual clarity is less forgivable because of their claims about the fundamental transformations that are affecting family and intimate life.

The individualisation thesis has also been criticised for operating at a high level of abstraction and as being 'data free'; this renders its efficacy in explaining changes in patterns of family formation moot.

Theoretical critiques: social capital

Concepts of social capital are potentially more useful for understanding change in the social environments of families, although there are problems here also, as we shall see. Theorists of social capital fall into two types, being concerned either with social integration or with issues of social inequality, social injustice and social struggle (Kovalainen, 2004; Adkins, 2005). Those of the integrationist variety define societies as consisting fundamentally of families and communities which are held together by trust and shared norms and values – 'a kind of social glue' (Adkins, 2005, 196; Franklin, 2007). Thus, for Coleman (1988), social capital is a resource which is generated in families and communities and can explain differences in children's educational attainment (Edwards, 2004). Parental support for children within the family and in relation to education is an important dimension of social capital; it provides children with access to parental resources which can be 'intellectual, material and emotional' (Lewis, 2001a, 162). Social capital therefore is seen in terms of investment and rational action, in other words, this is an economically based understanding of social capital dependent on the notion of a rational actor wishing to maximise returns from investment.

Putnam's focus is more on people's engagement in 'associations' and on the vibrancy of civic life (Putnam, 2000). Thus community-based associations create bonds of trust and reciprocal obligations which result in both increasing levels of participation in public life and greater economic prosperity. For him, the family is a crucial form of social capital 'and the massive evidence of the loosening of bonds within the family (both extended and nuclear) is well known. This trend, of course, is quite consistent with – and may help to explain – our theme of social decapitalisation' (Putnam, 1995, 73). For both Coleman and Putnam, changes in patterns of family formation, coupled with increasing levels of women's employment, are significantly undermining social capital and, for Coleman at least, 'a non-mobile, traditional nuclear family, with a working father, stay at home mother and one or at the most two children represent the ideal structure for maximising social capital' (Gillies and Edwards, 2006, 44).

Bourdieu, in contrast, conceptualises social capital as fundamentally about processes of reproduction of class inequality (Kovalainen, 2004). For him, social capital, as other forms of capital, functions 'as a social relation', it 'comprises sets of networks of relationships which may be mobilised as a resource in the process of class distinction' (Adkins, 2005, 197). He is not concerned with the decline of social capital but with the ways in which it contributes to social reproduction and, in particular, the reproduction of class inequalities, how access to other forms of capital affects its generation and how it in turn affects the generation of other forms of capital. His conceptual framework, therefore, rather than being integrative, is concerned with power and struggles over the distribution of capital. He is interested in how bourgeois families ensure that their economic capital is preserved and reproduced through the extensive networks which constitute social capital. 'Connections' are important in the maintenance and reproduction of class privilege and these connections are based on families' social networks. Indeed, social capital is 'the condition and the effect of successful management of the capital collectively possessed by the members of the domestic unit' (Bourdieu, 1998, 70–1). An individual's or family's access to the various types of capital is determined by and determines their social positioning and it is unequally distributed between agents. He is not therefore concerned with a story about the decline of social capital, but with how it is used in processes of class reproduction.

Despite their differences, what these conceptions share is a concern with 'networks and connectiveness' and a focus on the normative family as an important site for the generation of social capital (Edwards, 2004, 197; Gillies and Edwards, 2006). Moreover, social integrationist conceptions of social capital are criticised for their functionalist tendencies and their assumption of an optimal gendered division of labour.

A gendered subtext

Like the individualisation thesis, social capital theory has a gendered subtext (Adkins, 2005). Feminists are critical of social theorists for the failure to make explicit that the generation of social capital largely depends on women's networks, although, as we have seen, women are clearly identified as the ones who hold the key to its reproduction within families and communities (Hughes and Blaxter, 2007). Di Leonardo, for instance, argues that the work of kinship, which is largely undertaken by women, creates gendered networks of support which are both 'crucial to the functioning of kinship systems' and also 'sources of women's autonomous power and possible primary sites of emotional fulfilment, and, at times, ... the vehicles for actual survival and/or political resistance' (di Leonardo, 1987, 441). It is therefore women who create and maintain the networks through which families are connected to each other. They also create the social networks of which communities are made and are crucial to locality-based social capital (see also Gillies and Edwards, 2006). Others point out that social capital theorists assume that women's networks are only to be found at the local level, the possibility that women could be involved in networks of support and trust in the workplace seemingly not entering into their framework (Kovalainen, 2004). Thus, for Coleman and Putnam, women's employment is implicitly linked to the alleged decline in social capital that is besetting families and communities. Moreover, their conceptualisations of social capital are underpinned by an assumption of a gendered division of labour which extends women's domestic role to include involvement in local communities. They do not, however, acknowledge women's exclusion from more public and occupationally based male networks with their greater access to power. 'As a result women are viewed either as potential social capital saviours and targeted to undertake unpaid voluntary or community work, or they are held responsible for its perceived demise' (Gillies and Edwards, 2006, 50).

Even though feminists have sought to rescue the concept of social capital by insisting that its gender and class dimensions are recognised, there are those who see it as beyond rescue. Lisa Adkins argues, for instance, that 'in the current socio-theoretical imaginary' 'collective social goods ... are overwhelmingly associated with women, who are assumed to produce and circulate such goods in the context of caring, family and kin work' (Adkins, 2005, 204). In her view, feminist developments of the concept of social capital simply serve to shore up this association and fail to 'interrogate the association of women with collective goods' and with 'the social' (Adkins, 2005, 205). There is also the danger that the 'social organisation of moral responsibility' which expects 'women to seek personal development by caring for others and men to care for others by sharing the rewards of personal achievement' will remain unquestioned (Gerson, 1998, 8).

Thus, theorists of social capital fail to recognise the implications of the association of social capital with women and the way that it confines women to a situation that men have transcended. But, more fundamentally, women's role in families and communities is seen as vital to the generation of social capital. The logical implication of this is that the solidarity of families and communities is threatened by women's participation in paid employment, although, as we shall see, this assumption is not necessarily supported by empirical evidence (Charles and Davies, 2005).

Moral values

The other influential strand in theorising about families and social change relates to the moral values that guide social behaviour. Both Beck and Giddens agree that 'we have lost those cultural formations which once served to provide fundamental values; which once provided life-plans, identities and visions; which once determined a sense of worthwhile duty' (Heelas, 1996, 202). This is of concern because of its 'implications for the sources of moral commitments' and because declining normative prescriptions mean that morality has to come from within (Lewis, 2001a, 167). If it does not, individualisation may be seen as betokening the end of civilisation and indeed the end of society because of its association with anomic individualism (Durkheim, 1984).

The withdrawal of external regulation of social behaviour has taken the form of legal change which has gradually, during the early part of the 20th century, and rapidly, since the 1960s, removed itself from the regulation of personal and family life and the imposition of an external moral code (Lewis, 2001a, 172). A reduction in external constraints has been conceptualised by Elias as 'informalisation' (Elias, 1996). Elias's notion involves a movement between two different types of constraint on behaviour, namely from external, social restraints to internal, individual constraints (see also Therborn, 2004). Elias is anxious to insist that this shift is a new phase in the 'civilising process', not its reverse, and would not want to claim that informalisation involves the end of civilisation.

The reduction in the power of external constraints, together with processes of individualisation, is interpreted as leading inevitably to moral decline and to people pursuing their own self-interest. In this scenario men fail to make a commitment to women or children, women seek their own fulfilment rather than being willing to make the sacrifices necessary to bear and raise children, people lack commitment to long-term relationships and, as a result, the family declines, and with it, those moral values which can only be transmitted from parents to children in the bosom of 'the family' (Davies, 1993). Increasing individualisation can, however, be associated with the development of a moral individualism rather than with a state of moral decline and anomie. 'Whereas in the old value system, the self always had to be subordinated to patterns of collectivity, these new "we" orientations are creating something like a co-operative or altruistic individualism. Thinking of oneself and living for others, once considered a contradiction in terms, is revealed as an internal connection' (Beck and Beck-Gernsheim, 2002, 28). Others argue that an ethic which is based on a shared humanity is emerging, which provides a sort of community in a Durkheimian sense (Heelas, 1996, 211). These conceptualisations counterpose moral individualism (to use Durkheimian terminology) to anomic individualism. It is anomic individualism which is feared by social commentators who see it as the cause of family decline and social breakdown. Moral individualism, in contrast, involves the internalisation of moral rules rather than requiring external constraints to regulate behaviour. Individuals understand the importance of contributing to society and the inevitability and necessity of social connectedness but direct their own behaviour according to internalised standards rather than following externally imposed rules.

At the level of daily interaction there is also the argument, derived from symbolic interactionism, that social actors behave in ways that will protect and enhance their moral reputation (Goffman, 1969). Thus, in the negotiation of obligation and responsibility for self and others, care is taken to behave in such a way as to ensure that one's moral worth is not damaged. Indeed, it has been argued that it is negotiation according to a particular set of internalised norms and values rather than conformity to externally imposed rules which characterises kinship behaviour; the provenance of this is not recent (Finch, 1989; Finch and Mason, 1993). Duncan et al suggest that this type of theorising about families can be defined as 'moral negotiation in post-modernity' (Duncan et al, 2003, 325) and it involves the idea that through the negotiation of family ties and obligations people build moral reputations 'as a certain sort of person with particular competencies' (Duncan et al, 2003, 325). 'People negotiate these identities and reputations in understanding how they should act in relation to others' (Duncan et al, 2003, 325). As we have already indicated, this theoretical approach can be found in the work of Janet Finch and Jennifer Mason and suggests that the 'proper thing to do' is negotiated within families rather than being laid down in rules or ascribed on the basis of gender and generation. Duncan et al, however, argue, on the basis of their research, that 'the social prescription of what it is to be moral in contemporary society, as opposed to its negotiation, seems particularly important when mothers consider the care of their dependent children' (Duncan et al, 2003, 326). There is a suggestion here that social prescription (or gender culture) continues to operate as an external constraint on individual behaviour and, significantly, social prescriptions are found to vary with place and among different social groups. This perspective does not pretend to provide an overarching theory of social change, but it does inform empirical research into family practices, which is the focus of the next part of this chapter.

Empirical research

Much research on families and intimate life has been informed by the individualisation thesis, theories of social capital and conceptualisations of moral values. As Carol Smart has observed, individualisation 'has become a core metaphor through which sociological analysis of family life is now pursued' (Smart and Shipman, 2004, 492). Much of this analysis has taken issue with the individualisation thesis, arguing that social actors do not display selfish individualism in the way that they relate to others but, in contrast, are attentive to the needs of others in working out 'the proper thing to do' (Williams, 2004; Deacon and Williams, 2004). They conclude that individualisation has not progressed in the way that the individualisation thesis claims. This conclusion is, however, problematic on three counts. The first is that the individualisation thesis claims not to be based on the notion of a self-seeking individual, rather it argues that in reflexive modernity social agents are characterised by a moral individualism; second, it argues that individuals create connectedness to others, whether these others be kin or not; and third, it claims that it is a prediction of trends that will be unevenly realised. It is also difficult to refute the claims of the individualisation thesis through empirical research. This is because most findings can be interpreted either as demonstrating that individualisation and detraditionalisation have not occurred to the extent that is claimed, because people are connected to each other and do not demonstrate a self-seeking individualism, or that such connection demonstrates that individuals are busy creating communities and networks as part of the reflexive project of the self. Indeed, both these interpretations can be found in research that has taken the individualisation thesis as the lens through which to examine family and intimate life.

A substantial body of research claims to show that individualisation has not occurred in the way that Beck and Giddens predict. Thus, women and men do not operate as self-seeking individuals but work out 'the proper thing to do' in intimate relationships, behave in ways which reflect a feminist ethic of care and recognise connectedness. Neither do they behave in ways which would be associated with an individualised agent freed from all ascriptive ties, including those of gender (Smart and Neale, 1999; Ribbens McCarthy, Edwards and Gillies, 2003; Holmes, 2004; Smart and Shipman, 2004). Thus, women put the needs of their families before their own career and occupational aspirations and evaluate their labour market engagement in terms of its value for their families (Parry, 2003). There are also examples of men being 'kinscripted' into kin work which is defined as 'self-sacrificing hard work – work designed to insure the survival of the collective', which again suggests that people do not operate as 'free' individuals (Stack and Burton, 1993, 161). Such findings have been interpreted as a refutation of the individualisation thesis, but could just as easily be taken as evidence of the development of the moral individualism said to characterise reflexive modernity.

Similarly, issue has been taken with the idea that individualisation involves choice which is manifested in different patterns of family formation and living arrangements. Thus Duncan et al point out that there is more cohabitation, a 'non-traditional' form of family, to be found in circumstances of socioeconomic deprivation than among better-off sectors of the population in Britain, thereby suggesting that individualisation is not always chosen and that, among the working class, choice may be much less in evidence in patterns of family formation than among the middle class (Duncan and Smith, 2002). Indeed, so-called new family forms which are allegedly a product of processes of individualisation have long been characteristic of those 'oppressed by poverty and racism' (Lempert and deVault, 2000, 7). And, as we shall see, a relatively high proportion of single-person households are the result of bereavement rather than choice. The individualisation thesis, however, argues precisely that individualisation is not something that is chosen; it is an unavoidable, institutionally based feature of social existence in conditions of late modernity.

Attempts have also been made to measure the extent of individualisation by exploring the distribution of individualised households. These have been defined as those containing mothers who do not withdraw from paid employment, cohabiting couples with children and same-sex couple households (Duncan and Smith, 2006). The conclusion is that individualisation is hardly in evidence in the UK and that perhaps 'the whole edifice of individualisation has been erected on the specific experiences of particular minority groups (where the theorists themselves are located)' (Duncan and Smith, 2006, 19). Furthermore, geographical differences in patterns of family formation and the distribution of household types, together with the role played by place in maintaining kinship relations, suggest that, far from family and kinship networks being disembedded, thereby rendering place irrelevant to their maintenance and functioning, being together in a particular place remains an important dimension of kinship and may be relevant in explaining differences in patterns of family formation (Duncan and Smith, 2002; Mason, 2004; Duncan and Smith, 2006).

Conversely, research into people living without a partner but not necessarily alone, arguably the most individualised section of the population, found that they actively created diverse living situations involving networks of support (Roseneil and Budgeon, 2004). This is taken as evidence that the individualisation thesis describes how individualised social actors are reflexively creating a supportive network of social relations.

Although it may not be possible, therefore, to prove or disprove the individualisation thesis through empirical research, it is possible to show that self-seeking individualism is not what guides people in constructing their relations with others, that people are committed to each other and to their children, that gendered expectations, particularly about women's caring role, still guide behaviour, and that individuals operate according to a set of values that balance the needs of both self and other (Williams, 2004). These findings provide an important corrective to the pessimistic interpretation of family change in the 21st century, and point to the continuing vitality of family and intimate life alongside the considerable change in patterns of family and household formation that alarmed social commentators in the final decades of the 20th century. They are therefore socially and politically, as well as sociologically, significant.

A similar case can be made for research that has been guided by notions of social capital, although here the main outcome of research has been to show that, far from social capital being in decline, it is very much in evidence, not only among geographically stable populations but also among those whose kinship networks are transnational (Crozier and Davies, 2006; Mand, 2006; Zontini and Reynolds, 2007). Thus, a major body of research has shown

> the complex and multiple ways people rely on and trust each other; how class and gender still have a crucial impact on the capacity of individuals to create and access resources; and how families support and maintain relationships and interdependence across generations and global reaches. Perhaps above all, contrary to the social capital lost story, we have found a wealth of social capital as we define it in the families and communities we researched. (Franklin, 2007, 10)

One of the significant findings from research using this concept is that there are class differences in social capital, with working-class families being more likely to have high levels of bonding social capital and middle-class families having high levels of bridging social capital (Gillies and Edwards, 2006; Warr, 2006).[2] Furthermore, social capital is widespread among lone-parent families and parents on benefits, precisely those families where Coleman predicts that there will be a deficit of social capital (Gillies and Edwards, 2006). Other research has shown that when people are very socially isolated they become reliant on formal sources of support (Warr, 2006). Such isolation and a lack of social capital are found in areas of high socioeconomic deprivation and are associated with social exclusion.

Much empirical research raises the question of moral responsibility for care work, how it continues to be gendered, and how this gendering may be shifting in advanced capitalist societies. There has been a considerable amount of research into the moral values underpinning decisions about parenting and its relation to participation in paid employment (Duncan et al, 2003; McDowell et al, 2005). This suggests two things: first, that people make decisions 'with reference to moral and socially negotiated (not individual) views about what behaviour is right and proper, and this varies between particular social groups, neighbourhoods and welfare states' (Duncan et al, 2003, 310) and, second, that the requirement to care, particularly for children, is a 'deeply gendered moral requirement' (Duncan et al, 2003, 310). Furthermore, 'Women's moral commitment to care ... despite the variability in specific relationships in particular times and places, continues to exercise a powerful hold over individuals and is deeply implicated in the construction and maintenance of moral identity and reputation' (McDowell et al, 2005, 224). There is some evidence that this gender division of moral responsibility is being challenged among younger generations, who are more likely to regard 'autonomy as a prerequisite for commitment'; this could be seen as an indication of the existence of Beck's 'altruistic' individualism (Gerson, 1998, 24).

The significance of all this research, whatever its conceptual basis, is that it shows that individuals and families are embedded in networks which are often locally based; that people's relations with kin are guided by moral values which are underpinned by a relational practice of agency; and that selfish individualism does not appear to be widespread. It also suggests that the individualisation thesis and the associated integrationist concepts of social capital do not provide very effective tools for analysing family change.

An alternative approach

The preceding discussion suggests that it is time to move beyond the individualisation thesis and its more speculative claims and to develop an alternative way of understanding the relation between families and social change. We have already suggested that Bourdieu's conception of habitus, with its recognition of pre-reflexive aspects of identity, provides a way of understanding why it is that change may not be as radical as the individualisation thesis would have us believe. And it helps to explain the continuing strength of such things as gendered moral rationalities. It can also help to explain why, *contra* Beck and Giddens, notions of the family retain their discursive power and why family practices demonstrate high levels of continuity, even in circumstances of radical social change (Somerville, 2000, 244; Becker and Charles, 2006). The discursive power of the idea of family is apparent in the demand for the right to marry among same-sex couples and the naming of intimate relationships and a diverse range of living arrangements as 'families of choice' or 'elective families' (Weeks et al, 2001). Denoting a set of relationships as 'family' clearly retains significance, and the ability to have this officially recognised is seen as a right that has, until recently in western societies, been denied to non-heterosexuals. Within the variety of arrangements that are referred to as family, there remains an image of the 'normal' family and this, Bourdieu argues, retains its power because of its rootedness in habitus. It is an internalised, pre-reflexive category. His argument is important, so it is worth considering in some detail, as it brings together ideas of habitus, social practices, capital and institutionalisation.

Bourdieu argues that there are two assumptions made in family discourse. The first is that the family has an existence of its own, it is seen as a 'transpersonal person endowed with a common life and spirit and a particular vision of the world', much in the way of an individual. The second is that the family exists 'as a separate social universe, engaged in an effort to perpetuate its frontiers' and to separate itself off from the external world. Thus,

> in *family discourse*, the language that the family uses about the family, the domestic unit is conceived as an active agent, endowed with a will, capable of thought, feeling and action, and founded on a set of cognitive presuppositions and normative prescriptions about the proper way to conduct domestic relationships. (Bourdieu, 1996, 20)

It is conceived of as a realm where market principles do not operate, as 'a place of trusting and giving' (Bourdieu, 1996, 20).

Furthermore, although 'the family' is a category which is socially constructed, the principle of this social construction is internalised and forms part of our habitus, a habitus which is shared by all those socialised in a world that is 'organised according to the division into families' (Bourdieu, 1996, 21). It is therefore both individual and collective. Thus, rather as Marx speaks of commodities, Bourdieu argues that social categories are 'rooted both in the objectivity of social structures and in the subjectivity of objectively orchestrated mental structures, they present themselves to experience with the opacity and resistance of things' (Bourdieu, 1996, 21). Furthermore,

> the family as an objective social category (a structuring structure) is the basis of the family as a subjective social category (a structured structure), a mental category which is the matrix of countless representations and actions (e.g. marriages) which help to reproduce the objective social category. *The circle is that of reproduction of the social order.* (Bourdieu, 1996, 21, our emphasis)

The family has a permanence which is separable from the ebb and flow of individual family members' feelings, and this is achieved through social practice, or what Morgan has called family practices (Morgan, 1996; see also Harris, 1979; Charles and Kerr, 1988). These family practices involve ordinary, everyday activities as well as extraordinary family occasions – they include both 'practical and symbolic work'.

Thus, the exchange of gifts, support, visits and so on are the daily practices which turn the family 'from a nominal fiction into a real group whose members are united by intense affective bonds' (Bourdieu, 1996, 22). And family occasions such as weddings, birthdays and funerals involve more 'extraordinary and solemn exchanges'. He notes that the work involved in such exchanges is women's work. Furthermore, 'family categories as institutions' exist 'both in the objectivity of the world, in the form of the elementary social bodies that we call families, and in people's minds, in the form of principles of classification' (Bourdieu, 1996, 24).

Bourdieu defines the family as a field which is characterised by 'physical, economic and, above all, symbolic power relations' and linked to the different capitals 'possessed' by its members. He therefore recognises the power struggles that occur within families and has a means of theorising them. For him 'negotiation' and 'choice' within families are infused by relations of power and are outcomes of encounters and struggles within the domestic field. Within this field, we could add, access to different forms of capital is likely to be gendered and the access of some families to different forms of capital is likely to be much greater than others. McNay makes a suggestion that is significant for anyone researching families, and that is that the field of the domestic should be thought of separately from that of intimate relations. She does this in order to avoid 'the conflation of the private with the domestic'. Thus,

> the domestic might be viewed as a field governed by the logic of familial reproduction and characterised by struggles over child-care, domestic labour, division of resources, etc. While intimate relations – particularly parent-child relations – are predominantly reproduced within the domestic sphere it is no longer the exclusive site of the reproduction of these relations. (McNay, 1999, 113)

This is a similar distinction to that between family and household, and serves to underline the fact that the two parts of each pair are not necessarily coterminous; it is particularly important for a study of family relations extending between households.

Clearly, Bourdieu's focus is on social reproduction rather than social change, on the transmission of privilege and the ways in which families are able to do this. However, his notion of habitus and its relation to social practices enables us to understand the continuities in family life which, in much theorising about change, are neglected (cf Gross, 2005;

Uhlmann, 2006). It allows us to understand how the habitus inv
the internalisation of what is 'normal' about the family; this in
involves an internalisation and naturalisation of gender divisior.. ..
labour, particularly gender divisions of care, and the differently gendered
moral values that underpin this division of labour. There is a real sense,
therefore, that the family embodies moral values that are in opposition
to the values governing the market place (Bjornberg, 2001, 98). And if
we are to take McNay's argument seriously, these values are embedded
in individuals through the habitus and inscribed in gendered bodies.
Habitus therefore allows us to see how moral choices are gendered
and why it is that women continue to choose to look after their own
children if their circumstances allow (Duncan et al, 2003). In other
words, it explains the existence of gendered moral rationalities which
are relatively unaffected by structural changes in gender relations
and individualisation processes. Similarly, Bourdieu emphasises that
families reproduce both themselves and class privilege by means of
social practices, the ordinary everyday practices of family life and the
extraordinary and symbolic practices of family occasions. Such practices
also ensure the reproduction of a shared habitus which knows, without
being told, what it is that constitutes family practices and families. We
therefore agree with David Morgan that a focus on family practices is
more fruitful than endless debates about whether or not 'the family'
is in decline. For it is through family practices that family life is lived
and family practices can take place in many different forms of living
arrangement. We also agree that attention should be turned away from
the family *as institution* towards those practices which constitute family
and personal life (Roseneil, 2005; Smart, 2007).

Thus, while the individualisation thesis and associated stories of social
capital lost (Edwards, 2004) and declining moral values are all about
change, Bourdieu's focus on social practices and social reproduction
provides us with a framework for understanding continuity. We argue
that this is an important corrective to claims of dramatic change
and provides a more appropriate lens through which to explore the
continuities in family lives during this recent period of rapid social
change. It also allows us to bring into focus continuing solidarities
and connectedness, rather than viewing social processes as inevitably
involving fragmentation and loss.

The family and social change revisited

As we have already indicated, one way of investigating family change
is by means of a restudy, and this is the purpose of our book. In this

chapter we have pointed out the different theoretical contexts of 1960 and 2002, which inevitably colour the way in which questions about family change are formulated. However, there are some ways in which the theoretical landscape has remained the same. Thus, processes of individualisation, particularly women's individualisation, were seen as critical to family change in the baseline study where they were conceptualised as a process of de-domestication of women. The story is the same but the terminology is different. Similarly, in 1960 the social networks within which families were embedded were distinguished as either close knit or loose knit, they were gendered, had women at their heart and involved trust and shared norms and values (Bott, 1957). The difference between this and conceptions of social capital is that social capital is seen as a resource, whereas in the 1950s and 1960s social networks were understood primarily in terms of solidarity. Both, however, are underpinned by a Durkheimian conception of social norms and social solidarity (Furstenberg, 2006, 95) and see increasing differentiation within such networks as involving decreasing solidarity or the loss of social capital. This illustrates the affinity of integrationist theories of social capital with structural functionalism. Despite these similarities, studies which are framed in terms of contemporary theories of social change ask different questions from those that were asked in the 1950s and 1960s. A restudy, however, by definition asks, wherever possible, the same questions as the original study and as a result may provide a new perspective on the nature and extent of change.

In the next chapter we turn our attention to the sociostructural and cultural change of the last 50 years in order to paint a picture of the changed empirical context of family practices and to explore their implications for a restudy. In Chapter 3 we describe how patterns of family formation and kin relationships have changed between 1960 and 2002, showing that there is more differentiation within families than there was in 1960 and that there is greater geographical mobility. Despite this, there are still very high levels of contact between members of families living in different households and there is little evidence of disembedding processes except among the geographically mobile section of the middle class. In Chapter 4 we explore the relationship between family practices, cultural identity and cultural reproduction, investigating the symbolic importance of a particular type of 'traditional' family for diverse cultural groups and the continuing importance of family as a source of identity which endures over time and is linked to place. In Chapters 5 and 6 we focus on the support exchanged between kin, showing that individuals are embedded in kinship networks which provide support for their members. This is true even when families are separated by considerable distances. We also suggest that close-knit social networks (or high levels of social capital) mitigate the effects of social exclusion and that social exclusion, at least among our interviewees, was not very much in evidence even in areas characterised by high levels of male unemployment. Chapter 7 focuses on the ways in which family practices are modified when kin are geographically dispersed; we discuss the higher value placed on individualism and what could be regarded as the disembedding of kinship networks among some sectors of the middle class. At the same time we also find that place remains important for kinship networks and that being together in a particular place is a significant part of family life. In Chapter 8 we argue that the increase in single-person households is not necessarily an indication of choice and that the relative decrease in households consisting of a heterosexual couple with or without dependent children cannot unproblematically be taken as an indication of increasing individualisation and the decline of the family. We also explore the nature of family and community in contemporary Swansea, in terms of both social networks and social capital, and the extent to which all families are to some extent families of choice. In our final chapter we draw together our findings and discuss their policy implications, returning to the theoretical debates of our first chapter and evaluating them in the light of our findings. Throughout, we pay attention to the change and continuity in family practices since 1960 and the ways in which they are influenced by class, culture, gender and place.

Notes
[1] Thompson distinguishes four aspects: a hermeneutic aspect, which refers to the 'background assumptions that are taken for granted ... and transmitted inter-generationally' (Thompson, 1996, 91); tradition has a normative dimension which refers to the beliefs and patterns of action which are passed on intergenerationally and 'serve as a normative guide for actions and beliefs in the present' (Thompson, 1996, 92); there is also the 'legitimation aspect' (Thompson, 1996, 92), which refers to the way in which tradition may legitimate the 'exercise of power and authority'; and finally there is the 'identity aspect of tradition' (Thompson, 1996, 93).

[2] Bonding social capital denotes horizontal networks which tie people together and create solidarity between them. Network members tend to share similar circumstances. They are inward looking, reinforcing 'exclusive identities and homogeneous groups' (Putnam, 2000, 22–3). Bridging social capital, on the other hand, is outward looking and links

people across different social situations, it is useful for social mobility and can more often be found among middle-class than working-class families. Putnam refers to bonding capital as 'sociological superglue' and bridging capital as 'sociological WD-40' (Putnam, 2000).

TWO

Changing societies

Having explored the different ways in which social change and its effects on families have been theorised, in this chapter we turn our attention to the nature of the social change that has taken place between 1960 and the first decade of the 21st century. This provides a context for the exploration of patterns of family formation and kin relations that follows. We describe demographic, industrial and cultural change, looking particularly at the ways in which they have manifested themselves in Swansea, the setting for the research on which this book is based. We begin with an exploration of demographic change, as it is this which has led commentators to claim that 'the family' is in terminal decline. We then go on to look at the socioeconomic and cultural changes which, it is argued, have precipitated these changes. In the final part of the chapter we describe the research into families and social change which we carried out between 2001 and 2004 and consider some of the methodological difficulties that arise when conducting a restudy.

Structural and cultural change in the UK

Demographic change

According to Therborn, the 'second third of the twentieth century constitutes the Marriage Age in modern Western European history. Never before, ... since at least mid-sixteenth-century England ... had such a large proportion of the population married' (Therborn, 2004, 163). Indeed the 1950s have been characterised as the heyday of the male-breadwinner family (Seccombe, 1993). Since then marriage has changed from being a normative expectation for women to being one option among many, divorce rates have risen, marriage rates have fallen and cohabitation has increased. Along with this the mean age at first marriage, which fell throughout the first half of the century and bottomed out in the early 1970s, has been rising, reaching 29.7 years for men and 28.4 years for women in mid-2001 (ONS, 2002a). The rate of marriage (ONS, 2002a) and the proportion of over-16s married (ONS, 2001a) have also been falling since the early 1970s and there has been an increase in both cohabitation and lone parenting, particularly lone motherhood (Lewis, 2001b).

These trends can be related to four things. The first is the de-institutionalisation of reproductive partnerships, that is, the increasing replacement of 'partnership by marriage' by 'partnership by cohabitation'. The second is that cohabitation is now a prelude and sequel to, as well as substitute for, marriage. These two factors had resulted in an increase in the proportion of births outside marriage to nearly 40% by 2001 (ONS, 2002a). Cohabitation and births outside marriage are no longer stigmatised as they were in the first half of the 20th century; indeed many births outside marriage occur within a cohabiting relationship (Lewis, 2001b). The third is the postponement of partnership, which is reflected in the later age of 'partnership by marriage', and the fourth factor is the increased incidence of lifelong singleness and childlessness. As a consequence, the proportion of time potentially fertile women spend in a partnership has been falling with the result that the fertility of women in partnerships has fallen. By the early 1970s overall fertility had fallen to substantially below replacement level, where it has remained ever since (ONS, 2002a). The fertility of women aged 35–39 has, however, increased (ONS, 2001a). These changes have been characterised as involving two separations: the separation of sex from marriage in the aftermath of the 1960s, and the separation of marriage from parenting in the last decades of the 20th century (Lewis, 2001b). Over and above this, however, they entail a decline in the rate of family formation and a decline in the proportion of the adult population who are in partnerships that have generated or can reasonably be expected to generate children. This represents the 'decline of the family' (in the sense of a heterosexual partnership with children sanctioned by the state through marriage) from an institution in which adult participation was the norm, to one in which participation is regarded as a matter of personal choice.

The last demographic factor subject to continuous change is mortality. Here the trends established in the period before 1960 have not been reversed: expectation of life for both sexes continues to increase and, with it, the number and proportion of the population formed by the statutory old and, within that category, the proportion formed by the 'old' old. Increases in longevity have implications for the sex ratio of the population since women are more likely to live to a greater age than men. This means that the older the population, the more marriages are broken by the death of the man and hence the greater the number of single-person households inhabited by bereft women.

All these demographic changes necessarily have effects on household composition, producing an increase in the number of single-person households comprising family remnants among the old or, earlier in the life course, consisting of those who postpone or never engage in partnering and parenting; a decline in the proportion of households with children under 16 years; a decline in the proportion of nuclear-family households; and a transformation of the reproductive cycle of the domestic group. This cycle now starts relatively very late, has a short nuclear phase, and is likely to have a longer than expected time in its dispersal phase due to late partnership of the adult children. The original partners will spend a longer time in a household by themselves and the survivor will spend a longer time as a widowed person living alone. The increasing number of those who do not partner and parent means that once their parental generation is dead they will have far fewer kin in the descendant generation with which their household can be linked (Brannen, 2003). In contrast, one of the effects of high rates of partnership dissolution and reconstitution is to multiply and complicate the number of ties between households (Smart and Neale, 1999; Allan and Crow, 2001).

Changing patterns of employment

One of the developments often cited by those who argue that the family is in terminal decline, or conversely that it is undergoing a process of democratisation, is the increase in women's participation in the workforce. Indeed, in the post-war years the proportion of women of working age in the labour force has increased significantly and, between 1961 and 2001, it more than doubled from 33% to 70%. A significant part of this increase has been in part-time employment so that, by 2001, part-time women workers constituted 16.8% of the economically active population (ONS, 2001b, table 4.3). There are similar changes in the reverse direction in men's economic activity. Thus, in 1959 the male employment rate was 94% and by 1999 it had fallen to 79%, while the female employment rate had increased from 47% to 69% over the same period (ONS, 2001b, 75). These trends mean that by 2001 men's economic activity rate was 84%, while women's was 72% (ONS, 2002c, 32). And although men are much less likely to work part time than are women, part-time male employees in 2001 accounted for 4% of the economically active population (ONS, 2001b, table 4.3).

Changes in the gendering of employment and employment patterns are underpinned by economic and demographic change. Structural changes in the economy include the decline of manufacturing and heavy industry and the rise of the service sector, initially with the expansion of the welfare state and the retail sector and, more recently, with the growth of financial and leisure services. The proportion of the population engaged in manufacturing, for instance, fell from 33% in 1966 to 20% in 1991 (Gallie, 2000), and by 2001, 22% of male jobs were in manufacturing compared with 8% of female jobs (ONS, 2001b). The decline of manufacturing and heavy industry has had a significant impact on employment patterns in Swansea, particularly the decline in the steel industry, which was a major employer of men at the time of the 1960 study. Financial and leisure services, as well as retail, health and education, have expanded in Swansea, as elsewhere and, in recent years, as we shall see, women's employment has increased, albeit from a lower base than in the rest of the UK.

Cultural change

Cultural change, particularly changes in attitudes and values, is also seen as contributing towards changing patterns of family formation and gender relations and the 1960s are often pinpointed as a key moment in social change. This decade is associated with the 'permissive society' and a whole range of legislative reforms, including the legalisation of abortion and decriminalisation of homosexuality in 1967 and divorce reform in 1969. Together, this amounts to 'the deregulation of personal life' and a decline in 'the power of the state to impose a moral code' (Lewis, 1992, 41). Indeed the then Canadian prime minister is on record as saying that 'the state has no place in the bedrooms of the nation' (Lewis, 1992, 40). The 1960s marked a transition from a society characterised by unquestioning respect for authority and a strict formalism in language, etiquette and dress codes, to one which was characterised by idealism, protest and rebellion, permissiveness, a 'general audacity and frankness' and new social movements such as second-wave feminism and gay liberation (Marwick, 1998, 3).

One of the changes associated with this decade is the prevalence among post-1960 generations of post-materialist values. Among other things these values represent a shift in attitudes towards sexual behaviour and gender relations. Thus, post-materialists have more liberal attitudes towards abortion, sexuality, reproduction and gender equality; they do not think that marriage or even partnership is necessary in order to have children; neither do they think that motherhood is the only or main route to fulfilment for women (Inglehart, 1990). There is therefore a significant difference in values between pre- and post-1960s generations which is apparent not only in western Europe but also in many other parts of the world (Inglehart and Norris, 2003).

The other significant change between the early post-war years and the first decade of the 21st century is that Britain is a more culturally diverse society, and this cultural diversity is associated with different patterns of family formation. Thus it is well known that among Afro-Caribbeans, motherhood is not associated with withdrawal from full-time paid employment as it is among the white population, and among Asian families there is still an emphasis on women's full-time mothering although this seems to be changing with increasing levels of education among second-generation migrants (Dale et al, 2002).

The cultural diversity of British society is partly due to successive waves of migration, from Ireland in the 19th century and from former colonies in the years after the Second World War. However, Britain has prided itself on being a hybrid society for far longer than this (Strathern, 1992). Indeed, the fact that Britain consists of different nations – Wales, Scotland and England – means that it is, by definition, ethnically and culturally diverse. Ethnic diversity is, however, often understood as referring to the coexistence of different peoples of colour and the white population of Britain and seen as a result of post-war immigration. Such immigration was encouraged by the government, together with the encouraging of married women into the workforce, as a response to a shortage of labour. Indeed, in the post-war period, 'citizens of Commonwealth countries were granted special immigration status. The British Nationality Act of 1948 conferred on them the right freely to enter, work, and settle with their families' (Mason, 2000, 25). As a result, 'Commonwealth migrants began to arrive, first from the Caribbean and subsequently from India, Pakistan, parts of Africa, and the Far East' (Mason, 2000, 25). These migrants were often men who were employed in transport and in the metal and textile industries of the West Midlands and the North-West of England, although women came in large numbers to work in the National Health Service (Doyal, 1981). Subsequently these industries declined and led to further internal migration in search of work.

The socioeconomic and cultural changes that have affected Britain as a whole take a particular form in Swansea. In what follows we explore the changes that have taken place in Swansea between 1960 and 2001, looking in turn at industrial change and the labour market, the housing market, and the cultural context within which family lives take place.

Structural and cultural change in Swansea

Industrial change

Between 1900 and 1960, the decades with which the original study was concerned, a multitude of small metal-manufacturing plants in Swansea and its nearby valleys had been replaced by the building of three large-scale modern plants. Two were tin-plate works, one in neighbouring Llanelli and one slightly to the north of Swansea. The third, the basic steel-making plant, was located in Port Talbot, 9 miles from Swansea, and had its own harbour for the import of raw materials. This plant imported labour from all over south-west industrial Wales and became the workplace of most Swansea steel workers, many of whom, at the beginning of the century, had walked to work. Modern manufacturing methods had massively reduced the burden of manual labour from its 1900 levels and resulted in improved working conditions and high levels of wages.

These were all major changes. However, manufacturing processes in 1960 were, by 2002 standards, still relatively labour intensive. Between 1960 and 2002 this ceased to be the case. The largest single industrial employer in the Swansea region was and still is the Port Talbot plant. In 1968 it employed 18,000 workers. By 1984 it was employing fewer than 4,000 to make the same amount of steel (Harris, 1987). Census data show that in 1961 manufacturing accounted for a quarter of Swansea's workforce; today it constitutes little over a tenth (ONS, 2002b). In 1960, as in 1900, it was still true that the majority of the working population was 'traditional working class' inasmuch as it was male, manual and worked in the industrial sector of the economy. This is no longer true. Swansea's economy is now post-industrial in terms of employment and is characterised by much higher levels of women's and lower levels of men's employment. Changes in the distribution of occupations between industry groups in Swansea are shown in Table 2.1.

As we can see, between 1961 and 2001 there was a sharp decline in the proportion of the working population employed in manufacturing, construction, and transport and communication, and a corresponding increase in those employed in the service industries (Table 2.1A). The concentration of women in services increased between 1961 and 2001 but the domination of the service sector by women reached its peak in 1981, falling during the 1980s but rising again during the 1990s to its 1981 levels. The proportion of men in services jumped from two-fifths to two-thirds in the 1980s but declined with the economic recovery of

Table 2.1: Distribution of occupations between industries, Censuses 1961 and 2001

Industry (SIC)	1961 (%)			2001 (%)		
	Total	Men	Women	Total	Men	Women
1 Agricultural, mining, energy, water	3.7	4.7	1.5	1.6	2.5	0.5
2 Manufacturing	24.8	27.0	19.9	13.9	20.4	5.8
3 Construction	8.2	11.4	0.8	6.2	10.8	1.0
4 Distribution	20.5	15.9	30.7	23.2	21.2	25.5
5 Transport and communications	13.6	18.1	3.5	6.5	8.8	4.0
6 Services	28.8	22.5	42.8	44.6	32.4	58.5
No data	0.3	0.2	0.7	4.0	3.8	4.7
Total*	100	100	100	100	100	100

*Figures rounded to 100

Table 2.1A: Summary data 1961, 1981–2001

	1961	1981	1991	2001
% services 4 and 6	49.3	55.3	72.5	67.8
% women in services	73.5	80.0	87.0	84.0
% service workers who are women	46.5	57.9	36.0	58.0

the 1990s to half in 2001. The distribution of employment opportunities therefore changed significantly between 1961 and 2001.

Labour market participation

In Swansea, as in the rest of the UK, there was a massive increase in women's economic activity rates between the 1960s and the early years of the 21st century which relates to the changes in the distribution of employment opportunities; alongside this there has been a fall in men's economic activity rates. Thus, in Swansea in 1961 the economic activity rate for women was 29.4% as compared with 87.7% for men, while in 2001 the equivalent figures were 72.4% for women and 76.4% for men (www.statswales.wales.gov.uk). These changes mean that women's and men's economic activity rates are now far more similar than they were in the early 1960s. However, as in Britain as a whole, women are more inclined to work part time than are men. Thus in 1961, 18% of economically active women compared with 0.6% of economically active men were working part time while, in 2001, 36% of economically active women compared with 5.4% of economically active men were in part-time employment. This can be seen in Table 2.2.

Table 2.2: The structure of the Swansea labour force, Census 2001

	Percentages of total economically active		
	Men	Women	Total
Full time	37.2	22.0	59.2
Self-employed	7.2	2.6	9.8
Working, not part time	44.4	24.6	69.0
Part time	2.9	16.8	19.7
Off market	6.5	4.7	11.2
Total	53.8	46.1	100*

*Figure rounded to 100

This table shows that the labour market is quite clearly male dominated if non-part-time employment only is taken into account, with full-time and self-employed men together constituting 44.4% of the labour force as compared with a figure of 24.6% for women. Women, however, constitute one-third of the *non*-part-time sector in 2001 as compared with 28% in 1961. As might be expected, it is part-time work which pushes women's labour force participation up to near equality with that of men. It would of course be a mistake to suppose that the women recorded as part time are a breed apart who do special jobs called 'part-time jobs'. On the contrary, women's part-time status is highly family-phase sensitive and is the result of their negotiating between the needs and demands of other household members and employers.

The changing class structure

Changes in the industrial structure and labour market participation of women and men have implications in terms of the occupational class structure in Swansea as in the rest of the UK (Marshall et al, 1988). Here we compare the occupational structure of 1960s Swansea with that of

2001 bearing in mind the very considerable changes in occupational categories between these two dates which make exact comparisons between occupational distributions impossible. Moreover, Swansea has enlarged its boundaries twice since 1961. Enough can be done, however, by way of comparison to warrant the claims we wish to make as to the broad contours of change during the period considered. In order to investigate the way the occupational structure has changed we use data classified in terms of the Registrar General's Socio-Economic Group (SEG) for the 1961 to 1991 Censuses and the ONS's occupational groups for 2001. SEG data were available for men only in 1961. The results are presented in Table 2.3.

As this table shows, the proportion of economically active men in *manual* occupations has fallen since 1961 from two-thirds to a little below half in 2001, the remaining men being distributed equally between *managerial* and '*other non-manual*' occupations. In contrast, in spite of the near doubling of the female activity rate in the period, the proportion of economically active women in '*other non-manual*' occupations has remained fairly steady at around two-thirds for the last 20 years. The implication of this is that there has been an increase in the numbers of 'other non-manual' *jobs* which balances the increased *supply* of female labour concentrated in the 'other non-manual' sector. Only a quarter of men are in this sector of employment. Conversely, less than one-fifth of economically active women are in *manual* occupations. However, whereas in 1981 female representation in *managerial* occupations was only a third of men's, by 2001 it had increased to two-thirds. Overall the 2001 distribution of economically active women is skewed upwards as compared with 1981 in favour of the managerial occupations and to the slight disadvantage of both the 'other non-manual' and the manual group.

The shape of the occupational distribution taken as a whole has changed dramatically. The 1960 distribution was shaped like a pyramid. It was composed of a small elite group at the top, a large mass of 'ordinary working people' at the bottom and a medium-sized stratum composed of people who were 'in between'. The 2001 male occupational distribution echoes this: manual workers still constitute the largest group, though it is much shrunken, and the other two groups are enormously enlarged and of equal size. What makes the overall 2001 distribution depart so dramatically from that of 1960 is the distribution of women. Nearly two-thirds of women are 'in between'. Their distribution is 'oval' as is the distribution of the whole workforce when the distributions of the two sexes are added together (see Appendix I for a detailed discussion).

Table 2.3: Swansea's occupational structure: socioeconomic groups as percentages of the economically active

Census	Socioeconomic groups				Occupational groups		
	1961	1981			2001		
	Men only	Total	Men	Women	Total	Men	Women
Non-manual							
Employers, managers, professionals	11.8	13.4	21.8	6.8	23.4	27.5	18.8
Other non-manual							
Semi-professionals, non-manual, supervisory	4.0	9.9	4.4	14.7	13.8	13.2	13.4
Administrative and secretarial					13.9	6.3	22.4
Junior non-manual	12.0	21.3	11.6	41.0			
Sales and customer service					9.7	5.1	14.7
Personal service	0.6	5.3	1.4	12.0	7.1	2.5	12.2
Total other non-manual	16.6	36.5	17.4	67.7	44.5	27.1	62.7
Manual	65.6	41.0	43.3	18.8	32.3	45.4	17.5
Other	6.1	8.8	11.6	7.1	–	–	–
Percentage other non-manual who are women		71.0					68.0

The changes characterising the period 1960 to 2002 (the date of our survey), are therefore of a different order from those that occurred between 1900 and 1960. The class structure, for instance, has changed fundamentally. Thus, in 1900 it had at its base two fundamental distinctions: those who worked for a living and those who did not and, among those who worked, those who worked with their hands and those who did not. Reference to the manual/non-manual divide virtually defined what being 'middle class' or 'working class' meant. This division was expressed in dress so that class membership was instantly recognisable and interaction in public places was segregated according to these visible signs of class membership. In this sense, though the proportions had changed and wage differentials had changed (see Atkinson, 2000), 1900 and 1960 societies were societies that shared a major social division based on this distinction. However, even in 1960 there were signs of change with Rosser and Harris finding that there were 'too many socially mobile people in between' to make this two-part model 'a useful analytic device' (Rosser and Harris, 1965, 93). Such changes, in particular the increase of those who are 'in between', do not mean that hierarchical differentiation is any less important in explaining people's social behaviour or any less important an element of social structure. But at the structural level the locations of hierarchical distinctions have changed, as have the sizes of the groups that are demarcated by them, and at the level of social action, identity and consciousness, class distinctions are no longer as significant as they were in 1960. These changes are explored in Chapter 4.

Changes in the industrial structure and the associated increase in women's labour force participation, together with demographic change, are usually taken as underpinning changes in patterns of family formation. Rosser and Harris, however, attributed women's declining domesticity between 1900 and 1960 to demographic factors alone: principally the decline in female fertility in the first half of the 20th century. They recognised that demographic change was both cause and consequence of the decline in women's domestication. They did not, however, recognise that the decreasing domestication of women was an effect as well as a cause of the increasing entry of women into paid employment and that the transformation of the labour market was to play a similar role in the transformation of family life in the second part of the 20th century to that played by demography in the first.

Patterns of family formation and household composition are also affected by the supply of housing. We therefore discuss changes in the housing market between 1960 and 2002 before going on to explore the changing cultural context. We discuss demographic change in Swansea in Chapter 3.

The housing market in Swansea

By 1960 the intervention of the local state in the housing market, through the building of council estates on the periphery of the then built-up area – begun between the wars when it was combined with slum clearance – had resulted in a vast improvement of the total housing stock. It is impossible to overestimate the improvement in working–class housing in the first half of the 20th century. This was brought about by the combination of council house building with rising wages which made it possible for working–class people to pay rents for decent council accommodation. As a result, the occupants of council estates were spread over a wide range of strata within the working class. Nonetheless, in spite of these major differences, you would, if you were working class in the Swansea of both 1900 and 1960, almost certainly have rented your living accommodation.

By 2002, 70% of the population owned their own homes and council tenancies were increasingly concentrated among the most vulnerable members of society. Council houses were being pulled down (not put up) or sold off to housing associations (*SWEP*, 2003*)* which were also buying up and renovating existing centrally located properties. In addition, new estates were being built on the periphery of the built-up area for a prosperous middle class which values the diurnal mobility provided by the proximity of such estates to the M4 motorway.

In 1960 Swansea County Borough Council had a housing waiting list of 6,000, and 14% of all adults were either sharing a dwelling with another household or living in a household that included another couple. Eliminating these shared households by building the required number of extra houses would have taken the public and private sector between them 5 years at the 1960s rate of house building. In 1960, as in 1900, there was still a shortage of affordable working–class housing of a quality acceptable by the standards of the day, though the shortage had greatly diminished and the standards greatly improved (Rosser and Harris, 1965, 62).

By 2002 only 1.2% of the adult population was living in shared accommodation and the number on the housing list had fallen to 2,000. Most of those on the housing list were people who were not in urgent need of housing in the 1960s sense but people who wanted or needed to transfer to other locations, usually so that they could live nearer to relatives (Swansea City and County Housing Department:

private communication, 2002). Swansea did have housing problems, notably those of older people living in deteriorating accommodation that they own and cannot maintain. However, their plight can be seen as the result of what, in the view of one of Swansea's largest housing associations, was in 2002 the *over-supply* of housing which means a weak demand for older properties that otherwise would be bought for renovation. There was no *absolute* shortage of housing in contemporary Swansea. Rather one of the factors that is likely to cause families to double up is the inability of couples to find the deposit on a starter home. The housing market in 2002 was therefore very different from that in 1960 when the housing shortage meant a shortage of rented accommodation so that many newly married couples had to share the home of one or other of their parents (usually the wife's).

Cultural diversity in Swansea

Cultural change and the increasing cultural diversity of Swansea have also transformed the social context of family life. The cultural diversity which characterised Swansea in 1960 was associated with its being a Welsh city with a proportion of the population who were 'English'. Moreover, in South Wales during the 19th century there had been a huge influx of Irish labour and, in the early 20th century, from other European countries (Crow, 2002b), so in that sense also Swansea has always been ethnically and culturally diverse. It did not, however, have a significant minority ethnic population originating in Commonwealth countries and in the 1960 study, as in its precursor, the Bethnal Green study (Young and Willmott, 1957), ethnicity (apart from the Welsh–English distinction) was not the focus of attention.

In contemporary Swansea, Bangladeshis from the Sylhet region of Bangladesh constitute the largest minority ethnic group, followed by Chinese and then Arabs. An indication of the trajectory of the increase in the minority ethnic population between 1960 and 2002 was given to us by a representative of the Swansea Bay Race Equality Council who told us that, in 1953 there were 3 Indian (that is, Bangladeshi) restaurants in Swansea, in 1971 there were 45 and now there are over 85. This is an indication of how the Bangladeshi population has expanded, particularly since the late 1970s and early 1980s when men brought their wives and children over to join them (Phillipson et al, 2003, 19). The move to Swansea followed the decline of industries in Birmingham and the North-West of England. Most Sylheti men 'moved to London to seek employment in the garment or restaurant trades' (Gardner, 2002, 193); some, however, moved to Swansea, where they were involved in the restaurant trade. Whereas the 1961 Census had virtually no information on ethnicity (apart from place of birth and nationality), the 2001 Census showed that 1.65% of the population was Asian, Black, Chinese or from another minority ethnic group, with another 0.5% saying they were of 'mixed' ethnic origin. Thus 97.85% of the population described themselves as 'White'.

The fact that there was not an option allowing people to describe themselves as Welsh on the 2001 Census, although it was possible to indicate if they were Scottish or Irish, became a focus of considerable criticism and controversy at the time. Various groups provided stick-on labels to allow respondents to identify themselves as Welsh, although clearly the uptake was bound to be partial. In Swansea this produced the patently absurd result that, whereas 82% of the population were born in Wales, only 15.3% identified themselves as Welsh. Although the Census did not recognise the importance of Welsh as a cultural identity, it did collect data on the Welsh language and here there has been significant change since the time of the baseline study. In the 1961 Census 17.5% of the population of Swansea aged 3 and over were returned as able to speak Welsh. By 2001, the Census attempted to differentiate between levels of Welsh-language competence, so figures are not strictly comparable. However, the 2001 Census reported that the proportion of the population aged 3 and over able to speak Welsh in the City and County of Swansea had declined to 13.4%. This decline was not uniform across the age groups, and in fact the percentage of Welsh speakers in younger age groups has shown an increase since the 1991 Census; we discuss the significance of this further in Chapter 4.

There have also been significant changes with respect to religiosity. Since the 18th century religion has played an enormous part in the cultural and political life of Wales and membership of Welsh-speaking religious denominations has been a marker of Welsh cultural belonging. This was still true in the Swansea of the 1960s, with 97% of the 1960 survey reporting that they were affiliated with one or another Christian denomination. By 2002, however, there was no sense in which denominational affiliation constituted a social and cultural marker for the population as a whole. This notwithstanding, the 2001 Census found that 71% of the population of Swansea reported that they were Christian and the next largest religious category, Muslim, was reported for 1% of the population. A recent ethnographic study of religion, secularisation and social change in Swansea describes both the decline of Christian denominations and significant pockets of growth (Chambers 2005). These changes indicate increasing secularisation which is something that is linked to the spread of post-materialist values.

Our discussion thus far has highlighted the main dimensions of social change as they were experienced in Britain and manifested in Swansea between 1960 and 2001 and we are now in a position to describe the study we carried out in the early years of the 21st century. Our study was a restudy; we therefore provide some information on the baseline study before discussing our research.

The baseline study

The original Swansea study was carried out by Colin Rosser and Chris Harris at the very beginning of the 1960s. The society they describe is one which shares the characteristics of the 1950s when family and personal life was relatively untouched by the changes that the 1960s brought about. This means that our restudy has a baseline of what family life was like in a particular place before significant de-institutionalisation of 'the family' had taken place. It therefore provides a unique perspective on social change since 1960 and how family change and changes in personal relationships have been part of this. The 1960 Swansea study followed Young and Willmott's (1957) study of kinship in Bethnal Green and, like its predecessor, was an urban community study. It was designed to test Young and Willmott's conclusions, which had shown how related working-class family households in the East End were dependent on each other for their survival and were fearful of the failure of 'planners' to understand the social implications of the revolutionising of the built environment, namely the disruption of family support networks.

The Swansea study, in contrast, was centrally concerned with more general social change: the social changes that had occurred between the social world in which Swansea's 1960s old age pensioners had been raised (1880–1900) and the brash modern world of the 1950s with which the Swansea equivalent of Bethnal Green's 'mum'-centred extended families had to cope. The way the authors of the original Swansea study summed up these changes was by employing the contrast between a 'stable' and a relatively homogeneous society and a mobile and (on virtually all dimensions) heterogeneous one. These changes are those theorised by Beck and Giddens and took place in the *first half* of the 20th century. They consisted of a shift from a society made up of tightly knit local settlements with stable populations, strong cultural traditions and little cultural and economic differentiation to a new sort of society, which Rosser and Harris termed 'the mobile society'. Such a society was characterised by economic, educational, cultural, linguistic and residential mobility together with the divorce of place of work from place of residence. It was a society that had been transformed by global economic and technical change as a result of decisions made elsewhere by unknown persons, commonly referred to as 'the English'. The family retained its importance as a reproductive unit, but kin relationships, though still important at the level of individuals' social networks, no longer carried any structural weight: they were largely irrelevant to the economic and political spheres of social life (Rosser and Harris, 1965). The family was (in effect) a microcosm of society insofar as the cultural, occupational, linguistic and geographical mobility of younger generations within the family meant that the social solidarity of the three-generational kin group had been seriously weakened. Change internal to families and kin groups was therefore conceptualised in terms of mobility – occupational, geographic and cultural – which resulted from increasing differentiation of the occupational structure, increasing cultural differentiation and changes in the means of communication, specifically telephones and motor cars.

Despite these changes, and the fact that families were under strain, extended families continued to provide support and a source of social identification for their members. However, in recognising the significant social changes that were leading to increased differentiation and reduced solidarity within families, the conclusions of the Rosser and Harris study strongly suggested the value of a restudy which would investigate whether such changes had had the expected effects on families and kinship networks.

The restudy

Restudies are relatively rare in sociological research, in part because they raise methodological questions about the validity of comparison given the inevitable changes in both social and analytical contexts during the period between the original and the restudy. Sometimes no attempt is made at explicit comparison, even when the research is conducted in the same location as a previous study and addresses similar issues, as is the case with recent studies of family and community in London's East End (Mumford and Power 2003; Dench et al, 2006). Others make such comparison central to their research even building it into the original research design (Bryson and Winter, 1999). Restudies have, however, been carried out and have raised questions about the possibility of replication. Indeed, a restudy of three other classic family studies (Sheldon 1948; Townsend 1957; Young and Willmott 1957) concluded that replication was neither possible nor desirable, both because 'social science methods have moved on and different approaches are now available' and also because 'repeating particular questions at different time periods raises issues of comparability' (Phillipson et al 1998, 264; also cf Phillipson et al 2000). Thus, the fact that sociology as well as society will have changed in the intervening period can make it difficult to distinguish between sociological and social change (Bell, 1977; Crow, 2008).

While we accept, therefore, that exact replication of a study is neither desirable nor feasible, we have retained the research design of our baseline study as fully as possible and modified it where necessary in ways that continue to allow meaningful comparison. The original study consisted of a 2,000-household survey conducted in 1960 supplemented by ethnographic research. The survey carried out for the restudy was administered between May and September 2002 and retained most of the questions found in the original survey. It covered the electoral wards that correspond to the area included in the original survey and which, at that time, comprised the then County Borough of Swansea (see Appendix II for a discussion of boundary changes). The sample for the 1960 survey was a systematic random sample of the electoral register, constructed by taking every fiftieth name. The survey consisted of 1,962 completed interviews, an achieved sample of 87% (Rosser and Harris 1965, 37). The 2002 survey sample was also constructed from the electoral register using systematic random sampling. The survey consisted of 1,000 completed interviews which represented an achieved sample of 43%. The difference in the two percentages for achieved samples in 1960 and 2002 is a stark indication of the changes in the climate for social research over the past four decades. When compared to the 2001 Census data our survey sample over-represents the older age groups and under-represents the younger age groups. The age distribution of those whom we interviewed for the ethnographic part of the study, however, compensates for this as can be seen in Table 2.4.

The 2002 survey tried to remain as close as possible to the original survey, while making necessary adjustments as required by changes in both social and theoretical environments (see Davies and Charles 2002 for a full discussion). Those changes which we judged to be most significant were: technological changes that affected how family members maintained contact with one another; changes in the analytical context, in particular the treatment of social class and gender; and changes in the socioeconomic and cultural context, including the ethnic composition of the population of Swansea, the cultural indicators of social status and the significance of ethnic and cultural identities. The core of the questionnaire asked for detailed information about respondents' household composition, frequency and nature of contact

Table 2.4: Characteristics of the survey sample

A comparison of the age–sex distributions of household residents in the 2001 Census for the area corresponding to the 1960 County Borough of Swansea and the same distribution of the 2002 survey sample and ethnographic interviewees
(P = population parameter; S = sample statistic)

	Male (%)		Female (%)		Total (%)		Ethnographic interviewees (%)		
Age	P	S	P	S	P	S	Male	Female	Total
90+	0.5	2.0	1.0	2.0	0.5	2.0	1.4	–	0.5
80-89	3.5	6.0	6.0	8.0	5.0	7.0	5.6	5.7	5.7
70-79	10.0	15.0	11.5	14.0	11.0	15.0	21.1	8.2	13.0
60-69	13.5	20.0	13.0	15.5	13.0	17.5	18.3	9.8	13.0
50-59	16.0	15.0	16.0	16.5	16.0	16.0	16.9	13.9	15.0
40-49	17.0	13.5	16.0	15.5	16.5	14.5	19.7	18.0	18.7
30-39	18.0	11.5	17.0	13.5	17.5	12.5	8.5	23.8	18.1
20-29	18.0	15.0	16.5	14.0	17.5	14.5	8.5	17.2	14.0
18-19	3.5	2.5	3.5	1.5	3.5	1.5	–	3.3	2.1
Total	100	100	100	100	100	100	100	100	100

Sources: Census, courtesy Swansea County Council Planning Department.

with a broad range of relatives, patterns of residence since birth, and any marriage or marriage-like relationships. It also asked about employment, social class, religion, and ethnic and cultural identities.

The ethnographic research conducted in the baseline study consisted of some exploratory interviews and participant observation in two localities, one of which was primarily middle class and culturally 'English' while the other was more working class and culturally 'Welsh'. There were also some supplementary interviews which investigated people's attitudes towards class. We did not attempt to replicate the ethnographic part of the baseline study. Indeed, the inclusion of ethnographic research in a restudy is more problematic than is survey design, given that this methodology has undergone a thorough critique since the 1960s with resulting expectations about fieldwork practice and reporting conventions being quite substantially altered. Johnson et al, in their restudy of Townsend's (1962) *The Last Refuge*, note that his 'reports were produced in the positivist tradition prevalent at the time' but that 'fifty years on, we are inclined to take a more reflexive approach not only to the origins of the primary data but also to the production of our own reports' (2007, 97). Thus the ethnographic research for the project, while inspired by the significance of the ethnographic data in the baseline study and by the additional depth and insight they provided, was not as closely linked to the original study and was more extensive in terms of both the number of localities where we worked and the number of interviewees. We carried out ethnographic field research in four localities and in the process conducted 193 interviews with 122 women and 71 men aged between 19 and 92 years (Table 2.4). The interviews were tape recorded and transcribed verbatim. The samples in the four areas were constructed using a snowball technique with several different starting points such as churches, schools, community organisations, shops and personal contact. It was more difficult to find men than women who would agree to be interviewed and this is reflected in the gender composition of our samples. This is something that has been found by others conducting research on families and is an indication of the strong cultural association of families with women. The ethnographic interview topics included who counted as family, the importance of family, the nature of contact with family members, family occasions, social networks, the nature of support given and received, and questions of identity and family change. The social significance of friends and neighbours was also included in these interviews and attempts were made to ensure that interviews were conducted with respondents living in a variety of different household types and living arrangements. The qualitative data generated by the ethnographic studies supplement the survey data, allowing us to explore the meanings attached to the patterns of contact and exchange between kin that the survey identifies. They also provide in-depth information about social groups, such as minority ethnic groups, that are only present in small numbers in the survey.

The four ethnographic areas

We chose our ethnographic areas so as to ensure that they represented the socioeconomic and cultural mix which characterises Swansea. Fairview is affluent and culturally 'English', Pen-cwm is an area of social and economic deprivation, Parkfields is an inner-city area with a relatively high minority ethnic population, and Treforgan is mixed in socioeconomic terms and culturally Welsh. We have given all these areas pseudonyms. Here we describe each of them, presenting background data which provides a context for the chapters that follow.

Fairview

Fairview, with a population of 7,335, is situated on the bay, having at its heart an old fishing village. It is a popular destination for visitors to Swansea and provides a lively commercial and civic centre for the surrounding area. It has a regular farmers' market, banks and a post office as well as a wide range of places to eat, drink and shop. It has expanded enormously since 1960 with much new housing now joining it up with neighbouring villages; house prices are high and it is seen as a desirable residential area. It is prosperous and, as can be seen in Tables 2.7 and 2.8, a high proportion of its population is middle class. The housing in the original village of Fairview is dense and consists mainly of old terraced houses with small gardens and difficult parking. As would be expected, most accommodation (85%) is owner occupied and a good proportion (38%) of it consists of detached houses. There is some (13%) privately rented accommodation and students occupy a small proportion of this. The area has several primary schools, a secondary school with a good reputation and a range of community centres, sports facilities and local societies. The population is older than average and a higher proportion of those over 50 live in households comprising heterosexual couples; only 15% of households comprise two parents with dependent children with a further 4% consisting of lone parents and dependent children (Table 2.6).

Fairview is relatively homogeneous in terms of ethnicity and occupation. Thus, 98.7% described themselves as 'White' in the 2001 Census and almost two-thirds are in professional and managerial occupations, as compared with 16% in manual occupations. A relatively high proportion of women and men of working age are in employment and, as would be expected, men's economic activity rate is higher than women's. In comparison with Swansea as a whole, women's and men's economic activity rates are slightly higher, conversely unemployment rates are low and for men are lower in Fairview than in Swansea as a whole; there is no difference in women's unemployment rates (Table 2.5). Just over three-quarters of the population is religious, which is higher than in Swansea as a whole; similarly fewer subscribed to no religion. The vast majority of those who professed a religion were Christian. Only 11% of the population aged 3 and over were Welsh speaking which is the same as for the whole of Swansea.

Pen–cwm

Pen-cwm, in contrast, is one of the most deprived council estates in Swansea and has a reputation for crime and vandalism. In 2001 the electoral ward that contains Pen-cwm was among the top three in the City and County of Swansea in terms of entitlement to free school meals, and it is among the first 15 of 865 divisions in Wales on the index of multiple deprivation (City and County of Swansea, 2001). It was built in the 1950s when it was a popular destination for many families moving from multi-occupancy, inner city housing and has a population of 1,909. This was associated with a pioneer feeling which sparked off a strong sense of community that, to a certain extent, still remains. After the 1970s, conditions in Pen-cwm deteriorated, with unemployment, crime, joyriding and drugs becoming its hallmark. In the early 1990s the county council made an attempt to reshape the area by pulling down 900 houses that were deemed structurally unsound and, subsequently, a housing association built around 600 new houses. Now most (70%) of the housing consists of a mix of older-style council houses and new housing association houses with very few (21%) privately owned houses. Well-maintained streets alternate with corners of dereliction with boarded-up housing and overgrown gardens.

Pen-cwm has a couple of corner shops, a primary school and several community centres in which many of our interviewees were involved, either taking courses or working there in one capacity or another. The community centres are diverse in their aims and clientele, running playgroups and children's clubs, clubs for older people, sports activities and bingo as well as offering a range of adult education classes and advice on housing, health and employment. The population is younger than average, a lower proportion of those under 50 live in households comprising heterosexual couples and 18.7% of households comprise two parents with dependent children. Twenty-two percent of households consist of lone parents and dependent children which is a much higher proportion than in the other three case study areas (Table 2.6).

The population of Pen-cwm is relatively homogeneous in terms of ethnicity, with 99.5% describing themselves as 'White' in the 2001 Census, and of occupation, with over half the population in manual occupations (conversely only 14% are in professional or managerial occupations) (Table 2.7). Economic activity rates for men and women are considerably lower in Pen-cwm than in Swansea as a whole and are lower for women than men while unemployment rates are much higher in Pen-cwm for both women and men (Table 2.5). A lower proportion (53%) of the population is religious and more subscribed to no religion than in Swansea as a whole; the vast majority of those who professed a religion were Christian. Only 8% of the population spoke Welsh which is lower than the proportion in Swansea as a whole.

Parkfields

Parkfields, with a population of 5,152, is a heterogeneous, inner-city area spread out along both sides of a busy thoroughfare. It has a diverse range of retail outlets which include Asian, Chinese and Italian shops as well as long-established corner shops, small artisan workshops, charity shops and takeaways. The post office closed during the course of the fieldwork. In contrast to the social and cultural homogeneity of Fairview and Pen-cwm, it is much more heterogeneous. It is ethnically mixed, with 8.3% of its population being 'non-white', mainly Bangladeshi (4.3%) and although over two-thirds of the population is Christian, a significant 6% is Muslim. This is reflected in the fact that there are two mosques as well as a range of chapels and churches in the area.

At its heart is a long-established, 'respectable' working-class area and it is included in the Action for Jobs programme because of its status as a deprived area. Other parts of Parkfields are more middle class, houses are larger and some are multi-occupied and/or rented to students; indeed there is a relatively high proportion of student households (6.4%) in the area. Housing is a mixture of large and small terraced houses, 56.5% of which are owner occupied. The rest is either socially (13%) or privately (30.5%) rented. Only 9% of households consist of two parents with dependent children, with almost 5% of households consisting of lone parents and dependent children; a lower proportion of the population in all age groups lives in heterosexual couple households.

Occupationally Parkfields is also heterogeneous, with the population fairly evenly spread between managerial and professional, secretarial and clerical, and manual work. The one industrial group which is over-represented is hotels and restaurants; this reflects the presence of a significant minority ethnic population which is largely engaged in running restaurants and take-aways. Economic activity rates are lower in this area than in Swansea as a whole, particularly for men. Unemployment among men is higher than in Swansea as a whole but lower than in Pen-cwm and women's unemployment rates are much lower than in Pen-cwm. There are two primary schools, one of which is a church school. The ethnicity of the children attending these schools is markedly different. The vast majority of the children at the church school are White, while a majority (almost 70%) of children at the other school are from minority ethnic families; most of these are

Bangladeshi. The Bangladeshi population is now quite sizeable and is to be found partly in the fieldwork area and partly in another part of Swansea. Only 9% of the population over 3 years of age is Welsh speaking which is lower than for Swansea as a whole.

Treforgan

Treforgan, with a population of 17,422, is much more extensive than our other ethnographic areas. It is located in the old industrial area extending up the Swansea Valley which grew up with the major copper and tinplate industries of the 19th century. In the first half of the 20th century it was a traditional working-class community where men were employed in heavy industry and women ran the households. With the closure of virtually all the major industry in the lower Swansea Valley from the 1970s onwards, however, it began to experience unemployment, as well as a decrease in wages for those in employment, with a resultant decline in its overall prosperity.

Treforgan has a clearly defined and comparatively large centre, with a range of high street shops, banks and a post office, but it is far from prosperous, containing large numbers of charity shops and takeaway food outlets. Housing is mixed, with 35% being terraced houses concentrated in the centre of the area, and semi-detached (38%) and detached houses (20%) located on streets leading out of the centre and in the newer estates on the periphery. Most housing is owner occupied (74%) with another 12% being local authority housing. There are several primary schools and a large secondary school; the area also boasts a rugby club, several well-known choirs, community centres, numerous chapels and other local societies. The age structure is very similar to that of Swansea as a whole and a higher proportion of those under 50 live in heterosexual couple households. Two-parent households with dependent children account for 22.5% of households and a further 8.5% consist of lone parents and dependent children. Economic activity rates are slightly higher than for Swansea as a whole.

The population is quite homogeneous in terms of ethnicity, with 98% describing themselves as White. If place of birth is taken as an indicator of cultural identity, then the population is overwhelmingly Welsh, with 88% being born in Wales; a quarter of the population aged 3 or over were reported in the 2001 Census to have some knowledge of the Welsh language. This is much higher than in Swansea as a whole and in the other three areas. The occupational structure is heterogeneous, with 19% in professional or managerial occupations, 40% in manual occupations and the remaining 41% in intermediate white-collar occupations (Table 2.7).

These four areas therefore contrast with each other on a range of socioeconomic and cultural indicators. Pen-cwm stands out in terms of high levels of male and female unemployment and lone parenthood; this is what would be expected given the association of cohabitation with low male wages and economic insecurity and the fact that, in the UK, the majority of cohabitants 'with children are disproportionately ill-educated, young and poor' (Lewis, 2001b, 39). Their different levels of unemployment, economic activity rates and levels of lone parenthood are shown in Tables 2.5 and 2.6.

The areas also differ in terms of class with Fairview being overwhelmingly middle class. Treforgan has a smaller middle class and a larger lower middle and skilled working-class population; the middle-class population of Parkfields is similar to that of Treforgan but it has a more sizeable working-class population; and Pen-cwm has an overwhelmingly working-class population. Thus Fairview and Pen-cwm are at opposite ends of the spectrum in class terms while Treforgan and Parkfields are more mixed. What distinguishes Treforgan is the high proportion of people working in skilled trades and lower professions – a legacy of its industrial past. These differences can be seen in Tables 2.7 and 2.8.

Table 2.5: Unemployment and economic activity rates in ethnographic areas

	Economic activity rates (% all ages)			Unemployment (% economically active)		
	Male	Female	Total	Male	Female	Total
Fairview	65.1	52.6	58.7	5.5	4.5	5.0
Parkfields	51.5	45.5	48.5	15.6	3.6	7.2
Pen-cwm	56.0	38.0	46.0	18.5	12.8	16.0
Treforgan	69.8	58.6	64.0	5.7	3.3	4.6
Swansea	63.0	51.0	57.0	8.7	4.5	7.0

Source: Analysis of Census data for each area.

Table 2.6: Lone-parent households as percentage of all households in ethnographic areas

	Dependent children	Non-dependent children	All
Fairview	4.3	3.2	7.5
Parkfields	4.8	3.2	8.0
Pen-cwm	22.3	3.4	25.7
Treforgan	8.5	3.3	11.7
Swansea	8.1	3.5	11.6

Source: Analysis of Census data for each area.

Table 2.7: Occupational class structure of ethnographic areas (%)

	Fairview			Treforgan			Parkfields			Pen-cwm			Swansea*		
	All	Men	Women	All	Men	Women	All	Men	Women	All	Men	Women	All	Men	Women
1. Managers and senior officers	19.6	25.1	13.2	10.0	12.9	6.6	13.5	13.2	13.7	5.5	5.8	5.2	11.3	14.1	8.1
2. Professional occupations	25.1	25.5	24.7	8.6	9.5	7.6	10.2	11.2	9.1	2.8	3.8	1.7	11.2	12.3	9.9
3. Associated professional occupations	17.9	18.3	17.6	15.0	13.5	16.8	12.7	12.3	13.1	5.8	6.2	4.8	13.4	12.9	14.2
4. Administrative and secretarial	10.3	3.1	18.9	16.3	8.1	25.3	12.1	7.3	17.5	7.7	1.7	14.0	13.5	6.3	21.5
5. Skilled trades	7.2	11.6	1.8	11.5	20.5	1.7	12.3	20.9	2.7	13.5	25.1	1.3	11.3	19.7	1.8
6. Personal services	5.1	2.0	8.8	7.3	2.9	12.3	6.7	2.5	11.5	10	4.6	15.2	7.1	2.7	11.9
7. Sales and customer services	6.0	4.3	8.1	9.7	5.3	14.7	10.0	6.2	14.3	12.8	5.0	21.4	10.5	5.6	16.0
8. Operatives	2.3	4.1	0.2	9.2	15.1	2.6	5.0	8.0	2.0	16.6	26.4	6.1	8.0	13.1	2.4
9. Elementary occupations	6.3	5.9	6.7	12.4	12.2	12.6	17.3	18.4	16.2	25.4	21.3	30.0	13.7	13.3	14.3

* Area corresponding to the County Borough of Swansea as at 1960

Table 2.8: Collapsed occupational class structure of ethnographic areas (%)

	Fairview			Treforgan			Parkfields			Pen-cwm			Swansea*		
	All	Men	Women	All	Men	Women	All	Men	Women	All	Men	Women	All	Men	Women
Middle class 1, 2 and 3	62.6	68.9	55.5	33.6	35.9	31.0	36.4	36.7	35.9	14.1	15.8	11.7	35.9	39.3	32.2
'In between' 4, 6 and 7	21.4	9.4	35.8	33.3	16.3	52.3	28.8	16.0	43.3	30.5	11.3	50.6	31.1	14.6	49.4
Manual 5, 8 and 9	15.8	21.6	8.7	33.1	47.8	16.9	34.6	47.3	20.9	55.5	72.8	37.4	33.0	46.1	18.5

* Area corresponding to the County Borough of Swansea as at 1960

In terms of cultural identity, Parkfields stands out as having a significant minority ethnic population while Treforgan has the highest proportion of Welsh speakers. The areas therefore contrast both in socioeconomic terms and in terms of cultural identity. Perhaps most significantly for this book, they also differ in terms of the proportion of the population engaged in bringing up children – it is highest in Treforgan and Pen-cwm and lowest in Parkfields – and in terms of household composition. In Chapter 4 we explore the links between patterns of family formation and cultural identity in more depth.

A note on class

In the baseline study Rosser and Harris constructed a class variable which was 'concerned less with the economic or status aspects of class than with the different styles of life associated with economic and status groups' (Rosser and Harris, 1965, 99). They did this by developing a complex and innovative procedure using three dimensions: the occupation of the respondent (or husband's occupation in the case of married women); the occupation of the respondent's father; and the respondent's self-assessment of the class to which they belonged (Rosser and Harris, 1965, 99–105). They did this because they recognised that classes, as well as being based on 'broad economic divisions', 'are also cultural groupings marked by distinctive standards and styles of living, and by characteristic values and social attitudes' (Rosser and Harris, 1965, 95). They also recognised that feelings of belonging to a particular class were affected as much by social and family background as by current occupation, and that family practices may relate to the attitudes and values underpinning such belonging. To deal with the 'background' problem, they included as criteria of class membership the occupation of respondents' fathers as well as that of respondents, and to deal with the 'social attitude' issue they included respondents' self-ascribed social class membership. From these decisions the problem arose of how to classify respondents whose attributed class locations contradicted one another and who could not therefore be unambiguously placed since they fell *in between* the categories of a two-category system.

For Rosser and Harris there was, however, a more fundamental problem arising from the nature of the occupational hierarchy itself. The Registrar General divided occupations into five 'social classes': I & II included professional and managerial occupations ('middle'); IV & V included those in semi-skilled and unskilled manual ('working'). But what 'social class' should be attributed to the members of the Registrar General's 'social class' III? The Registrar General solved this problem by splitting III into 'IIIa – other non-manual' and 'IIIb – skilled manual'. This Rosser and Harris felt to be inadequate. A well-paid skilled worker might, in the 1960s, have had a level and pattern of consumption indistinguishable from that of a clerical worker though have been regarded as inferior in terms of social prestige. In other words, IIIa and IIIb were *in themselves* contradictory class locations and truly *intermediate* between the managerial and professional occupations which Rosser and Harris termed '*managerial*', on the one hand, and the manual occupations which Rosser and Harris termed '*artisanal*', on the other. Rosser and Harris put IIIb (skilled manual) in with the 'artisanal'. They left IIIa on its own and termed it '*clerical*'.

These distinctions led Rosser and Harris to form their own (because two-generational) system of occupationally based classification of people which classified 68% as artisanal, 14% as managerial and 18% as intermediate, that is, 'in between'. They then cross-tabulated self-ascribed social class ('middle class' versus 'working class') against the threefold occupational classification above which yielded 11% middle class, 53% working class and 36% 'in between'.

In order to be able to compare our findings with those of the original study we needed to construct a contemporary version of Rosser and Harris's social class. This we did (a detailed discussion of how this was done can be found in Appendix I). For us, however, the proportion of people 'in between' was much greater (45%) than in 1960 (36%) and renders the middle-class/working-class distinction more problematic than it was for Rosser and Harris. For purposes of comparison, however, unless we state otherwise, in the analysis that follows we use a modified version of the Rosser and Harris class schema which, like theirs, incorporates a subjective measure of class as well as one based on respondent's occupation.

In this chapter we have described the significant structural and cultural changes that have taken place in the UK and Swansea between 1960 and 2002. As well as providing a context for family life in the first years of the 21st century, these changes highlight some of the methodological difficulties encountered by a restudy (see Charles, Davies and Harris, 2008 for further discussion). In the chapters that follow we present our findings, exploring the nature and extent of continuity and change in family practices. In the next chapter we focus on how patterns of residence and contact between members of extended families have changed since 1960, drawing mainly on our survey data. In subsequent chapters we focus to a greater extent on our ethnographic data; this allows us to provide a more nuanced account of the ways in which family practices have changed and how they have remained the same.

THREE

Changing families

In this chapter we turn our attention to the ways in which family practices have changed since 1960 and the sense in which such change can be understood as the decline of 'the family'. In the baseline study, Rosser and Harris conceptualised social change in terms of increasing differentiation and the move from a cohesive to a mobile society. They also spoke about the ways in which demographic change was associated with the 'de-domestication', or increasing individualisation, of women. Since 1960, as we saw in the last chapter, there have been considerable changes in the occupational structure which have created more employment opportunities for women and a greater occupational differentiation of society. This is likely to have led to further occupational differentiation within extended kinship networks leading, in Durkheimian terms, to greater heterogeneity and decreased solidarity within them. Decreasing solidarity within social networks is also conceptualised in terms of declining social capital and/or disembedding; in either case, social networks are said to be less dense and less able to provide support, a sense of identity and a source of moral values for their members. In what follows we explore the extent to which the changes outlined in Chapter 2 have led to a reduction in the connectedness of kinship networks. We look at the major patterns of continuity and change in family lives between 1960 and 2002, describing how families and households have changed, how far away from each other family members live and how often they see each other. Our focus is on extended family networks, the extent to which they form kin groups, and their increased heterogeneity in terms of residence and occupation. In particular we discuss the frequency with which members of kin networks see each other and how close to each other they live. We show that, despite the significant socioeconomic and cultural changes since the 1960s, the patterns of residence and contact found in 1960 have changed much less than we might have supposed. This is particularly surprising given claims of radical family change during this period.

The family in decline?

It is often argued that the family is in terminal decline. Our findings, however, show that the situation is more complicated than this and that, as well as change, there is also continuity. In support of the argument that the family is in decline we find in Swansea, as in Britain as a whole, that there have been significant changes in patterns of marriage and the formation of reproductive partnerships. One of the most striking changes is the decrease in the proportion of people who are in coresidential, heterosexual partnerships. Thus, in 1960 the vast majority of people married (76.2% of respondents) and had children. This meant that the majority of the population spent a large part of their lives in nuclear family households: either those of their parents or their own. In 2002, however, just over half our respondents were married (Table 3.1), the proportion of the population which was unpartnered had increased to almost a fifth, the number of children born to a given couple had decreased, the proportion of survey respondents with children had fallen by nearly 10 percentage points (from 83% to 73.7%) and 9.2% of married respondents had no children. Just over one-third of respondents had children living with them, and of this third 69.9% were married with another 7.1% cohabiting. Alongside these changes, life expectancy has increased and, as a result, the time that will be spent by a typical younger (under 50) member of the population in nuclear family households is now unprecedentedly short. It is *in this sense* that the nuclear family in Swansea is, as it is everywhere else, in decline.

Table 3.1: Marital status of 2002 survey respondents

	Number	Percentage
Married	538	53.8
Cohabiting	55	5.5
Single	196	19.6
Widowed	120	12.0
Divorced	76	7.6
Separated	15	1.5
Total	1,000	100.0

Changing households

Along with changes in partnering and parenting there have also been significant changes in household composition. Thus the proportion of single-person households has increased from 5% to 19.9% while the classic extended family consisting of three generations living under the same roof has declined. In 1960 1 in 5 households contained three generations of the same family, in 2002 this had fallen to 1 in 200. The extended family *household* is therefore all but extinct. Almost the only sector of the population where three-generation households remain is among the minority ethnic population, particularly among Bangladeshis. Here, three-generation, patrilocal family households are common, although our interviewees told us that such households were unlikely to survive for long, as younger generations preferred to establish their own households on marriage. This patrilocal family structure contrasts with the two-generation neo- or uxorilocal family households of the majority ethnic population and also with the female-centred kinship networks that are common in areas of high socioeconomic deprivation.

Table 3.2 shows some of the changes in household composition between the two surveys and, at first glance, suggests a *reduction* in the variety of households between the two surveys. The original intention of this table was to measure the incidence of extended family households and to differentiate between households where couples lived with the wife's parents and those where couples lived with the husband's parents. As we can see, there has been a reduction in the number of households shared by parents and their partnered children. This is because in 1960s Swansea there was a shortage of housing which meant that young couples were unable to set up independent households.

What Table 3.2 also shows is that the category 'Parent(s) and unmarried child(ren), with or without relatives, but not married children', has become a catch-all category insofar as it includes single-parent households and households containing reconstituted families; indeed 3% of this category consisted of respondents living in reconstituted families. Furthermore, 16.5% of respondents who had children living with them were single, divorced or separated. And although just over 80% of respondents were presently either in a marriage (92.1%) or long-term cohabitation (7.9%) or had been at some time in the past, 15.8% of this group reported having been in two or more such relationships.

This suggests that although the variety of extended-family households has declined between 1960 and 2002, there is now a range of living arrangements, some of which involve reconstituted families and others which involve non-kin. Thus, our ethnographic data show that 5% of our interviewees were living in extended-family households, most of

Table 3.2: Household composition (%)

	1960	2002 (survey respondents)	2002 (ethnographic interviewees)
Person living on own	5.0	19.9	15.3
Married couples alone without children or other relatives	19.4	31.9	23.3
Widowed and/or unmarried siblings without other relatives	1.5	0.1	–
Parent(s) and unmarried child(ren), with or without other relatives, but not married children	49.2	43.2	51.7
Parent(s) and married son(s), with or without others, but not married daughter(s)	5.5	0.2	1.1
Parent(s) and married daughter(s), with or without others, but not married son(s)	14.8	0.3	2.3
Married couples with other relatives, other than own children	2.6	0.5	0.6
Other relatives living together, not any of above*	1.1	0.5	1.7
Unrelated persons	1.1	3.4	4.0
Total	100.0	100.0	100.0

Note: For 2002 sample married and cohabiting couples included in married category
*For ethnographic interviewees, this category includes two extended family
households with both married son(s) and married daughter(s) in the same household.

them from the Bengali population; 5% were living in unrelated-person households, just under half being students; and 2% could be described as 'living apart together'.

Along with the decline in extended-family households, the other major change between 1960 and 2002 is the increase in divorce rates and in the frequency of reconstituted families (McRae, 1999). Although we cannot compare the number of reconstituted families in 2002 and 1960 and our data are only indicative, our interviewees commented on changing patterns of divorce and remarriage. Many of our older interviewees found it hard to understand the living arrangements of their adult children and were saddened by the instability of heterosexual partnerships (cf Smart, 2005). What comes across in these discussions is the concern and puzzlement voiced by our older interviewees about the instability of their children's relationships, and many of them wished for their sons and daughters the stability and security of a long-lasting marriage such as they had themselves experienced. One of our interviewees, who was in her 70s and who lived with her daughter and daughter's partner now that her husband had died, was puzzled by her other daughter's living arrangements. Currently she was staying with them until her new house was ready for her to move into.

> She's separated after 25 years. But friendly again [with her ex-husband]. Ridiculous.... It's strange, isn't it? I don't understand really. She's staying with us now whilst this house is going through now isn't it? ... Within what distance from him? Close. After 25 years. I think it's very difficult to cut the cords or something isn't it? ... but it's very strange.... They go out for meals, don't they? They go to the cinema. Like they're courting again. No one knows what's happening.... I just find it very strange. I don't know what my husband would have thought, he'd have been totally confused. (Female, 76, Parkfields)

She was asked later whether any of her children were still married and replied, 'No, isn't it sad? ... I find it terrible, find it awful. But we are used to it now.' She compared their experiences with her parents' marriage:

> My mother and father were married for, oh gosh, they were both 86 when they died and ... she was only 18 when she got married. She had 10 children and they were absolutely devoted to each other. Absolutely devoted. (Female, 76, Parkfields)

Despite feeling sad and wondering why 'children' were not inclined to stay with their partners, there was an acceptance that things had changed. Indeed one woman, when we asked her about her children, replied:

> They've all been divorced.... One has got remarried, the
> other one has got a partner and the other one just wanders
> around. (Female, 63, Parkfields)

Indeed it is from our ethnographic interviews rather than the survey that we gain an insight into the complexity of the kin relationships of reconstituted families and the way that relationships between ex-in-laws are often maintained because of childcare needs and grandchildren (see Chapter 6).

The family, in the sense of the proportion of the population living as a heterosexual couple with children, has declined between the two surveys. Families, however, remain of great importance to people and, as we shall see, adult children still tend to live close to their parents and see them almost as frequently as they did four decades ago. Indeed one of our major findings is that although the proportion of the population 'doing' family, as in heterosexual partnering and parenting, has declined significantly, the way they do it, as indicated by patterns of contact and support between kin, has changed remarkably little between the two studies. This reflects trends in Britain as a whole. Thus a recent discussion of gender and kinship in Britain concluded that 'The mother–daughter link is still strong; full-time working women appear to have less time for kin-contact; grandparents, particularly grandmothers, are an important source of childcare; men are more likely to provide financial support to adult children' (Nolan and Scott, 2006).

Continuity in the face of change

Alongside these changes there is a surprising degree of continuity in terms of how far away kin live from each other and how often they meet. If we look at where adult children live in relation to their parents and the frequency with which they see them we find that the patterns of contact and residence that were found in 1960 have changed relatively little. Women and their daughters are still at the heart of kinship groupings and there is an exchange of domestic services which maintains high rates of face-to-face contact. Mothers and, to a lesser extent, fathers are involved in caring for their grandchildren and fathers often provide practical support for their adult children when they move into their own homes or when they need home improvements. Adult children are also involved in caring for their parents; indeed almost a quarter of our survey population was involved in caring for someone outside their own household and most often this was parents. We explore exchange of care between kin living in different households in Chapter 6; here we look in detail at our findings on patterns of residence and contact in order to assess how social change has affected family practices.

Residence

Our survey findings show a high degree of geographical stability which is comparable with that found in 1960. For instance, 5.1% of respondents had lived in their present house since birth, this compares with 4.6% in 1960. Several of our interviewees commented on this, telling us stories of their childhood and showing us how the house in which we were interviewing had changed over their lifetimes. One of our older interviewees told us how, during the Second World War, when her parents' house had been bombed, her

> auntie lived round the corner there and she walked around and when she saw this house empty ... and found out who the landlord was she went up and saw the landlord... and we moved in and we've been here ever since... 62 years, yes, since we came here. (Female, 63, Parkfields)

She had moved into the house in which she was currently living at the age of 11 months and her brother and sister had both been born there. She went on,

> We were never out late anyway... my aunt made sure of that. My mother's sister. She'd be on the door. [*So she was living with you as well?*] Yes. Extended family. We had my grandmother, all my mother's side. My father's side, no, we didn't have them. But we had my mother's side at one time or another. We had my auntie and her husband in here. They lived in here, they had a little boy. (Female, 63, Parkfields)

The proportion of respondents living at their present address for over 20 years had increased by 5 percentage points since 1960 to 35.6%, and a third (39%), as in 1960, had lived in the same part of Swansea before moving to their current address. Overall, then, almost 80% of our respondents had lived in the same part of Swansea or in the same house for a considerable length of time. In contrast, the proportion who had lived somewhere other than in Swansea or its immediate environs before moving to their current address had increased from 10.3% in 1960 to 17.9% in 2002. Thus, stability for the majority of our respondents coexists with an increase in geographical mobility for a substantial minority.

It is also useful to look at where our respondents were brought up as this gives a better idea of the increase in geographical mobility between the two surveys. Thus, the proportion of respondents who had been brought up in and around Swansea fell by 10% between the two surveys while those who had been brought up outside Wales increased from 12.5% to 20%. We also asked respondents where they had spent most of their lives. In 1960 the proportion who had spent most of their lives in Swansea was 54% and in 2002 it was 59%; this may reflect the greater age of the sample population in 2002 when compared with 1960 rather than any greater geographical stability. Conversely, the proportion who had spent most of their lives outside Swansea in 1960 was 5.2% and, by 2002, had risen to 18.5%. These figures suggest a high level of geographical stability but an increase in migration into Swansea. Historically there has been population movement from Wales to England but our findings show that increased in-migration to Swansea between the two surveys has resulted in a higher proportion of respondents with parents in other parts of Wales and Britain. This small change reflects the increasing integration of Swansea into the British labour market, particularly at the higher occupational levels. Our ethnographic interviews include several respondents, particularly among the minority ethnic population, who have parents residing outside Britain and, for some of our respondents, their kinship networks are transnational.

Parents and adult children

This provides a context for our discussion of how close kin live to each other and, unsurprisingly, we find that the geographical dispersion of *different generations* of kin shows only a minor increase between 1960 and 2002. Members of potential extended family groupings,[1] however, tend to live further away from each other than they did in 1960. There are two ways of measuring this: (1) by taking respondent as parent and exploring their geographical closeness to the child that they have seen most recently (or the child that they mention first during the interview) and (2) by taking the respondent as child and exploring their geographical closeness to their parents. Here we look first at the respondent as parent and, as Table 3.3 shows, the proximity of parents to children, as reported by parents, has not changed very much between 1960 and 2002.

Table 3.3: Proximity of parents and children (respondent as parent) (%)

Residence of last-seen child and first-mentioned child, percentages of respondents with children outside household

Residence	Last seen 1960	Last seen 2002	First mentioned 2002
Same part of Swansea	32	34	27
Other part of Swansea	40	35	32
Region around Swansea	4	6	5
Elsewhere in Wales	–	8	10
Elsewhere in Britain	24	16	19
Outside Britain	–	2	6
Numbers	603	482	483

Although parent–child proximity measured in this way shows little change between 1960 and 2002, the change is greater if the child that parents mention first during the interview is taken as a measure. This is almost bound to be the case as the child that has been seen most recently is likely to be the one living closest to parents. If we take the second way of measuring proximity, by looking at where respondents report their parents to be living, we find three things. The first is that there is a gender difference in proximity. Thus daughters are more likely to live close to their parents than are sons, and a greater proportion of sons have parents living outside Wales. Second, partnered respondents live closer to their parents than do those who are unpartnered and, for partnered respondents, the gender difference is smaller. This can be seen in Table 3.4.

Third, if we compare the findings of the two surveys, we find a decrease in proximity of parents to partnered respondents between 1960 and 2002 which is more marked for daughters than it is for sons. It is still the case, however, that daughters tend to live closer to their parents than do sons. There is also a substantial increase in the proportion of respondents having parents living elsewhere. The figures can be seen in Table 3.5.

What this discussion shows is that there has been a widening of the geographical range of kin, increased geographical mobility, and increased migration into Swansea between the two surveys. However, we should not lose sight of the fact that 72.5% of partnered sons and 77.5% of partnered daughters have parents living in Swansea or the

Table 3.4: Proximity of parents to respondent (respondent as child) (%)

Percentages of all and partnered respondents with parent living outside the dwelling

Parent respondent	Father to son		Father to daughter		Mother to son		Mother to daughter	
	All	Partnered	All	Partnered	All	Partnered	All	Partnered
Same part of Swansea	28.5	33.5	31.5	31.5	26.5	29.5	33.0	31.0
Other part of Swansea	26.5	33.5	33.5	37.0	32.0	36.5	35.0	38.5
Total within Swansea	**55.0**	**67.0**	**65.0**	**68.5**	**58.5**	**66.0**	**68.0**	**69.5**
Region around Swansea	4.5	7.0	5.0	4.5	3.5	5.0	4.5	5.5
Another part of Wales	14.0	10.0	10.0	8.5	15.0	14.0	7.5	5.0
Another part of Britain	23.0	11.5	16.0	14.0	20.5	13.0	15.5	13.0
Outside Britain	3.5	4.5	4.0	3.5	2.0	2.0	4.5	5.0
Total outside Wales	**26.5**	**16.0**	**20.0**	**17.5**	**22.5**	**15.0**	**20.0**	**18.0**
Numbers	109	69	177	108	135	101	214	141

Table 3.5: Proximity of parents to partnered respondents (%)

Data for 2002 reworked to make a direct comparison possible

Parents' residence	1960 Married sons	2002 Married sons	1960 Married daughters	2002 Married daughters
Same part of Swansea	26	31.5	42	31
Other part of Swansea	45	36.5	38	41
Region around Swansea	9	4.5	5	5.5
Elsewhere	20	27.5	15	22.5
Numbers	383	112	408	150

region around Swansea. Well over two-thirds of women and men, therefore, live close enough to their parents to make weekly, if not daily, face-to-face contact possible. This compares with national data which show that over 65% of people live within an hour's drive of their mother and that this has not changed significantly over the past 15 years (Nolan and Scott, 2006). The original study predicted that increasing geographical mobility would reduce the proximity of extended family members to such an extent that frequent contact would become more difficult. This would then have an impact on the ability of extended families to form a group. Our findings show that this has not happened to any significant extent.

Contact

National data show that 82% of women living within an hour's journey time from their mothers see them weekly (this compares with 68% of men) (Nolan and Scott, 2006). These findings reflect those of both the baseline study and our own. The baseline study found that increasing geographical mobility made little difference to frequency of contact between parents and adult children and, in our survey, we found that for those with parents living in and around Swansea, which was the majority of our respondents, frequency of contact remained high. A comparison of the frequency of face-to-face contact between the two studies for partnered respondents and parents shows that it has fallen by an average of only 5%. This can be seen in Table 3.6 which also shows that 24-hour contact has fallen, particularly for daughters. The ranking of the different pairs remains the same as in 1960, with

Table 3.6: Frequency of contact between partnered respondents and parents (respondent as child) (%)

Last seen respondents	Mothers				Fathers			
	Sons		Daughters		Sons		Daughters	
	1960	2002	1960	2002	1960	2002	1960	2002
24 hours	31	25.5	54	41	29	26	47	35.5
24 hours to week	40	42.5	27	38	41	38	30	38.5
Within week	**71**	**68**	**81**	**79**	**70**	**64**	**77**	**74**
Week to month	14	17	7	10	15	18.5	9	8.5
Over a month (1960 survey only)	15	–	12	–	15	–	14	–
Month to year (2002 survey only)	–	13	–	5	–	13	–	7.5
Over a year (2002 survey only)	–	2	–	5	–	4.5	–	10
Numbers	345	101	348	139	237	69	254	107

Note: The 1960 figures refer to all married respondents with parents alive; the 2002 figures refer to all married or cohabiting respondents with parents alive.

Source: 1960 figures: Rosser and Harris, 1965, 219, Table 6.3.

frequency of mother–daughter (whether partnered or not) contact being the highest.

This slight decline can be explained by the increased geographical dispersion of extended family members. If those with parents outside Swansea are excluded, then weekly contact rates with parents rise to around 80% for sons and 90% for daughters which can be compared with the figure of 82% nationally. And, although we can agree with Nolan and Scott (2006) when they say that 'geographical distance is not a major impediment to kin contact', there is no doubt that geographical proximity is related to frequency of face-to-face contact. One of our interviewees lamented the distance she lived from her parents.

> I think the only thing I do miss, and it's nothing to do with
> Fairview, is the fact that we are a long way from the family.
> And both Colin's parents and my parents live in [town],

so it's a five-hour journey down, so it's a long way, and I would like to be within two hours. If I could be within two hours then you know you can go for the day or meet up over night, or go after school at a push, but five hours it has to be a special trip. A bit of an expedition. (Female, 36, Fairview)

Despite this she sees a lot of her parents, who are able to spend time with them because they are retired.

We do see a lot of each other. In fact I think I see more of mum and dad than some people here, whose parents are local. And that's nice, because when they come down they are here for a week, so we've got the whole week to just be together. Spend time and they can do all the ordinary things with the girls. Rather than just you know, meeting up for a treat or whatever. So, yeah no it's good. (Female, 36, Fairview)

These comparisons show that, despite increased geographical mobility, the most frequent contact continues to be that between partnered daughters and their mothers and that partnered daughters see their parents significantly more frequently than do partnered sons. This goes along with the other continuity between the two surveys which is that, once partnered, men tend to live closer to their partner's parents than to their own. We return to this later in the chapter.

Siblings

The only category of kin where there has been a significant fall in geographical proximity and frequency of contact is between siblings. This has two consequences: (1) it affects the internal structure of potential extended family groupings which can now be represented diagrammatically as a star (with parents at the centre having contact with children but the children having reduced contact with each other) rather than a net, and (2) it weakens the kin connectedness of the society, especially that of the locality. This finding is reflected in British data (see Nolan and Scott, 2006; see also Pescosolido and Rubin, 2000).

There are various factors which have an impact on how frequently siblings see each other. One of our interviewees related the lack of contact between him and his sister to the fact that he has a child while she does not, and to their work commitments.

> We haven't had a lot of contact really over the last year or
> so, I think mainly pressure of work on both sides and also
> us being more concerned with [child] and my sister not
> being pregnant or having a family at that time,… once they
> have got a child, then they probably will be interacting a lot
> more. I think it's going to be convenient for us to babysit
> for each other and to go out together to, you know, child-
> orientated places. (Male, 33, Fairview)

Another of our older interviewees describes the contact he has with
one of his brothers:

> We are great friends, but every time I ring my brother up, he
> says 'I was just gonna ring you', and that was about, I haven't
> heard from him for about twelve months, but he was always
> gonna ring me when I ring him. We've got good friendship,
> but he's got his family, we've got ours, and he does his things,
> yeah we meet up and have a good time, but uh, not every
> week or every month, no, it's only about once, twice a year
> we might meet up with each other. But we still got a lot of
> affection for each other, even though we are lazy in writing
> and corresponding. (Male, 72, Pen-cwm)

Some siblings, in contrast, saw each other frequently. A woman in her
sixties talked about the close contact with her sisters and sister-in-
law:

> We really, we keep in touch every week, we are very close,
> yeah.… That's the four of us going away now next Monday
> to Butlin's. [*Oh I see.*] All of us are going. [Her husband
> interjects, *To Bournemouth, Butlin's.*] Bournemouth rather
> not Butlin's. Yeah we keep in touch you know. [*So you meet
> up every week.*] Yeah we phone one another, you know, yeah,
> oh we keep in touch, yeah. (Female, 64, Pen-cwm)

These findings confirm that the trends identified in the baseline study
– increasing geographical mobility and decreasing density of kinship
networks – have continued into the present but that, despite these
trends, adult children and parents continue to see each other frequently.
Of course it could be argued that those children who have moved
away from Swansea are, de facto, excluded from the survey and that
this, in and of itself, inflates the frequency of contact between parents

and adult children that we have observed. Three things can be said in this context: the first is that our findings are not out of line with national trends; the second is that the measure of parent–child contact we are using is based on respondent as child not parent; the third is that our ethnographic interviews and our survey material give us a chance to explore the extent to which adult children have moved away. We find that greater distances are involved for middle-class families, especially when children have been upwardly mobile and have moved away, first to university and then to a job (see Chapter 7 for further discussion). But what comes across in the interviews is the closeness of kin networks and the importance attached to regular and frequent contact with kin.

Our findings also show that, despite women's increasing economic activity, patterns of residence and contact are still gendered such that women live closer to their parents and see them more frequently than do men. The impact of women's employment on patterns of contact is explored more fully in Chapter 6.

Children

Having children makes a difference to how often parents and adult children see each other. In the baseline study, proximity and contact tables are not available for those who do not have children; they constituted 17% of the 1960 survey sample as compared with 26.7% of the restudy sample which is a significant increase. Our data show that those with children live closer to and see their parents more frequently than those without children, but we are unable to make a comparison with 1960 patterns as the data are no longer available.

Normative expectations

These patterns of residence and contact are brought to life by our ethnographic data which also reveal the normative expectations underpinning them. One of our interviewees told us that he sees his daughter more often than he sees his son, even though his son lives in Swansea and his daughter lives in England. He explains this with reference to the fact that his daughter has children and he anticipates that this is likely to change as his son and partner are now 'trying for' a baby.

> We're waiting to hear now. I think if this happens then I would see a lot more of him then. [*Why?*] Well simply

> because they would be, with the baby you tend to want to go out for a break. (Male, 55, Parkfields)

He compares this with his own experience.

> When my kids were young I'd see my mum a lot more then because it was somewhere to visit, somewhere to take them out. Summer, beach, walking, and then the winter then you'd visit and from that point of view, yes, that's what families are there for. (Male, 55, Parkfields)

Another interviewee, when asked if there was anyone that she was particularly close to replied, 'Mother' to which her mother, who was present during the interview, responded, 'Well, since you've had the kids really isn't it?' (Female, 29, Pen-cwm). And one of the men we interviewed told us how his relationship with his parents had changed since having children.

> I think their attitudes to me and Gillian have changed since we've had the children.... I think it's probably brought us closer as a family then, since we've had children and they've been more included in our lives. Before we didn't need them an awful lot. (Male, 33, Fairview)

This suggests that having children creates a 'need' for parental help which draws parents and adult children closer together.

Half (50.4%) of the survey respondents who did not have children were under 30 which means that many had not yet reached the stage of family formation if, indeed, they were going to at all. Furthermore, a substantial proportion of those who were unpartnered and childless were still living in the parental home (49.5% of men and 35% of women). Those who had left home were living on their own (38% of men and 37.5% of women), with other relatives (2% of men and 3.5% of women) or with unrelated persons (10.5% of men and 24% of women). If proximity to and contact with parents varies with stage in the life course, then it can be anticipated that when and if they become parents themselves, contact with their own parents is likely to increase. Increased geographical mobility, however, may militate against this, and it was our middle-class respondents who were more likely to live at a distance from their parents. For instance, 56.1% of middle-class daughters had mothers living in Swansea as compared with 87.1% of working-class daughters, and generally the parents of working-class respondents were more likely to be living in Swansea than those of middle-class respondents.

Our qualitative data show that provision of support and frequency of contact are critical in defining who is counted as 'family'. Kin could lose the status of family members if they failed to provide support and contact was infrequent. Similarly, friends could become 'family' if they were seen frequently and provided and received support, and similar processes could turn distant relatives into 'close' family (Becker and Charles, 2006). This is discussed more fully in Chapter 8. Moreover, normative expectations of frequency of contact depend to some extent upon degree of affinity. Thus parents and adult children are generally expected to be in close and frequent contact, while more distant kin, like cousins, aunts and uncles, are still considered to be family even if they are only seen at weddings and funerals. Phrases such as 'we don't live in each other's pockets' were often used to sum up the subtle norms and expectations surrounding contact. Such phrases emphasised the independence of interviewees and their households when describing frequent contact and/or close relationships. Maintaining the appropriate level of contact enables a balance to be struck between social isolation and an invasion of privacy. What that appropriate level is, however, differs depending on the nature of the relationship and expectations.

Mothers and daughters

Rosser and Harris argued that the strength of extended family groupings depended not only on the degree of homogeneity of their members but also on the mother–daughter relationship which was at the heart of kinship groupings (cf. Young and Wilmott, 1957). The strength of the mother–daughter tie was measured in terms of contact within the previous 24 hours which was much higher for mothers and partnered daughters (54%) than for other categories of kin. In the intervening years women's employment has increased and their domesticity has decreased; these changes can also be understood in terms of increasing individualisation. This has resulted in the proportion of mothers and partnered daughters having daily contact falling from 54% in 1960 to 41% in 2002 although, as we have seen, their levels of contact are still higher than those for other categories of kin. This suggests that, although the frequency of contact has fallen since 1960, the mother–daughter relationship remains crucial for the functioning of kin groups. For those who are unpartnered and without children rates of contact are lower but mother–daughter contact is still the highest.

There is a class dimension to mother–daughter, contact with it being higher for the working class than for the middle class. In 1960, 24–hour mother and daughter contact was 56% for working-class daughters but only 44 % for middle-class daughters. In 2002 we found the same class difference but much diminished for *weekly* contact (working class 82%; middle class 78%), and that 24–hour contact had suffered a greater decline in the working class than in the middle class. This was to be expected, given that 24–hour contact is associated with domestic assistance and that domestic assistance is less often provided in 2002 due to what Rosser and Harris called the de-domestication of women. However, we also find that, although women's full–time employment reduces their frequency of contact with kin overall, it increases their need for support with childcare which is most often provided by mothers or mothers-in-law. The exchange of assistance between women is evidenced by the continuing relatively high levels of contact between mothers and daughters. One of our interviewees, who was in her thirties, with two pre-school-age children, explained how her mother adapted her own activity to her daughter's hours of work and childcare needs.

> So mum does voluntary work, which is regular days, so she tries to plan around, basically they have to wait, find out whether she can do it, depending on what I'm working. So she is very good with that. They don't, they babysit very rarely other than work. And occasionally might babysit in the evenings. But I spend a lot of time with them with the children. And they help me out with that. (Female, 31, Fairview)

Another of our interviewees told us how every weekday, after taking her oldest child to school, she goes to her mother's house and spends the mornings there.

> Every day I come here. Monday to Friday I'm here, Saturday and Sunday I'm in my own house. [*So with the two younger children you normally come here?*] Yeah, and she is in afternoons so, that's why I normally come here because they go to Pen–cwm school, so rather than go all the way home I just come here then. Take them to school and come here to wait for them. (Female, 26, Pen–cwm)

The continuing strength of the mother–daughter tie is also reflected in the fact that partnered heterosexual men have greater contact with their partner's than with their own parents. In the original study it was noted that there was a bias towards the wife's kin due to the strength of the relationship between mothers and daughters. This was reflected in the location where a couple lived on marriage and the frequency with which they saw their parents and parents-in-law. We look at each of these in turn, showing that although there is still a bias towards the wife's side of the family, it is less marked than it was in 1960 and that this relates to changing class patterns of contact.

Sharing a home with parents

As we have already noted, in 1960s Swansea there was a tendency for young couples to live with one or another set of parents in the early days of their partnership (usually marriage) and it was more likely to be the wife's parents' home that they lived in. Thus, in 1960, 53% of newly married couples shared a house with one or another set of parents; by 2002 this had fallen to just over a third. There has also been a change in which set of parents young couples choose to share with, such that in 1960 they overwhelmingly shared with the wife's parents while, in 2002, although there was still a preference to share with wife's parents, this had been considerably reduced (Table 3.7). It should be remembered that these figures are for all our respondents, those who were first married in the 1950s and 1960s as well as those first partnered in the 1990s. In fact, a much higher proportion of our older respondents started off married life with one or other set of parents, and the biggest fall has taken place among those starting off married life with the wife's parents (Table 3.8). In the oldest generation (those born before 1934) 30.5% started married life with the wife's parents, while in the youngest generation this had fallen to 8.5%.

Table 3.7: Household composition after marriage/cohabitation (%)

Least recent (usually first) partnerships of respondents living in Swansea at partnership

	1960	2002
With husband's parents	14.5	14.5
With wife's parents	31.0	21.0
With other relatives	7.5	2.5
On own	47.0	62.0

Table 3.8: Household composition after marriage/cohabitation by generation, 2002 sample (%)

Least recent (usually first) partnerships of all ever-partnered respondents

Born	Before 1934	1934 –49	1950 –64	1965 –84	Total
Sharing with husband's parents	17.5	14.5	13.3	12.5	14.5
Sharing with wife's parents	30.5	22.0	16.3	8.5	21.0
Total sharing with parents	48.0	36.5	29.6	21.0	35.5
Sharing with other relatives	7.0	1.0	1.0	0.0	2.5
On own	45.0	62.5	69.5	79.0	62.0

Even though heterosexual couples are much less likely to share a house with their parents in 2002, and the marked preference for sharing with the wife's parents has fallen, there is still a tendency for them to live closer to the wife's parents than to the husband's. Thus, sons live closer to their partner's parents than to their own and daughters live closer to their own parents than to their partner's parents. Women also live closer to and see their own siblings more frequently than they do their partner's siblings.

The two sides of the family

If we look at the proportion of respondents seeing their own and their partner's mother during the last week we find a continuing bias towards mother's kin. Thus, daughters see more of their own mothers (with 78% seeing them on a weekly basis) than of their partner's mothers (58.5%), and more of their own fathers (72%) than of their partner's fathers (55%). They therefore maintain stronger ties with their family of origin than with their affines. This is reflected in those whom they 'count' as family. Thus, in an earlier paper, we discussed the way family of origin tends to be counted as 'family' with in-laws being seen — at least by women — as not so close (Becker and Charles, 2006).

> [*Whom would you count as family, whom do you count as your family?*] Immediately I would say, my husband and children. But I would involve my parents, and my brother and sister, but I quite happily leave out my in-laws, despite, if someone said to me, you know if you were to take your family on holiday with you, I'd only take Ben [her husband] and the children, because I couldn't bear to have the in-laws. (Female, 31, Fairview)

Sons, in contrast, see slightly more of their partner's mother (69%) than of their own mother (63%) and substantially more of their partner's father (67%) than of their own father (56%).

Rosser and Harris pointed out that the man's vacation of his natal group and his absorption into his partner's group did not prevent the retention of a strong relationship between him and his mother and these figures are consistent with this interpretation. The inclusion of the man within his partner's family therefore does not take place at the expense of contact with members of his own family. The expected uxorilateral bias is manifested in the relationship between wife's mother and husband's mother, the husband's mother being interactionally relatively excluded. We find a similar pattern for contact with siblings. There is only a small difference in weekly rates for men's contact with their own siblings (38%) and with their partner's siblings (42.6%), but the figures for women show markedly different rates of contact with their own siblings (54.2%) and with their partner's siblings (28.8%). The weakest relationships are therefore between women and their affines – their partner's parents and siblings.

If we compare the two sides of the family then we find the expected bias towards the woman's side of the family, what Rosser and Harris termed uxorilocality or uxorilaterality, in patterns of residence and contact, with closer relationships (in the sense of living nearer and seeing more frequently) between a husband and his wife's parents than with his own. The relatively low level of contact between wives and their husbands' families was reflected in the experience of one of our interviewees.

> And I mean I've got a lot of cousins, and I do see them, you know if there is anything going on, I always see them. So I see you know plenty of family, they are all my family. My husband's family I don't see, unless anything happens and one dies and they phone me to tell me and I've got to go to the funeral. That's the only time I see my husband's family. (Female, 66, Parkfields)

In the original study Rosser and Harris found that the stress on uxorilocality was stronger among the working class than the middle class and that patterns of residence and contact reflected this. They also found that kin relations were generally closer among the working class than the middle class. In the following section we explore class differences in patterns of contact to investigate the extent of change between the two surveys.

Class differences in patterns of contact

As we have seen, overall levels of contact, although slightly lower in 2002 than in 1960, do not differ significantly. There are, however, some subtle changes which serve to reduce class differences such that patterns found previously among the working class are now found in the middle class. In order to explore this we look first at partnered, working-class respondents and then at partnered, middle-class respondents. The reason we are taking partnered respondents is for purposes of comparison with the original study.

Working class

The original study found that, among partnered respondents in the working class, contact between mothers and daughters was more frequent than that between fathers and sons. It also found that relations between a husband and his wife's kin were closer than those between a husband and his own kin, and that, within the extended family, husbands lived closer to their wives' than to their own kin. In other words, there was a bias towards the wife's side of the family in both residence and contact which was termed uxorilocality. In 2002 we found that working-class husbands lived closer to their mothers-in-law than did working-class wives to theirs; a finding which confirms a continuing uxorilocal bias. We also found that contact with own kin was highest between mothers and daughters, followed closely by sons and mothers and by fathers and daughters. It was lowest between fathers and sons. Further, contact with partner's kin was highest between husbands and their mothers-in-law and fathers-in-law, followed by wives with their mothers-in-law. Contact was lowest between wives and their fathers-in-law. In the original study Rosser and Harris concluded that working-class husbands were more closely involved with their wife's kin than with their own but that, despite this involvement, they retained close links with their own kin.

Middle class

In contrast to the working class, Rosser and Harris concluded that 'the middle-class family shows a very even balance in the strength of relationships between parents and sons and daughters' (1965, 220–21). In a kinship system based on uxorilocal residence, the relationships between a daughter (wife) and her parents would be stronger than between a son (husband) and his parents. So what the 1960 study is saying is that the bias of the couple towards wife's kin, characteristic of the working class, is absent in the middle class. In 1960 there was a slight difference between weekly contact rates for middle-class daughters and parents and middle-class sons and parents. In 2002, however, there is a major difference between sons' and daughters' contact rates with their mothers. The highest frequency of contact is found between mothers and daughters but the lowest is not between father and son, as it was in 1960, but between mother and son. This difference does not relate to geographical distance between middle-class sons and mothers but, in our view, to changes in the occupational structure and the transformation of gender relations within the domestic group. Changes in the occupational structure between 1960 and 2002 have led to an increase in the degree of upward occupational mobility over the life course. This means that the middle class now contains a proportion of older people who have moved rapidly up the occupational ladder, carrying with them the tendency to exhibit the relatively low rate of mother–son contact characteristic of the 1960 study's 'working class'. Since even today partnership is likely to precede the attainment of relatively high occupational status, this effect is likely to be exaggerated by the fact that the 2002 sample, as we have seen, is older than the 1960 sample: a greater proportion of respondents in 2002 will have had time for substantial life-course mobility.

The figures also suggest a transformation of gender relations within the domestic group. Thus, middle-class partnered sons have a negative bias to their own kin. This negative bias is unequalled even by working-class sons' relations with their fathers. They also show that husbands have the highest rate of contact with spouse's parents and that middle-class wives have the highest positive bias to their own kin. These figures suggest a changing balance of power within the middle-class marital household. This can best be explained by changes in the occupational structure and increases in women's participation in the workforce.

There has therefore been an important change between the studies. Middle-class sons are seeing mothers less and fathers more. Working-class sons are seeing mothers more and fathers less. Other relationships show little change. In other words, the patterns of relationship in the two classes, though still different, have become more like each other. Thus 'the very even balance of middle class families between sons and daughters' observed by Rosser and Harris (1965, 220) now only exists for middle-class sons' and daughters' contact with fathers; the emphasis is now on the mother–daughter tie, as it is in the working class, an emphasis which has arisen because of the significant decline in middle-class sons' contact with mothers. For all sets of relationships (with the exception of middle-class sons' and daughters' contact with fathers) daughters' contact with parents is higher than that of sons. The class patterns identified by Rosser and Harris in 1960 have therefore changed such that the emphasis on daughters' ties with parents can now be seen throughout the class structure rather than being a characteristic only of the working class (see Table 3.9). In addition, the pattern of relatively high involvement of working-class husbands with their wives' kin is still in evidence and is now found among middle-class husbands.

Table 3.9: Frequency of contact with parents by social class of subject, 1960 and 2002

Married (1960)/partnered (2002) subjects only (%)

	Mothers				Fathers			
	Middle classes		Working classes		Middle classes		Working classes	
	Sons	Daughters	Sons	Daughters	Sons	Daughters	Sons	Daughters
1960								
Within 24 hours	39	44	27	**56**	37	39	26	**48**
24 hours–1 week	35	32	43	27	26	28	45	31
Total % in 1 week	74	76	70	**83**	63	67	71	**79**
2002								
Within 24 hours	16	41	36	41	29	27	23	**40**
24 hours–1 week	39	33	42	41	38	37	40	37.5
Total % in 1 week	55	74	78	82	67	64	63	**77.5**

Note: Bold figures highlight highest frequencies.
Source: Rosser and Harris, 1965, 220, Table 6.4

Cultural identity

There was also a difference between the 'Welsh' and the 'non-Welsh' in patterns of residence and contact. In the baseline study Rosser and Harris constructed a 'Welsh' category by asking about respondents' and respondents' parents' ability to speak Welsh. If either the respondent or one of their parents was Welsh-speaking, either fluently or partly, then the respondent was deemed to be culturally Welsh, that is, they had a Welsh-language background. Those who came from an English-language background were defined as non-Welsh; Rosser and Harris neither assumed nor asked questions about their self-identification as

Welsh. In the restudy we included the same questions for purposes of comparison and, using this constructed Welsh category, we found (as anticipated) that the proportion of the survey sample who were Welsh had declined between 1960 and 2002 from 46% to 33%. In the baseline study no significant differences in patterns of residence and contact between the 'Welsh' and the 'non-Welsh' had been found. In the restudy, however, we found that 'Welsh' daughters tended to live closer to their parents than 'non-Welsh' daughters and that 'Welsh' daughters' contact with their mothers was higher than that of 'non-Welsh' daughters. 'Welsh' respondents had also seen their siblings slightly more frequently than had the 'non-Welsh'. There is, however, a problem in drawing firm conclusions from this data, given that the 'non-Welsh' category of the 2002 sample includes a higher proportion of respondents who have moved to Swansea from outside Wales than does the original study. This may increase the differences between the 'Welsh' and 'non-Welsh' categories as those who are more geographically mobile are likely to be included in the 'non-Welsh' category. These methodological problems notwithstanding, it seems that our findings may point to cultural differences in family practices which define Welshness and non-Welshness. This issue is explored in more detail in Chapter 4.

Increased occupational differentiation within kinship groups

The trend towards occupational heterogeneity within kinship groups identified in the 1960s study is confirmed by our research. As we have seen, there has been a slight increase in geographical dispersion, but what is particularly striking is the increased occupational differentiation which is characteristic not only of extended kin groups but also of heterosexual couples. Rosser and Harris (1965) noted increasing occupational heterogeneity within extended families, specifically between fathers and sons. Since 1960 there has been considerable change in the industrial and occupational structure of Swansea which has resulted in an increasingly differentiated occupational structure. This, together with women's increased labour market participation, must of necessity generate greater occupational intergenerational heterogeneity within extended family networks, whether or not occupational mobility between generations has also taken place. This can be seen if we compare respondents' and their fathers' occupations. In the original study 31% of male respondents were in different occupational classes from their fathers (classified according to the Registrar General's Occupational

Classification). The corresponding figure for 2002 is 56% and for all respondents is 65% (a comparison of women's and their fathers' occupations was not made in the original study). This increase should not be seen as an indication of massive social mobility because of the changes in the occupational structure which have taken place in the intervening period. Rather, it is the change in the occupational structure which has increased the differentiation within Swansea's potential kin groupings as measured by fathers' and sons' occupations.

The chief change in the occupational structure relates to the greater economic activity levels of women; 69% of our women respondents under retirement age were economically active as compared with 78% of men. As we have seen, 59.2% of our respondents were partnered at the time of the survey and of them just over a third were couples where both partners were in employment: 58% of this third had partners of different occupational statuses. This figure may be compared with the figure of 65% for different statuses between respondents and living fathers in the 2002 sample, and the figure for all fathers and sons cited above for the 1960 sample of 31%. A more detailed analysis shows that the differentiation within kinship groups noted by Rosser and Harris now extends to the heart of the elementary family and, in a significant proportion of couples where both partners are in paid employment (36%), women's occupational status is higher than that of their partners. Just under half of this 36% were in the 'traditional' situation of heterosexual couples where women's jobs are of higher status than men's, that is, where the man is in a manual occupation (IIIM) and the woman in a clerical occupation (IIIN). There is also evidence of a generational trend towards an increasing likelihood of women's occupational status being higher than that of their partners and a decreasing likelihood of this difference being of the 'traditional' kind (see Charles and Harris, 2007 for a more detailed analysis). These findings suggest that the trend towards increasing differentiation within extended family networks, identified by Rosser and Harris, has continued and is now to be found within the reproductive partnership at the heart of the elementary family as well as in the wider kinship network. They also tie in with the changing patterns of contact between middle-class sons and their parents and parents-in-law and our view that this can be explained by changes in the occupational structure and the related transformation of gender relations within domestic groups.

Discussion

What this discussion shows is that, although a smaller proportion of the population is engaged in partnering and parenting in 2002, for those that are there has been remarkably little change in patterns of residence and contact between 1960 and 2002. This is particularly evident in contact between mothers and their adult daughters which remains the most frequent; it is still the case that women are at the heart of kinship networks.

There has, however, been a continuing decline in residential and occupational homogeneity. The increase in geographical mobility has resulted in a widening of the geographical range of kin which could be interpreted as a disembedding of kinship networks from place; this process has both class and gender dimensions, with men being less likely than women, and middle-class respondents less likely than their working-class counterparts, to have parents living in Swansea. There has also been a fall in the frequency of contact between siblings which weakens the potential extended family grouping and, hence, the kin-connectedness of society. Furthermore, occupational differentiation has increased and can now be found within the elementary as well as extended family. This increased occupational differentiation is also associated with signs of a transformation in gender relations within domestic groups such that occupational inequality between heterosexual partners is reduced. Thus, the trend of increasing heterogeneity within families which was identified in the baseline study has continued and is underpinned by women's increasing participation in the workforce and the structural changes that make this possible. Women's increasing employment, however, does not necessarily reduce kin-connectedness and can be associated with more frequent contact because of the need for help with childcare. This is explored more fully in Chapter 6.

Despite these changes, the majority of our respondents continue to live near to kin and to see each other frequently, although these patterns vary by class and gender and, to some extent, ethnicity. In the next chapter we explore the ways in which these patterns relate to cultural identity, how personal and cultural identities relate to family practices, and the importance of tradition to the reproduction of cultural identity within families.

Note
[1] Potential extended family grouping refers to those kin from whom an extended family grouping might be formed.

FOUR

Families and cultural identity

In the last chapter we explored the degree to which societal change since 1960 has affected the connectedness of kin networks. We found that, in spite of the increased heterogeneity of extended family networks, in terms of both residence and occupation, most of our respondents still lived close to other members of their extended family and had regular contact with them. Looking at their patterns of residence and contact more carefully revealed some differences, with both 'Welsh' and working-class respondents being likely to live closer to their parents and to see them more frequently than their 'non-Welsh' and middle-class counterparts. For Rosser and Harris investigating family practices in Swansea in 1960, cultural identity had these two salient dimensions of class and Welshness, and cultural differentiation, along with occupational and geographical differentiation, was associated with decreasing solidarity within families. The cultural diversity of Swansea in 2002 is considerably more complex and the potential for increased cultural heterogeneity correspondingly greater. In this chapter we consider how different ways of 'doing' family symbolise different cultural identities and whether families continue to provide a sense of identity for their members. Families and identities, both personal and collective, are interrelated in a complex fashion. Thus, family forms and family relationships, particularly the influence of parents on children, shape the personal identities of their members while broader collective identities – such as those based on ethnicity and class – affect the ways in which families are organised. This chapter explores these relationships between families and cultural identities and how they have changed over the past 40 years. First, however, we discuss the way class and cultural identities relate to our four ethnographic areas and the different patterns of family formation which characterise them.

Place and cultural identity

Rosser and Harris noted that the distinctive neighbourhoods with strong local identities that they found in Swansea were frequently used by their respondents as symbols of class distinctions, with those in the west of Swansea being associated with 'social superiority' and those in the east with a lower social class; they felt that their respondents' tendency to speak of class using a simple twofold division into middle and working class was 'reinforced by the basic geographical dichotomy of Swansea into east and west in the popular image of the town' (1965, 86). This dichotomy, which is related to the occupational structure and economic history of different parts of the city, persists today in spite of the significant changes in the industrial structure, and is reflected in the differences between our four ethnographic areas, with Fairview and Parkfields identified as west and Treforgan and Pen-cwm as east Swansea. However, we have to stress – as indeed did Rosser and Harris – that these broad identifications linking class, as well as ethnicity ('Welshness' in the 1960 study), with location gloss over the very substantial internal complexities of these localities.

We have already described the characteristics of these four ethnographic areas in Chapter 2, looking at how they differ in their occupational structures, economic activity rates and distribution of housing types; we also noted their differences in terms of cultural indicators, in particular, the ethnic composition of the population and the prevalence of Welsh speaking which was the indicator of 'Welshness' used in the baseline study. Moreover, our different ethnographic areas demonstrate variations in patterns of family formation and kinship networks. Thus, broadly speaking, in the relatively affluent, middle-class area of Fairview, families generally consisted of a heterosexual couple where the man was the main provider and the woman the main carer. In the older industrial area, Treforgan, families also consisted of heterosexual couples but there seemed to be more frequent interaction with extended kin. In the inner-city area, Parkfields, amongst the Bangladeshi population, men were central to kinship networks as providers and heads of extended family households. This pattern was modified in some cases, with sons and their partners forming separate households in the same street as their parents. There were also more single-person households. In the socioeconomically deprived area of Pen-Cwm, men were notable by their absence from kin groups as well as their lack of participation in paid employment; women and their mothers and children were at the heart of kin groups, and kinship networks extended between households. In this area the structure of kin groups was that of strong intergenerational and inter-household ties between women.

These differences relate to differences in class and culture, with those areas which were more working class and/or Welsh being characterised by a greater frequency of contact between kin. They were also reflected in how interviewees talked about their own families, the areas in which they lived, and their identification in terms of wider collectivities, such as those based on class and ethnicity. We now turn our attention to the ways in which these collective identities are imagined and experienced by our interviewees and their relationship to different ways of 'doing' family. We begin with a review of the most significant cultural identities present in our dataset, explaining how we investigated these identities, how they have altered since the original baseline study in 1960 and how their representations differed across our ethnographic areas. We then consider how these cultural identities both influence and are influenced by family practices and examine culturally based ideas about family associated with these collectivities. Culturally determined expressions of family are transmitted through, and have an impact on, individual family members and we look at such familial influences on personal identities. Finally, we recognise that individuals within families often identify with different cultural traditions, families frequently are not 'pure' representations of a given culture, and we consider how families 'do' culture under such circumstances. This allows us to consider the effects of cultural differentiation on family solidarity.

Cultural identities in Swansea, 1960 and 2002

In their study of extended family networks in Swansea in the early 1960s, Rosser and Harris looked at how they might be affected by the horizontal divisions of social class. They also considered a vertical division of the population based on cultural difference between the 'Welsh' on the one hand and the 'non-Welsh' on the other and compared these various collectivities, determined by class and culture, on a wide range of factors relevant for understanding the nature of family and kinship relations. In order to examine the behavioural attributes of these divisions of class and culture, they first had to define them so as to be able to assign individual respondents to a social class and a cultural collectivity ('Welsh' or 'non-Welsh').

They found class determination based on occupational criteria to be problematic and, as we described in Chapter 2, developed a procedure that incorporated both occupational mobility and self-assessment into their determinations. This allowed for class to be as much about values, attitudes and styles of living as it was about income and occupation. It also produced an 'in between' group, comprising 36% of their respondents, whose class position was ambiguous and whose cultural identity was less secure. Given the increase in occupational mobility over the past 40 years, along with the influence of public debate about a classless society, we have found the determination of class to be equally, if not more, problematic as there is an increased reluctance to adopt a class identity; this is something that other researchers have also observed (Savage et al, 2001). Here we consider how people discuss class, in particular how they assess their own class positions and how this relates to family and cultural identities.

Class

In the 1960 survey, respondents' self-assessments of class suggested that the vast majority (93%) operated with a model of two classes, working and middle. However, a comparison of respondents' self-assessments with their occupations revealed widely varying ideas behind how they assigned class membership and called into question this twofold model as accurately representing their interpretations of class. Thus, Rosser and Harris found both solicitors and shop assistants describing themselves as middle class, both university lecturers and dock workers saying they were working class. The evidence from their ethnographic interviews (1965, 82–5) revealed the complexities of the thinking behind informants' interpretations of social class and the range of cultural indicators that informants drew upon in applying the label 'working class' or 'middle class' to themselves or others. In the 2002 survey we asked the same question about self-assessment of social class and found that the difficulties some respondents apparently experienced in selecting a conventional class label that had been observed in 1960 had escalated, so that by 2002 the percentage of respondents in the survey who said they did not know or refused to answer the question had increased from 2.6% to 13.5%; those who gave a description that could not be linked to a conventional class label had increased from 4.4% to 11.3%.[1] There was virtually no difference in the responses of men and women to this question (see Table 4.1). Furthermore, as the table makes clear, the vast majority (75%) of our respondents did

Table 4.1: Self-assessment of social class by survey respondents (%)

Class label	1960[1]			2002		
	Men	Women	Total	Men	Women	Total
Middle	32	36	33.6	32.0	32.6	32.3
Working	62	57	59.5	43.2	42.6	42.9
Other	4	5	4.4	12.2	10.6	11.3
Refuse/Don't know	2	2	2.6	12.6	14.2	13.5

Note: [1] 1960 figures calculated from Rosser and Harris, 1965, 86.

provide an unambiguous class identification, with 42.9% identifying as working class, a drop of 16.3% from 1960, and 32.3% identifying as middle class, a decrease of only 1.3% since 1960. Our ethnographic data provide an insight into the meanings people give to these class labels and their reasons for selecting or rejecting them.

Our ethnographic research revealed considerable variation – in terms of social indicators such as occupation and income – among those who identified themselves as either working or middle class. To a degree, locality appeared to affect interviewees' self-assessments of class: for example, two women in Treforgan who worked as a secretary and a teaching assistant described themselves as working class; in Fairview women in the same occupations said they were middle class; and in Parkfields and Pen-cwm the self-assessments of women in these occupations were divided between working and middle class. Thus, it is likely that local understandings of the character of particular neighbourhoods and communities, which probably relate to the east–west division noted by Rosser and Harris, have an effect on self-assessments of class. Indeed several of our interviewees, when asked about social class, discussed it entirely in terms of different neighbourhoods. One woman, who said she did not think in terms of class and that it was just 'snobbery', nevertheless admitted that when they had lived in another neighbourhood, similar to Pen-cwm, she 'was embarrassed to tell people I lived [there] … But it's just because people look down at you' (Female, 30, Parkfields). Another interviewee compared three different neighbourhoods, including the one where she was currently living, but without using class terminology. Her initial response was hesitant.

> I don't know. I don't think about it.… I feel I fit in. I feel, although Alan [her husband] was saying 'Don't fit in down here', I didn't fit in, in [middle-class area], I didn't fit in there. [*Oh, right. So, you weren't at home there?*] Not quite. I know where I feel completely at home would be an area like [neighbourhood bordering Parkfields]. I don't know why. I seem to get on with people very well up there.… There's a lot of racism down here, which I don't like. I find that difficult. (Female, 52, Parkfields)

Family background was also a significant factor in self-assessments of class. Many of our interviewees felt that, in order to explain their class position, they had to clarify not just their current circumstances but those of their families of origin. One married couple, in their late 60s, whose economic circumstances, occupation prior to retirement and residential location (in Fairview) would all be considered solidly middle class, debated between themselves whether they were working class or 'lower middle class' and discussed their class identity in terms of their respective natal families' circumstances and political background:

> *Wife*: I wouldn't like to say that I'm not working class because we come from strong Labour working-class backgrounds.... I wouldn't like to deny our work backgrounds, either of us. My father was a miner. Leighton's [her husband's] father was a red. (Female, 67, Fairview)

Another woman contrasted her husband's background, which she described as 'middle-class upbringing, with very fortunate parents', with her own rural roots:

> My upbringing was far lower. We had a farm, my parents were not wealthy, we didn't have the opportunity. There was no opportunity to go to university, they couldn't afford for any of us four children to go to university, so therefore we had to find jobs. (Female, 63, Fairview)

She regarded her current middle-class identity as deriving from her marriage.

Others who did specify a class position in accordance with their occupation nevertheless made it clear that they regarded this as being closely linked to cultural difference rather than simply socioeconomic indicators. For example, a primary school head teacher acknowledged that her occupation placed her in the middle class but, like many of our informants, resisted this classification on the grounds of her family background:

> I was obviously born working class. I obviously have, if you are thinking in more, sort of, social categories, typical of Welsh working class, aspired to be a teacher and so on. Typical class sort of thing. In lots of ways it's ... to me, see, I'm not a fan of class. It's one thing I don't like really. (Female, 58, Treforgan)

As with our survey respondents, a significant proportion of our interviewees responded to our question about their social class with comments that avoided conventional working- or middle-class labels.

This tendency was evident across all four of our ethnographic study areas (see Table 4.2 for a breakdown by age group and gender for each area) and was particularly apparent in Pen-cwm – the area with the highest level of social deprivation – where over one-third of our ethnographic interviewees rejected any conventional class label, preferring to describe themselves as 'normal', 'down to earth' or 'definitely not snobby'. In part, this was linked to the large number of interviewees who were unemployed, and was especially widespread among young women, some of whom had never been employed. Thus, one woman who was unemployed, when asked about her social class, said 'Not working class any more, common' (Female, 34, Pen-cwm). And her friend, who was being interviewed with her, also unemployed, elaborated:

> I wouldn't think I was better than anybody else, you know, if somebody is, you know, better off than me or hasn't got as much or whatever, I wouldn't say, 'Look I've got more than you so I'm better than you'. No, I wouldn't have thought so. (Female, 31, Pen-cwm)

These responses suggest a rejection of conventional class labels as a defensive reaction by interviewees to a concept that threatens to undermine them as individuals, something that other researchers have also observed (Reay, 1998; Savage et al, 2001). A second group of interviewees, mainly found in the other three ethnographic areas, also refused to assign a class label to themselves, but their reasons for this were very different from those quoted above, tending to be based on general arguments rejecting the concept of class. For example, nearly one-fifth of our interviewees in Fairview, the most middle class of our four areas, were unwilling to assign themselves a conventional class label, frequently going on to question the meaning and significance of class: 'I don't, for me it doesn't exist. Because I just think it's a ridiculous thing. Class' (Female, 47, Fairview); or to reject assigning any such label to themselves: 'I never really categorise myself, I don't know' (Male, 41, Fairview). Another interviewee, living in Treforgan, said that he was 'classless', then elaborated:

> I don't think it's the slightest bit important. I've seen people try to be very self important and I've, how can I put it? I'd been perhaps having lunch with well, 2 or 3 members of the House of Lords, Army Officer or whatever the case may be and they're all Bert, Fred, John and whatever. There's no question of any rank or anything involved. The ones

involved in rank are usually the ones that are very insecure, you know? They are the ones that are so important although they've got their stripes on their, on their shoulders or whatever the case may be. But they, they consider that that's important. I couldn't care less. It doesn't worry me in the slightest, you know. (Male, 78, Treforgan)

Table 4.2: Self-assessment of social class by ethnographic interviewees[1] (number, % in brackets) by area, age group and gender

	Age under 40		Age 40-60		Age over 60		Totals
	Male	Female	Male	Female	Male	Female	(%)
Fairview (n=55)							
Middle	4	6	3	8	4	3	28 (51%)
Between[2]	2	3	-	-	2	5	12 (22%)
Working	-	1	2	1	1	-	5 (9%)
Other[3]	-	1	1	3	3	2	10 (18%)
Parkfields (n=43)							
Middle	1	6	2	2	2	2	15 (35%)
Between[2]	-	1	-	1	-	-	2 (5%)
Working	-	2	2	1	3	5	13 (30%)
Other[3]	-	6	3	4	-	-	13 (30%)
Pen-cwm (n=53)							
Middle	-	-	1	2	1	1	5 (9%)
Between[2]	-	-	-	-	1	-	1 (2%)
Working	4	9	1	4	6	-	24 (45%)
Other[3]	-	11	4	3	2	2	22 (42%)
Upper	-	1	-	-	-	-	1 (2%)
Treforgan (n=32)							
Middle	1	1	1	1	2	2	8 (25%)
Between[2]	-	1	1	1	1	-	4 (13%)
Working	-	3	2	6	4	2	17 (53%)
Other[3]	-	-	-	-	2	1	3 (9%)

Notes:
[1] Totals do not include a small number of informants who were not asked about social class
[2] Informants used conventional class labels but saw their own position as intermediate
[3] Informants refused the class concept, used other labels (e.g. 'normal')

This second form of rejection of class labels has also been reported in other studies. In particular, Savage et al found a similar dichotomy among their interviewees in a study carried out in the Manchester area: 'The main variation in the way people responded to questions on class identity was between those who had the cultural capital to play around reflexively with ideas of class, compared to those who felt threatened by the idea of class and lacked the cultural confidence to reflect on these terms' (2001, 885).

Besides these two groups, we also found a group – the majority of our interviewees – who were comfortable identifying with one of the conventional class labels. Again, these individuals were to be found in all our ethnographic areas, but Treforgan was the area where the proportion of interviewees unable or unwilling to identify themselves in terms of class was lowest, less than one-tenth, and over half unambiguously defined themselves as working class. This is probably linked to the industrial history of the area; some of our interviewees referred either to the nature of their own work or to a family history of employment in the heavy industry of the Upper Swansea Valley. Thus, one man in his fifties, who had moved into management and described his lifestyle, referring particularly to his house and his new BMW, as a 'sort of middle class living', nevertheless emphasised his working-class origins based in his industrial occupation:

> I'm an industrial worker. We are a dirty worker, aren't we? You are a dirty worker.... I'm in dirty work. All right. I'm staff and I'm middle management staff, right? That's my grading. I am middle management but I still look at myself as no one. I've come from the shop floor. I've been down there. I've worked down there. (Male, 50, Treforgan)

Thus, our ethnographic data suggest that, while the majority still relate to conventional class labels, those who have experienced occupational mobility often find it difficult to identify unambiguously as either working or middle class, and they often develop a discourse about their family of origin and its effect on their assessments of their class identity. Furthermore, there are two categories of interviewees who reject conventional class labels: those who seem to do so as a defensive measure because of the personally undermining nature of such assessments; and those who have the confidence to play with the concept of class, using this strategy 'to try to evade social fixing' (Savage et al, 2001, 889). Another category of interviewees, those with origins from outside Britain, also found it difficult to address the issue of class labelling, often commenting on the cultural dimensions of class. Thus, one of our interviewees, who was from Italy, when asked whether she thought of herself in terms of class, said:

> I've been asking this question to myself much more often since I came to Britain. Because I think Britain is more, it's part of their culture, they think of social class much more than we tend to do, at least in Italy. (Female, 31, Fairview)

Another, from Bangladesh said,

> Well, class, the British people, they make the class. See? My opinion, everybody human being, everybody in one class and British, they make the class. (Male, 47, Parkfields)

And several other Bangladeshi interviewees said they found it easier to place themselves in terms of Bangladeshi social divisions.

The complexity of interviewees' interpretations of class, and their interrelationship with culture, locality and ethnicity, is strikingly illustrated by the only one of our interviewees who claimed to be 'upper' class, a 32-year-old unemployed woman living in Pen-cwm. This woman, who described herself as 'definitely English', explained her class position almost entirely in terms of her speech style, contrasting the way she spoke with the language of her Welsh partner and his friends: 'it's like, well, effing this and effing that, you know everybody is like swearing and the language that comes out'. She went on to explain:

> I am upper class, because of the way, how I speak, and everything, people, I am upper class. I don't like to say that I am, but I'm not, I am upper class. Because of the way I was brought up and everything as well. [*Yeah. So do you think that's the way people see you?*] People, oh yeah, a lot of people don't know how to interact with me because of the way, how I talk, and the way, how I speak, people don't know how to interact with me sometimes. People think I should say, 'oh, dunno', do you know what I mean, as long as, if I'm swearing and mouthing off and stuff, that's how most people are around here. You know because I don't mouth off and I say 'yes, please' and 'no, thank you', you know, and all this kind of thing, people don't know how to interact with me. [*Yeah. So in a way you are different from them.*] I'm different from them, and some people don't understand

me, 'Oh where do you come from?' You know, and all this kind of thing. (Female, 32, Pen–cwm)

Ethnicity

The emphasis on speech style and accent, as in the above example, was used by other interviewees when discussing cultural difference, in particular Welsh cultural identity. Hence the following exchange with an interviewee, a Welsh speaker, who was born and had lived all his life in Wales: [*Would you say you were Welsh?*] 'Definitely.' [*Can you explain why to me?*] 'I think I might have a Welsh accent' [grinning] (Male, 40, Treforgan). Some interviewees regarded a local Welsh accent as a negative cultural marker and associated proper speech with English identity. For example, a 74-year-old man from Fairview, who identified as 'Welsh by birth, but I regard myself as European', reported making common cause with English evacuees during the war:

> My allegiance should have been with the Welsh, but it wasn't. I think it had to do with the way they spoke. In my household when I was quite small, it was very important to speak correctly. You know, if you spoke badly, it was common. It was described as being common. Like they do in Swansea. (Male, 74, Fairview)

This leads us to the second salient cultural division that was considered in the baseline study, that between the 'Welsh' and the 'non-Welsh'. As we have already seen (Chapter 3), in order to place respondents in one of these two collectivities, Rosser and Harris used a procedure based on two dimensions: Welsh-speaking ability of the respondent and Welsh-speaking ability of the respondent's parents. In contrast to their procedure for determining class, they did not include the dimension of self-assessment, remarking that they were 'not here concerned with Welsh as a nationality ... but with Welsh as a distinctive regional culture within Britain' (1965, 118). Thus, respondents were deemed culturally 'Welsh' if either they or at least one parent were Welsh speaking, fluently or partly. This produced a 'Welsh' category of 896 (46% of the sample) and a 'non-Welsh' category of 1,061 (54%). Although Rosser and Harris did sometimes refer to their 'non-Welsh' category as 'English', they recognised that this large collectivity was 'a very mixed bag of English, Irish, and Scots immigrants (or their descendants) together with a substantial – and annually increasing – proportion of anglicized Welsh at least "twice removed" by the test of language from Welsh cultural traditions' (1965, 121). When we applied the Rosser and Harris definitions of 'Welsh' and 'non-Welsh' to the 2002 survey, we found a 'Welsh' category of 331 (33.5%) and a 'non-Welsh' category of 658 (66.5%).

Since the 1960s the theoretical treatment of ethnic and cultural difference has shifted from a focus on cultural indicators (such as language, religion, food practices, etc) that might identify ethnic groups to an interest in how individuals understand, and indeed construct, their ethnic and cultural identities, which are assumed to be multiple, and how these identities affect social interaction. For this reason, in the 2002 survey we included questions designed to provide some insight into the self-assessment of respondents' identity in terms of their identification with Welshness and any alternative, or complementary, ethnic or cultural identities. These questions were as follows:

- Do you consider yourself to be Welsh?
- Do you consider that you have any other cultural, ethnic or national identity?
- If yes, what is this identity?

A large majority of our respondents, 78.8%, identified as Welsh, and 81.6% of these did not lay claim to any other 'cultural, ethnic or national identity'. That is, 64.3% of the entire sample identified as Welsh only. Among the category that we constructed as culturally 'Welsh', following Rosser and Harris (that is, respondents who spoke Welsh or had a Welsh-speaking parent), a significantly higher percentage, 92.4%, identified as Welsh. This was slightly higher again (94.7%) among fluent Welsh speakers but slightly lower (91.0%) among all Welsh speakers. Among the 314 respondents who selected another 'cultural, ethnic or national' identity – whether they identified as Welsh or not – the most frequent choice was 'British' (44.3%), followed by 'English' (25.8%) and 'Scottish, Irish or other European identity' (13.3%).

Turning to our ethnographic data, there was a noticeable contrast in the relative ease with which our interviewees discussed their cultural identity as compared to their responses to the questions about social class. Fewer than 4% responded in ways that suggested they rejected the concept of cultural identity and, in two of the four ethnographic case study areas (Treforgan and Parkfields), no one refused to engage with our questions about Welshness and other cultural identities. Furthermore, the responses in this section of the interview tended to be comparatively fuller than in our discussions of class. Among our ethnographic interviewees, 61% said they were Welsh and did not invoke any other cultural identity, while another 9% described themselves as Welsh with another identity (usually British). The fact that these percentages are slightly lower than our survey results is probably due to the fact that we deliberately sought a disproportionately high number of minority ethnic interviewees in one of our study areas (Parkfields). As with class identity, there was some variation across the four case study areas but it was much less pronounced. For example, the percentages of those claiming only Welsh identity were 73% in Treforgan, 67% in Pen-cwm, 55% in Fairview and 53% in Parkfields. These differences reflect the different cultural make-up of the areas, with Treforgan generally regarded as being more 'Welsh' than Fairview, both Treforgan and Pen-cwm having relatively higher percentages of people born in Swansea, and Parkfields having a larger minority ethnic population.

Our ethnographic data allow us to look behind these statistics for a better understanding of the meanings people attach to these various identities, as well as their reasons for selecting or rejecting them. There was considerable variation in how people responded to this question, ranging from those who said unequivocally that they were Welsh to those who rejected the idea of ethnicity (or nationality) altogether. Some of the latter seemed almost to adopt a self-consciously 'cosmopolitan' position on issues of cultural identity, particularly if they had moved about a lot. One told us that he thought of himself as European: 'You got to be, a European is just [laughs] an awareness that Britain isn't the centre of the world and that we are actually on this corner of the world where there are lots of other cultures and countries as well' (Male, 41, Fairview).

Several interviewees claimed a British identity for similar reasons, using it as a way of rejecting 'separatism' rather than having a sense of Britishness as the basis for a cultural identity.

> Yes, I am Welsh, but I consider myself Welsh but British. To me it's a load of nonsense splitting up the country. We should be living in harmony as British people. Altogether, as a family. Not splitting up. To me it's more important, I think these nationalists coming, look what it's cost in this country, having signs in Welsh, you know, what have you. (Male, 75, Fairview)

Others saw British identity as a convenient label for what they regarded as mixed parentage or as a recognition of the hybrid background of the Welsh population more generally.

> I'm Welsh–Scottish. Half-and-half blood, born in Wales, I'm Welsh. Yeah it's, you know, to fill in forms or anything, nationality, I usually, British. Yeah British I'd say first. I see all of us as British not just separate, but saying that, British, but if I go to Spain or somewhere, and usually you know they say, 'You're English', and I say, 'No, I'm not English, I'm Welsh'. Yeah. They just see everyone from Britain as English, but British really, yeah. (Female, 45, Pen-cwm)

As with discussions of class, interviewees often responded to our questions about ethnicity by reflecting on their ancestry, mainly their parents and grandparents, although others did not view ancestry as determinative and instead spoke of becoming Welsh, some using the metaphor of adoption, others by virtue of length of residence.

> I'm English, but I feel more Welsh than English, do you know that? And I often think I'd like to be known as an English lady that became a Welsh lady. Because I'm more Welsh than English. How long have I been down here? For over sixty years. That's a long time, isn't it? (Female, 89, Fairview)

This tendency to negotiate identity with reference to place of birth, ancestry and residence, as did so many of our interviewees, as well as the flexibility they displayed in the application of these considerations, has also been observed in a study of Scottish identity which looked at the way this identity was negotiated by arts and landed elites (McCrone et al, 1998), both groups having been involved in recent controversies about the effect of English incomers on Scottish institutions.

Welsh identity

There were three main themes in the meanings that people attached to Welsh identity: the importance of the Welsh language for Welsh identity; the expression of Welsh identity through support for national sports teams, especially rugby; and opposition to English, or occasionally British, identity. For those who spoke Welsh, the language was usually quite a prominent feature in their explanation of why they considered themselves to be Welsh. One woman said she was Welsh, 'Because I was born in Wales and I speak Welsh. Welsh is my first language' (Female, 57, Treforgan). Another said,

I speak Welsh. I'm very much a part of Welsh culture. I went to a Welsh primary school and a Welsh secondary school. I went to the only university, well, in the world I guess, who offer courses or a lot of their courses through the medium of Welsh. I protest quite a bit for the language, especially for university to try and get more modules or more diversity of choices through the medium of Welsh. (Female, 20, Treforgan)

Others, also Welsh speakers, emphasised that

Well, I come from a, a Welsh-speaking family. Well, but I, I don't believe, people think that they're more Welsh because they, they can speak the language but I, I, me personally, I don't, I don't think. Of course it's a form of Welshness but one person without being, being able to speak the language can feel just as passionate or if not more passionate about being Welsh with not being able to speak the Welsh language. (Male, 40, Treforgan)

Very many of our interviewees, in claiming Welsh identity, felt obliged to explain their relationship to the Welsh language in terms of competence as well as their attitude towards it. One said,

I am Welsh. And I feel ashamed of myself that I don't speak Welsh. Unfortunately I put that down to education. Education policy at school, there is no point starting teaching languages at eleven, and this is a very un-Welsh-speaking area. (Female, 34, Fairview)

Another, asked whether he saw himself as Welsh, told us,

Yes. Even though I sort of go into Welsh mother and toddlers and not being able to speak Welsh is embarrassing, I've always said, I feel I ought to speak Welsh if I call myself Welsh. And I've always said I'm going to learn, but I get nowhere.... But yeah, I still see myself as Welsh even though I can't necessarily speak Welsh. (Male, 33, Fairview)

Most of our interviewees regarded the Welsh language as a positive attribute of Welshness and included some reference to it in their expressions of Welsh identity, often an explanation of why they did not speak Welsh, sometimes just an expression of support for the language. They did not, however, maintain that inability to speak Welsh disqualified them from claiming a Welsh identity, in the way that interviewees frequently did regarding ancestral roots outside Wales. Most seemed to have a proprietary view of the language, regarding it as part of their identity whether they were Welsh speaking or not. Two interviewees, both non-Welsh speakers, made specific reference to Welsh road signs as a symbol of home: 'When I come over the Severn Bridge and I see the signs in Welsh, I'm happy' (Female, 67, Fairview); and

> I'm Welsh and I'm proud that I'm Welsh. When I go over to England, because I mean I do travel around the country, when I go across to England, I say uh, that's England, but as soon as I come to it, I say yes I'm home. As soon as you see that Welsh sign you're home. Yeah. Very important that I'm Welsh. I mean I don't speak Welsh. (Female, 37, Pen-cwm)

There were a few who were not so positive about the language. One of our working-class interviewees, for instance, said that she hated the Welsh language; this mainly seemed to express her frustration at being unable to speak it, even though 'I've always wanted that, but I just can't get hold of, you know, the language. I couldn't do it in school' (Female, 34, Pen-cwm). And one of our middle-class interviewees, although a Welsh speaker herself, did not see it as useful in terms of children's education and aspirations. The vast majority of those who claimed a Welsh identity, however, referred to the language in positive terms.

The second prominent theme raised in our discussions of Welsh identity was sports, particularly rugby, with interviewees often using support for national teams as a kind of touchstone of identity (cf Jones, 2003). One man said he was 'as Welsh as the hills', an identity he shared with his father 'because he is part of the culture, the rugby and stuff like that, and you know I've grown up in that as well' (Male, 31, Pen-cwm).

Others used the medium of sport to elucidate personal identity: 'I'm a naturalised Welshman. All four of my grandparents were born in England.... essentially I'm British. I mean, if Wales are playing England, I support Wales. If England are playing Germany, I support England' (Male, 64, Fairview). This theme tended to be gendered, with men more likely than women to use it to explain their own identity.

The third theme that emerged from the interviews was that of Welsh identity being defined in terms of opposition to English identity and, less frequently, to British identity (cf Kiely et al, 2006). As we have already seen, several people spoke of having to correct assumptions that they were English when they travelled abroad.

> I do regard myself as Welsh, certainly when I'm abroad, I tend to automatically say I am Welsh, because there are a lot of things about the English that I'm uncomfortable with. I don't identify that much with the English. So I suppose I feel Welsh. But it's just being a sort of London Welshman you know it's not that clear cut. And I'm not a sort of beer and rugby type Welshman. (Male, 46, Fairview)

Interestingly, a few interviewees who identified as English also reported a sensitivity to this distinction: 'When I go abroad I feel more British than when I'm here. Talking to Welsh people here, like my Welsh friends, then I feel English, compared to them' (Male, 21, Fairview). Those who spoke of Welsh identity in opposition to Britishness generally felt that British identity was in some way undermining Welsh culture and identity. One spoke of Wales as 'a conquered nation' (Male, 69, Fairview). Another provided yet another example of the role of sports in defining national identities:

> It annoys me, in things, the Commonwealth games now, any bloody sports as far as that goes, where a Welsh athlete will do well and he [sic] suddenly becomes a British athlete. Right? Where an English athlete always stays an English athlete. (Male, 49, Pen-cwm).

Minority ethnic identities

As we have already seen, the cultural diversity of Swansea increased between the two surveys. Thus, by 2002 there was a small but significant minority ethnic population in the city. The 2001 Census reported 1.65% of the population in one of the Black and minority ethnic categories and a further 0.5% as 'mixed'. Eighteen of our survey respondents (1.8%) identified as Black or as having another minority ethnic identity, with another seven (0.7%) identifying themselves as 'mixed'. Of the eighteen minority ethnic respondents, only one (a black African) also identified as Welsh; three of the seven 'mixed' ethnicity respondents identified themselves as Welsh. Because the numbers of minority ethnic respondents in our survey were bound to be small, reflecting their proportion in the population as a whole, we selected Parkfields, where minority ethnic groups made up a higher proportion of the population (8.3%), as one of our ethnographic areas; we did this in order to increase the representation of minority ethnic families in our study. The vast majority of our minority ethnic interviewees were from Parkfields, although one or two came from the other areas, being either interviewees or their partners. The opportunity to discuss cultural identity in the context of a semi-structured interview, rather than responding to a more structured survey questionnaire, produced a higher proportion of minority ethnic interviewees in our ethnographic study identifying as Welsh (3 out of 18, or 17%). The ethnographic data also provide access to a much more nuanced understanding of the range of relationships to Welsh identity among ethnic minorities. Thus one young woman, born in Bangladesh but who came to Wales when she was a toddler, still felt that her primary identity was Bangladeshi Muslim: 'Because although I'm living here, I can't speak Welsh, I don't look like a Welsh person [laughter], I can speak English but I would still say I'm a Bangladeshi Muslim' (Female, 28, Parkfields). In contrast to this a Bangladeshi man, a restaurant worker, who had lived for a time in London, and had adult children there, told us:

> I can say I am the Welsh because ... I can talk a little bit of Welsh. Because I'm 36, 37 years in Swansea and I am a Welsh man. I am a Welsh man. Because my children also, feel they Welsh, feel they're English. Because some of them born in London, and some of them born in the Welsh. You know? Then I'm a Welsh. I am Welsh. I *siarad Cymraeg un, dau, tri, pedawr, pump* [I speak Welsh, one, two, three, four, five], you know, I can count. Not bad for people from London. (Male, 47, Parkfields)

A Bengali woman, born in Britain but taken to live in Bangladesh until she was 10, initially rejected any idea that she was Welsh but then reflected further: 'But if I live here, I mean, I should say I'm Welsh because I've stayed that long here. Then I should say I'm Welsh because I stay here. I'm not going to go anywhere!' (Female, 31, Parkfields). However, she also felt herself to be Bengali. Another woman said, 'I would say I was a Welsh Bangladeshi person. I'd have to say that I'm, sort of, in the middle. I'm not complete, you know Asian person or I'm not a complete Welsh person. I'm sort of, I've got both cultures in me, you see' (Female, 28, Parkfields).

Several people talked about their children's identity. One woman who said she was Indian with a British passport added that 'my children don't think anything else rather than Welsh really' (Female, 48, Parkfields). And a man who was clear that his own identity was Bangladeshi decided, on reflection, that his children were free to adopt a Welsh identity.

> [*So, this is a question about ethnicity, because we are in Wales would you say …*] Bangladeshi is my ethnicity. [*You wouldn't say you were Welsh then?*] No, me, no. Because I cannot. Even though, you know, I respect the people of Wales, I'm happy that I'm living in Wales. But my ethnicity always will be Bangladeshi. [*Yes*] Because that was my country of origin. Because there's a difference between ethnicity and nationality. My nationality can be British, I'm a British subject, I've got a British passport. Yes I may be British citizen, but my ethnicity and my children's ethnicity always will be Bangladeshi, because that's my country of origin. [*And your culture as well?*] Yes, but saying that, if my children wanted to describe themselves as Welsh, I'd have no control to that. They are quite free to what you want to describe them as. This is a choice of individual. (Male, 39, Parkfields)

As well as considering that his children may choose to describe themselves as Welsh rather than Bangladeshi, this interviewee also distinguishes between ethnicity and nationality. For him nationality seems to be about having a British passport and British citizenship rather than being about his cultural identity. Other interviewees, such as the woman above who described herself as Welsh Bangladeshi, seemed to be using an idea of Welsh nationality in a similar way. This use of territorially based identities by black and minority ethnic individuals, along with a cultural identity based in their country of origin, has also been reported in Scotland (McCrone, 2002; see also Modood et al, 1997).

Cultural identities and family relations

We now turn to a consideration of how these different cultural identities, based on class and ethnicity, influence family relationships and family forms and affect understandings of the nature and function of families. We explore how different ways of 'doing' family acquire important symbolic significance for different cultural identities. Our data reveal some interesting convergences in family practices, as well as differences between the culturally defined collectivities we have been discussing.

'Very Welsh' families

As we have seen, Rosser and Harris developed variables for both social class and a 'Welsh'/'non-Welsh' cultural distinction that provided a rich characterisation of the cultural context of family life in Swansea. They did not find these variables useful indicators of patterns of family formation, concluding that 'the differences in the organization of the extended family by social class in Swansea, or by the Welsh/non-Welsh distinction, are slight, and only barely discernible' (1965, 290). However, they did find important differences between social classes in patterns of residence and contact, something that we have also found.

We also found a slight difference in patterns of residence and contact between the 'Welsh' and the 'non-Welsh' in that 'Welsh' daughters tended to live closer to their parents and to have more contact with their mothers than 'non-Welsh' daughters. This finding can be linked to the widely held perception among interviewees that 'very Welsh' families, often interpreted as those having Welsh-language links if not necessarily being Welsh-speaking households, place greater importance on extended family ties which are commonly seen to be maintained principally by women. One woman in her fifties described how her extended family had been centred on her grandmother.

> It was a matriarchal, I think that's probably a Welsh way actually, the mother probably does rule. But it certainly was in our house, and we were all very close to my grandmother. She was the nucleus, and we all, we were all very close to her. My mother, my sister, and my cousins, all girls, all women, very close to my grandmother. And she was the centre, she was the nucleus, yes. And she lived until she was 96, so yes, and her mother before her had been the same, and she'd lived until she was 95, so it is that sort of family unit. Yes. And they were all based in Swansea. (Female, 50s, Fairview)

This extended family had been entirely Welsh speaking – including the grandfather who had come to Wales from Ireland – until this interviewee's generation: 'My grandparents, both my grandparents, both sides of grandparents and my parents and all the aunts, they all spoke Welsh. We can understand it, but don't speak it very well. No. Which is a shame.' What is interesting about her comments is that she talks about the mother ruling and the extended family being 'matriarchal'. This suggests that a specific gender division of labour is associated with the Welsh family and that this involves the powerful figure of the 'mam' holding the family together; when she dies, the family can easily fragment (see also Rosser and Harris, 1965, 14).

Several of our Welsh-speaking interviewees in Treforgan provided examples of this kind of extended family network which was still operative, often in spite of family members being scattered over a wider geographic area and in one instance even surviving a divorce. Thus one woman, in her late 50s, remembered a post-war childhood of 'very communal living, you know, even though we had houses separately', in which her natal family lived with her maternal grandparents and her paternal grandparents and their daughter's family lived next door. In spite of her divorce, and with four grown children living outside Swansea but in South Wales, she described the regular contact and support extending throughout this family network: up a generation to an elderly aunt and uncle; down two generations to her children and grandchildren; and her own generation of her brother and his family. She also maintained close ties with her ex-husband's parents and siblings and their families, seeing them regularly and being included in family gatherings.

> Until the day he died, I was always invited to, [my father-in-law] had a birthday in December, you see?... So, then we all went for a meal then because it was like a Christmas get-together in a way ... I was always there, and I used to go, why not? Shouldn't keep away ... [*Where was your, where was your ex? He wasn't invited?*] He was there, oh yes. (Female, 58, Treforgan)

For this woman the extended family network was clearly still vibrant, in spite of changes in circumstances such as proximity of households, employment of women and even marital breakdown. Thus she concluded:

> You think of family, because your, your husband's left, and it's getting smaller, but it's not, it gets bigger, I find. Mine's much bigger, I've got 2 sons [her daughters' husbands] along with my [own children]. Lovely. And there's extra grandchildren, it's growing and growing and growing.

Another interviewee felt that such close extended families, which she linked to Welshness, were disappearing in her part of west Swansea but could still be found in other nearby areas.

> I think all that Welshness has gone. You know, you go and there'd be, everything would be out for you, you know, they'd be baking, and you'd have these big family teas, you know, ... I think you'll find this part of Swansea totally different to some parts of Swansea, where it's still, even parts of Mayhill I would think and Townhill, they are far more family orientated there, they have big families there, and they all, you know, intermingle and intermarry, and that's more like this part of Swansea was years ago. You know, and Neath is another place.... if you go to parts of Neath, that is like Swansea was years ago. And, you know, they, I go there quite a lot and I find that they are still very Welsh. In their family life, family outlook. (Female, 67, Fairview)

Thus, family practices such as these, including regular gatherings for members of extended family networks that were spread over a sizeable geographic area, are clearly linked to Welsh cultural identity. They can also be seen as generating a form of social capital for those who are embedded in these networks.

Two other interviewees contrasted the importance of extended family networks in Welsh culture with what they perceived to be their lesser role in English culture. One, referring to his experience of attending the funeral of a family member in England, noted, 'So all their family with wives came. Actually in much more, smaller numbers than our family. Because English people, I don't think on the whole the English members of the family have quite the same kind of family attachment as the Welsh do' (Male, 51, Fairview). The second said that the importance of family may remain in some parts of England, 'but in the bigger conurbations, you know, Manchester, the Midlands and London, where I have had friends and met them, and spent time with them, I didn't feel that they had the same sort of attitude towards their family connections that I had towards mine' (Female, 70s, Fairview). Clearly these family practices, carrying the expectation that family members attend ceremonial occasions such as funerals, as well as important birthdays, weddings, and other family events, are marked as culturally Welsh by these interviewees and this is emphasised by contrasting them with what they regarded as 'English' practices.

These extended family networks, whether remembered from the past or described in the present, were often gendered in that women tended to be central to their functioning. One man, a widower in his 70s with grown children living away from Swansea, acknowledged the key role his wife had played, even though she had also been employed:

> I mean, when the wife was alive, I, I had a, I had a 'dolly' of an existence because she made, everything was, she ran the show like a, like a clock. And she would work in order to help, but it, it helped keep us together, keep the family together but basically she was working for the children.... And I, of course, when she did die, I found out the extent of what that meant. (Male, 70, Treforgan)

Such extended family networks, with women at the centre, were particularly common among working-class interviewees; their networks tended to be less dispersed geographically than those of our middle-class interviewees and they typically provided more practical support on a day-to-day basis for family members. For example, one woman in her 30s, married with three children, described her close family network: 'I've got two sisters here, my sister-in-law lives a couple of doors away from me where I am, so, and my husband's family you know are relatively close as well, so it's, we are all pretty close.' Her mother also lived nearby and contact with her and her sisters was very frequent:

> I see her [mother] more now that she is on the sick, I mean obviously when she was working I'd see her about twice a week, but now she is on the sick it's daily mainly. [*Yeah. And your sisters?*] About the same. [*So it's also like you pop in or they...*] Yeah I pop in or they pop, you know. (Female, 39, Pen-cwm)

Thus, for many of our interviewees large extended families that retained fairly close ties were seen as a defining feature of Welsh culture. For many, this type of family is archetypically Welsh and may include an association with the Welsh language. Several felt that it was less characteristic of present-day Welsh culture, or at least that it was to be found in other nearby areas rather than in their own neighbourhood, although others provided examples of precisely this kind of extended family network adapting to changing residential and employment patterns; a few interviewees explicitly contrasted this aspect of Welshness with English culture.

The 'Asian' family

Many of our Bangladeshi interviewees lived in close-knit extended family networks which resembled those in our working-class areas. Several of them spoke about there being an 'Asian family' in similar terms to those in which people spoke about the 'Welsh family', with both being characterised by extensive and close-knit kinship networks (see also Becker and Charles, 2006). One young woman said that, for her, 'family is something that is with you all the time, or you have a regular contact with them and they know what you are doing tomorrow or the day after' (Female, 28, Parkfields). And she contrasted this with the much looser kinship networks she associated with 'white' families. Another young woman talked about the considerable informal power that older women may hold within kinship networks as paternal grandmothers:

> With my gran on my dad's side, she's controlling. She likes to be in charge of things.... And in our culture the husband's mother has more priority over the grandchildren, everything, than the wife's mother and father, you know? (Female, 28, Parkfields)

This informal power of older women which, in patrilineal kinship systems, is invested in the paternal grandmother, was mentioned by several of our interviewees and is reminiscent of the informal power attributed to the mam in Welsh households. The extended kinship networks of our Bangladeshi interviewees were patrilineal and patrilocal. This meant that on marriage the norm was for young women to move to the home of their husbands' parents, although this was not always realised in practice. In this sense they contrasted with the extended kinship networks of the native population which, as we have seen, are uxorilocal.

Some of our Bangladeshi interviewees lived in extended family households which were seen as embodying traditional family and cultural values. However, the cultural expectations surrounding residence on marriage are undergoing change and this was reflected in the experiences of our Bangladeshi interviewees. Extended family households either took the traditional form of patrilocal residence in what was usually an arrangement which lasted until the death of the parental generation (Khanum, 2001), or they took a modified form with a husband moving into his wife's parents' home on marriage; this was usually because he had come from Bangladesh where his parents were still living. This was often a temporary arrangement until the couple could move into a separate house, a process which sometimes involved financial help from the wife's brothers. This, and evidence from other studies (Khanum, 2001; Shaw, 2000), suggests that, in spite of cultural expectations, the extended family household with patrilocal residence is undergoing change for a number of reasons. These include patterns of transnational migration which involve men marrying Bangladeshi women who are resident in Britain and subsequently themselves moving to Britain; the fact that houses are not large enough to accommodate households which may include several families (see also Khanum, 2001; Phillipson et al, 2003); and the preference of some second-generation Bangladeshis to move into their own home on marriage. Cultural heterogeneity is therefore part of the experience of family life for our Bangladeshi interviewees and is leading to changes in family practices. One of our interviewees, who was married and living in her parents' house, talked about this.

> Because with our culture, when a girl gets married [pause] – I've broken that rule you see? – But when a girl gets married she moves to her husband's house and she lives there. So the husbands have more priority over things. (Female, 28, Parkfields)

But when asked whether she felt that living with her own parents was preferable to this arrangement, she said, 'I don't know, I'd rather have it so that everyone just lives on their own or whatever. But, you see, mum and dad, they would like us to live all together. Stay all connected' (Female, 28, Parkfields). Another young Bangladeshi woman told us,

> Our mentality is different from our parents' mentality. It's like we've grown up in a society that emphasises a lot on space, individuality, and sometimes it can be a bit clashing with our system.... And sometimes, I think growing up here makes you a bit resentful of not having that space. (Female, 25, Parkfields)

This suggests that the experience of growing up in Britain is likely to result in some changes in cultural practices within the families and households of the younger generation.

Despite such changes, difficulties sometimes arose when cultural norms were breached. A young woman who lived with her husband and children in his parents' house, and who was supportive of the cultural norms which stipulated that she move into her husband's family's home after marriage, was unhappy about the continuing presence of her husband's married sister and the married sister's husband which transgressed these norms.

> Once the sisters get married they should go. To their husband's. Financially. But she's still living here, paying for nothing, doing nothing or helping, which is not really right. (Female, 28, Parkfields)

This transgression of expected residence patterns was due to the sister's husband's parents being in Bangladesh. It was, however, temporary, as the couple were soon to move out into a house of their own. These findings suggest that there are various factors that are modifying the cultural practices associated with patrilocal residence on marriage and can be understood in terms of increasing cultural heterogeneity within families.

This was also evident in discussion of the merits and demerits of arranged and free-choice marriage, another cultural practice which was undergoing change (see also Phillipson et al, 2003). Some of our Asian interviewees were very much in favour of parental involvement in the choice of marriage partner and others were not. Likewise some thought that free-choice marriage was a good thing and others thought that it was fraught with risk. One of our interviewees anticipated that her sons would have arranged marriages (they were still in primary school at the time of interview). She thought that arranged marriages 'worked out better' and that it was particularly important because, if things went wrong, then 'the family would try and work things out'. If it was not an arranged marriage this sort of support would not be there. She felt herself to be 'old fashioned' in this view although she was not alone among our interviewees (Female, 28, Parkfields).

The different family practices associated with different cultures were evident in the experience of one of our Asian interviewees whose partner was Welsh. She found that her relations with her in-laws, while not corresponding to her cultural expectations, were easily accommodated: 'They are very average white in-laws. I mean, you see them occasionally. They don't interfere, they let you do whatever, you know?' On the other hand, she acknowledged that her Welsh husband 'finds it a bit suffocating, the Asian culture. Because it's too much. Whereas to me it's very bizarre, his family. They are just TOO relaxed.' She felt that her husband had 'taken Asian value of family from us' and was spending more time with his own family, especially his brothers. This couple was also in the process of working out how to accommodate their different cultural traditions in their daughter's upbringing. However, she felt that her husband had 'taken a lot of Asian culture on board. So there's not a lot of conflict that we have' (Female, 28, Parkfields). Indeed he had also converted to Islam.

Thus, distinctive family practices are seen as defining families as 'Welsh', 'Asian' or 'white' and sometimes they coexist within both elementary families and extended family networks. There is also some indication in the experiences of our minority ethnic interviewees that cultural heterogeneity within families is associated with changing family practices. We investigate this further by considering the relation between families and cultural identity and how this is affected when different cultures are brought together within families, not only through generational change but also through partnering and parenting, as in the example above.

Families and the reproduction of cultural identity

Cultural identity is often associated with religion and language and many of our interviewees saw the maintenance of religious or linguistic practices as critical to the survival of their culture. Families were often seen as important to the intergenerational transmission of culture and this was particularly apparent in the way parents talked about their children and children talked about their differences from their parents.

Religion

In the baseline study, religion, in the form of adherence to a particular Christian denomination, was an important cultural indicator with observed differences between 'Welsh' and 'non-Welsh' categories. Our main finding in the 2002 survey with respect to religious indicators was that these were no longer particularly relevant. In the 1960 survey, respondents were asked 'Which denomination do you belong to?' and 98% responded by giving their denomination. In 2002 we asked a much weaker question, namely 'Do you feel any sense of belonging to or connection with any religious group or organisation?' and only one-third of our respondents said 'yes'. When we examined this subset of 327 respondents who claimed some religious affiliation for differences between 'Welsh' and 'non-Welsh' categories, there was only one significant change since the 1960 survey, namely the collapse of membership in Welsh nonconformist denominations. This had fallen from 30% of the 'Welsh' category in 1960, to 6% of those in the 'Welsh' category who said they had some religious attachment in 2002. This collapse occurred in spite of the fact that the percentage of the 'Welsh' category with one or both parents who had belonged to a Welsh-speaking church or chapel showed a decrease of only 11%, from 57% to 46%. Our ethnographic interviews produced a deeper understanding of this decline. One interviewee, a 22-year-old man, a Welsh speaker and the son of a minister, said: 'my parents would have liked if we [he and his four siblings] would have had more of a religious nature to us but we, we stopped going to chapel and that [in their mid teens]'. However, he also reported that one of his brothers had started attending again after he married and had children; 'they've got children so they take those, the whole family go' (Male, 22, Treforgan).

Among our minority ethnic interviewees there were divergent views on the significance of religion. Some suggested that it was a matter of individual conscience rather than a social or familial obligation, while others saw it as a fundamental part of their personal and cultural identity. One woman, for instance, said,

> My husband is Hindu, I'm Buddhist. We did not insist that they follow our religion. If there is a prayer meeting they [children] come along. They believe or accept as well. I don't know ... Whatever divinity, religion, they have no objection. They just come along. But at the end of the day is up to them. (Female, 53, Parkfields)

While another told us:

> To me, Islam is a way of life. And if I'm going to live that way of life anything that contradicts it can't really be a way of life as well. So if Bengali culture says, traditional Bengali culture says, education isn't important for a girl and Islam says it's VERY important for a girl, then to me, Islam is most important. So I'd rather follow the Islamic way which is going to give me my rights. Which is due to me as a human being. And a female. (Female, 25, Parkfields)

Islam was the religion of most of our minority ethnic interviewees, and the Imam, in our interview with him, placed family values at the centre of this faith. The mosque provided a social and religious centre for almost all our Muslim interviewees, both women and men, and several defined themselves as Muslim when asked about their ethnicity. For the young woman quoted above, Islam was being used to develop a critical position on aspects of tradition, including family practices such as not valuing girls' education or paid employment and assuming that they will marry at a young age; this use of Islam by the younger generation has been noted in other studies (see, for example, Dale et al, 2002).

Language

Families are also seen as having an important role to play in the transmission of culture through their practices in relation to language. This was the case for many of our minority ethnic interviewees. One of them, who was Chinese, explained why she placed so much emphasis on speaking her language to her young son:

> I try to keep [him] to speak the language. If they can't speak the language, and you tell everybody you are Chinese, although he was born in Wales. But I think to be able to speak the language, make you that person. Or make you that Chinese person. (Female, 31, Parkfields)

And many of our Bangladeshi interviewees, who mostly originate from the Sylhet region of Bangladesh, said that they spoke Sylheti to their children at home. This was talked about in terms of maintaining their cultural identity and enabling children who were being brought up in Swansea to relate to their grandparents on visits home (see Chapter 7). Indeed the ability to speak more than one language was often seen as an advantage.

The issue of language and its relation to culture has a particular resonance in Swansea because of the importance attached to the Welsh language, both individually, as a marker of cultural identity, and collectively, as something that is supported through an explicit Welsh language policy. This was an issue which was explored in the baseline study, where attention was focused on the effect of cultural heterogeneity within families on the fortunes of the Welsh language. It is therefore important to look at the extent to which Welsh is a language which is spoken within families in Swansea and how it relates to cultural heterogeneity.

Between the two surveys, the proportion of respondents who spoke Welsh has declined. In the 1960 survey, 28.5% of respondents said that they could speak Welsh, 16% fluently and 12.5% partly. When we repeated this question in 2002 we found 15.5% to be Welsh speaking,

7.5% fluently and 8.0% partly. However, whereas Rosser and Harris reported a steady decline in the percentage of Welsh speakers across the generations (Rosser and Harris, 1965, 118–19), we found an increase of 4% in fluent Welsh speakers in the youngest generation in our survey (born 1965–84) over the previous generation (born 1950–64). This increase over the past four decades in the proportion of the population who can speak Welsh, particularly among the younger generation, can be attributed primarily to the growth of Welsh-medium education. Whereas in the sample as a whole 40% of fluent Welsh speakers had attended Welsh-medium schools, among those in our youngest generation (born 1965–84) the proportion rose to 71%. However, when we look at the transmission of the Welsh language through its use within families, the picture regarding the situation of the language is very different indeed. Our findings show that only eight of our 1,000 respondents reported that Welsh was the primary language of the household, with another 11 saying that both Welsh and English were normally spoken. Thus, although 15.5% of Swansea households in our survey contained at least one Welsh speaker, only 1.9% used Welsh as a normal household language, either as the primary language or alongside English. Certainly, in some instances our respondent was the only Welsh-speaking member of the household. However, when we looked only at Welsh-speaking respondents who lived in a household with at least one other Welsh speaker, we found that Welsh was either the primary language or one of the languages of the household in only 11 out of 45 cases (24.4%). Thus the Welsh language is symbolically important and regarded as a central marker of Welsh culture, yet it is not actually a part of current family practices for most families in Swansea.

To a large degree this is a consequence of the decreasing likelihood of both partners being Welsh speakers, an accelerating trend that was observed by Rosser and Harris in 1960. When they looked at the frequency of occurrence, among both Welsh speakers and non-Welsh speakers, of what they termed 'cross-cultural marriages', that is, marriages with one partner Welsh speaking and the other not, they found that the frequency of such marriages was significantly greater for Welsh speakers than for non-Welsh speakers and, furthermore, that this frequency increased among those Welsh speakers who were more recently married while remaining virtually unchanged for non-Welsh speakers. When we introduced data from the 2002 survey, it was clear that this trend had continued to accelerate over the past 40 years (see Table 4.3). In our sample of 25 Welsh-speaking men in a heterosexual partnership that had begun since 1960, 17 (68%) were in

Table 4.3: Changing proportion of cross-language marriage/ cohabitation

Date of marriage	1914–1939		1940–1960		1961–2002	
Language	Welsh speaking (fluent or part)	Non-Welsh speaking	Welsh speaking (fluent or part)	Non-Welsh speaking	Welsh speaking (fluent or part)	Non-Welsh speaking
Men (%)	26	12	43	15	68	10
Women (%)	23	15	48	13	75	7
Total number	231	382	202	523	49	390

Note: 1914–1939 and 1940–1960 figures from Rosser and Harris, 1965, 24.

'cross-cultural' partnerships, and out of 24 Welsh-speaking women in a heterosexual partnership that had begun since 1960, 18 (75%) were in 'cross-cultural' partnerships. Thus the cultural heterogeneity of the heterosexual partnerships of Welsh speakers has increased between 1960 and 2002. The comparable percentages for non-Welsh speaking men and women were 10.4% and 6.8%, respectively.

Some of our interviewees were in cross-cultural partnerships of this kind and spoke about the language. One man, who was not a Welsh speaker but whose wife was Welsh speaking, said they both wanted their children to speak Welsh; both children were attending a Welsh playgroup but English remained the language of the household (Male, 33, Fairview). In a different example, one of our Asian interviewees, who was married to a Welsh man, discussed her husband's concern that their young daughter be aware of the Welsh side of her identity:

> He can't speak Welsh.... So he feels sometimes that he can't give her enough of the culture. So he does do extras, you know? Like he'll make sure she has Celtic jewellery, or he'll just, whatever few words he knows of Welsh he'll try and speak to her in that. But at the end of the day he's competing with this mighty Asian culture that's around her all the time [laughter]. But he always says, 'I'll send her to Welsh school'. And I don't have a problem, great, as many languages as she knows, I'm happy with that. (Female, 28, Parkfields)

This woman spoke her own language with her daughter as well as with her mother; her quite positive attitude about acceptance of Welsh as an additional language for her child was typical of our minority ethnic interviewees. However, what this also suggests is that cultural heterogeneity within families may make the transmission of language and culture more problematic, particularly if it is not spoken at home.

As these examples illustrate, families that are culturally heterogeneous find that the expression and transmission of cultural identities is complex and may require considerable negotiation. Thus one of our minority ethnic interviewees who was in a culturally heterogeneous marriage found it difficult to accept her husband's family's way of doing things. She told us that, during the early years of their marriage, when they had lived in London with his mother and sister, there had been tensions: 'Because I'm not used to living with family, especially from India, whose views are totally different. And I find that there – a lot of influence on his family to him. Which affected our relationship. But when we are together he's normal! [laughter] Is that the right word?' Another source of tension was her commitment to continuing her career, even with the birth of their two children: 'I feel I don't want as a housewife. Because of my career. I'd rather be out and about working.' The tensions were resolved after a move to Swansea, away from his family, although they continued for a while over childcare and her return to work. (Female, 52, Parkfields)

The most common culturally heterogeneous families among our interviewees, unsurprisingly, were those where one partner was Welsh and the other 'English', at least in relation to place of birth. Many interviewees who were English born but had lived for most, or all of their adult lives in Wales with a Welsh partner, would identify as Welsh, sometimes talking of having adopted Welsh culture or themselves been adopted. One 74-year-old woman, a widow, living alone, who had been born and brought up in England but identified as Welsh, exemplified this:

> It was the traditions, the customs that I felt proud of, the culture of Wales....And of course, [my late husband, a Welsh speaker] was delighted because that proved to him then that I was Welsh. [Laughter] ... And the Eisteddfod, I went every time with him.... And I loved it and, and I loved being on the, the *maes* as they refer to the Eisteddfod field, you know. (Female, 74, Treforgan)

Her experience shows that cultural identity is not fixed and that as well as transmitting culture intergenerationally, moving to a place with distinct cultural traditions and becoming involved in them through family relationships can influence cultural identity.

In other families, in contrast, different cultural identities were steadfastly maintained and sometimes came into conflict. By far the most common medium for the expression of any such conflict was via sport, mainly through support for different national teams. One woman with three children said that she was English, but

> I look at these [the two younger children] as Welsh. And [my brother] sees himself as English as well, I must admit. And my other two see themselves as Welsh now, and it's hard, because they, with the rugby, it's me and [my brother] for England, and then there is three of them, well one English boy [her older son] and two Welsh boys, and they are supporting Wales, you know, so it's quite comical at times I must admit. (Female, 27, Pen-cwm)

Cultural differentiation

This evidence suggests that the relation between family practices and the reproduction of culture and cultural identities is complicated and that this complexity has increased since 1960. This relates to the increase in cultural differentiation, since 1960, in terms of both class cultures and cultures relating to ethnicity, religion and language, and raises questions about the effect of cultural differentiation on family solidarity, particularly intergenerational solidarity, and the relation between cultural heterogeneity within families and the reproduction of culture and cultural identities.

Our evidence seems to suggest that cultural heterogeneity is not necessarily associated with a reduction in intergenerational solidarity within families and, it could be argued, that generational change inevitably involves differences between older and younger generations and that these differences have to be negotiated. This was clearest among our minority ethnic interviewees, particularly when the younger generation was the first in the family to have been brought up in Britain. There was evidence that these differences were negotiated, with the result that children made choices about those aspects of cultural traditions that they wished to maintain and those that they challenged. The reproduction of culture is therefore not a one-way process and change as well as continuity can result from the active engagement of children in this process. There was also evidence that children exercised choice with great care and awareness of the effect that their behaviour would have on their families and often modified their behaviour accordingly. In this way family solidarity is maintained even though cultural traditions may be subject to change. In particular, cultural heterogeneity can create difficulties for the transmission of culture in the form of language. This is exemplified in the reduction in Welsh speaking within families between the two surveys. On the other hand, a diversity of languages within families can be regarded positively insofar as it enables children to speak more than one language. And as long as they are able to communicate with older generations in the older family members' language then it does not undermine intergenerational solidarity. There is some evidence in our ethnographic material, however, that cultural heterogeneity can create difficulties when it exists between couples, especially if there are different cultural expectations about women's behaviour and their obligations to other family members. This can also be the case if family practices are modified thereby no longer conforming to traditional expectations.

It is also clear from our evidence that ideas about 'the family' are culturally specific and assume a symbolic importance. Thus people talked about 'very Welsh' families, which are matriarchal, and 'the Asian family', which is patriarchal (and patrilocal); both family forms are seen as traditional and both are characterised by close-knit extended family networks. They were also understood as undergoing a process of change which was sometimes seen in terms of decline; we return to ideas of decline and how they need to be treated with caution in Chapter 8. Different family forms and cultural identities are also linked with place, both symbolically and in terms of actual demographic differences. Thus our four ethnographic areas, while containing significant internal variation, nevertheless provide us with contrasting cultural identities, related family types and expectations about gendered family obligations.

Note
[1] For these figures we have included the category 'no response' in the total respondents in order to compare with the category 'refuse/don't know' used by Rosser and Harris (1965, 86). For this reason the percentages for self-assessed class differ from those found in Charles, Davies and Harris (2003) and Charles, Davies and Harris (2008) which treated the 'no response' category as 'missing'. When this is done the proportion of respondents identifying as working class becomes 49.6% (as compared with 59.4% in 1960) while the proportion identifying as middle class is 35.8% (as compared with 31.9% in 1960).

FIVE

Families in and out of work

In this chapter and the next we explore the ways in which employment and unemployment, together with changing gender divisions of labour, affect the support that is exchanged within extended family networks. It has been argued that this support is lessening because of women's increased participation in paid employment and that there is a weakening of the connectedness of local social networks because of increasing occupational and geographical differentiation. This, as we have seen, has been conceptualised in terms of a reduction in social cohesion and/or social capital and increasing individualisation. There is also considerable debate about the effect of unemployment on families, the association of unemployment with social exclusion, and the moral values guiding choices about participation in paid employment. We therefore begin this chapter with a brief overview of this debate before discussing the type of support exchanged within kinship networks and the way it is affected by unemployment. In the following chapter we look at how family members care for each other and the impact of employment, particularly women's employment, on their ability to do so. Taken together, these two chapters provide a picture of the support exchanged by family members, how this support is affected by employment and its lack, and how it relates to class and gender.

Unemployment, social exclusion and gender divisions of labour

There is a tension in much debate about family change which hinges on different conceptualisations of social inclusion and social cohesion and their relationship to women's and men's employment. Thus, within the western social democratic tradition participation in paid work has come to be seen as the main way to ensure social inclusion (Lewis, 2002), while social capital theorists point to the negative impact of women's employment on the cohesiveness of families and communities (see Chapter 1). We have already considered the social capital argument so here we briefly look at the ways in which employment and social inclusion are linked in policy debates. We also highlight the difficulties of pursuing a policy based on the full integration of women and men in the workforce given the gendered moral values underpinning people's decisions about the balance between market and care work; this is an issue to which we return at the end of the book.

Those who are unemployed are variously regarded as forming an 'underclass' or 'lumpenproletariat', or as living in a culture of poverty which is distinct from the culture of mainstream society (Barlow et al, 2002). In order to counter social exclusion thus conceived, policies have been developed to encourage people into the workforce with scant regard either for the values underpinning the mode of participation in the workforce or for how the care needs of children and other dependent people will be met. The contradictions to which this gives rise are particularly apparent in the case of lone mothers but are by no means confined to them. Thus, in Britain in recent years lone parents have been targeted in order to encourage them into paid work. Given the fact that the vast majority (90%) of lone parents are mothers, this represents a shift in policy from 'treating lone mothers as mothers to treating them as workers' (Lewis, 2002, 54; Daycare Trust, 2007). It has been argued that attempts to integrate lone mothers into the workforce do not take into account the gendered moral rationalities which guide decisions about both women's and men's participation in paid work (Duncan and Edwards, 1999). There are three points to make here. The first is that policies designed to enable all adults to participate in the workforce do not take into account how women and men negotiate care work and paid work within families and the value which mothers attach to 'being there' for their children and which fathers attach to being able to provide for them (Ball, 2006). They therefore fall into the same trap as earlier policies insofar as they assume a 'universalised adult worker model [which] no more fits the social reality than did the male breadwinner model of the past' (Lewis, 2002, 52). Second, women and men make decisions about how to balance paid work with caring for children in the context of what they see as 'the proper thing to do', but what is regarded as the 'proper thing to do' is socially negotiated and 'varies between particular social groups, neighbourhoods and welfare states' (Barlow et al, 2002, 111); it is also gendered. Thus 'culture – the dimension of societal ideas, meanings and values' has to be taken seriously in exploring how social actors come to decide about their participation in paid work, particularly when they are parents (Pfau-Effinger and Geissler, 2002, 77). Third, there is empirical evidence that 'unemployed lone mothers are not "socially excluded" or in some sense "outside society"' (Barlow et al, 2002, 114). On the contrary, they are fulfilling a socially accepted and normatively prescribed social role. Furthermore, value may be attached not only to prioritising mothering over paid employment but also to fathers fulfilling the provider role.

Recent research has, for instance, found that this role is highly valued although, in practice, it is often difficult to attain (Charles and James, 2005). And although the male-breadwinner family may be in decline, it is far from clear that it is being replaced by a dual-earner family, at least within the UK, or that the male-provider role no longer guides people's aspirations for family living (Yeandle, 1999; Lewis, 2002; Charles and James, 2005).

In our survey we were interested in exploring the extent to which the provider role was still important and, if so, how it related to gender divisions of labour. In the baseline study an assumption had been made that there would be a head of household and, given the low levels of married women's employment, it had been reasonable to suppose that this head of household would be male. In the restudy we did not make any assumption about there being a head of household and, as we have seen, women's employment rates were much higher and men's much lower than in 1960. In order to investigate the prevalence of male-breadwinner ideology, we asked whether or not respondents would say that there was a main breadwinner in the household. In response, 71% of our respondents (n=612) said that there was a main breadwinner in their household. In 55% of cases there was a male breadwinner, in 16% there was a female breadwinner and in the other 29% the breadwinning role was shared. Furthermore, despite the vastly changed economic activity rates of women and men, far more men than women regarded themselves as the main breadwinner and just over half of respondents nominated men as the main breadwinners. This, we would suggest, is an indication that male-breadwinner ideology still has some purchase in this particular part of the UK and it is likely to inform people's decisions about participation in paid work (see Charles and James, 2005 for a discussion of this).

Responses were affected by the relative occupational status of heterosexual partners. For instance, when we compared the occupational status of heterosexual couples with claims about breadwinner status we found that, where the man's occupational status was two levels higher than that of the woman, the male partner was defined as breadwinner by 92% of men and 75% of women; where the woman's occupational status was two levels higher than her male partner's, only 8% of men and 18% of women defined the woman as the main breadwinner. We were not able to compare claims about breadwinner status with the relative earnings of heterosexual partners, although we discuss this in conjunction with findings from another piece of research carried out in the same area elsewhere (Charles and Harris, 2007). These findings support our contention that there is an underlying value orientation such that breadwinner status is claimed for men even when their occupational status is significantly lower than their partners'. Clearly, however, relative occupational status has some effect on whether or not heterosexual couples define the male partner as breadwinner.

This context helps us to understand the significance of the renegotiations of domestic divisions of labour that sometimes occurred when women took up full-time employment. One of our married women interviewees said:

> When I decided that I would take a full-time position we did obviously sit down to discuss it. And I said he's going to have to pull his weight a little bit more and do certain things, and fair dos, he's stuck to it. I don't do the breakfast dishes in the morning, he does it. And I'm very meticulous about my home, it's got to be hoovered before I leave for work in the morning and he'll hoover before he goes to work in the morning. So yeah, I think at the end of the day you've got to be more of a partnership. It's not going to work otherwise. (Female, 38, Parkfields)

This renegotiated domestic division of labour did not affect her husband's position as main provider for the family and cannot therefore be seen as necessarily undermining the value accorded to men's ability to provide for their families. The corollary of this is that women place a high value on their ability to care which is often expressed in terms of 'being there'. Even though there is some generational change in the strength of male-breadwinner ideology (Charles and James, 2005; Charles and Harris, 2007), there remains an underlying value orientation in Swansea such that men's provider and women's caring roles are highly valued and socially sanctioned.

Types of support

This gender division of labour is reflected in gender differences in the type of support that is provided within families, with women being more likely to provide kin with support which involves labour and time and men more likely to provide financial support (Finch, 1989; Finch and Mason, 1993). Underlying these patterns are domestic divisions of labour, gendered participation in the workforce, gendered moral rationalities and institutionalised heterosexuality (Duncan and Edwards, 1999; Dunne, 1997), all of which lead to women's greater involvement in the domestic sphere and 'care work' and men's greater involvement in paid employment. This means that, even taking into account the changes of the last 50 years in women's and men's participation in paid employment, women are likely to have more time at their disposal than men for the provision of support and men are more likely to have greater access to money. Women's full-time employment, however, has an effect on the availability of time and is associated with a reduction in their frequency of contact with kin (McGlone, Park and Roberts, 1999) although, as we shall see, this may be mitigated by the need for help with childcare.

Support has been characterised in various ways by different researchers. Thus, Finch lists five types of support: economic, accommodation, personal, practical and childcare, and emotional and moral (Finch, 1989; Baldassar et al, 2007). Similarly Uhlmann, drawing on his own and other research, lists the main types of support as 'material (money, goods, emergency shelter or use rights in goods and capital), physical (labour power), emotional (love, counsel), legal (guardianship) or spiritual (religious duties)' (Uhlmann, 2006, 39–40). Support within families tends to flow from parents to children; this includes financial support from fathers to sons in middle-class families as well as mothers' practical support for their daughters across the social spectrum (Bell, 1968; Leonard, 1980; Finch and Mason, 1993; Uhlmann, 2006). We found that there are two main aspects of support: that given to adult children by parents and that given to parents by adult children. For purposes of analysis we divide support into five main categories which are, in practice, inextricably intertwined. They are care, practical support, financial support, employment or labour, and emotional support. In this chapter our focus is on all forms of support except care which is discussed in Chapter 6. These two chapters taken together provide a detailed analysis of the types of support exchanged between members of extended family households.

Contact and support

In the baseline study one of the main findings was that extended families provide their members with support and a sense of identity. The types of support that were exchanged were assistance with domestic labour, such as mothers and daughters helping each other with the weekly wash; babysitting, which was provided by family members for each other; children staying with their grandparents or with their parents' siblings; parents and adult children going on holiday together; practical help with such things as sorting out overgrown gardens; and care for older relatives which was provided by their younger, female relatives, usually daughters. Rosser and Harris suggested that families' ability to provide support for their members would be adversely affected by increased geographical mobility, the shift from a cohesive to a mobile society, and that increased occupational and cultural as well as geographical differentiation within family networks would lead to less solidarity (and hence support) within them. They also suggested that women's changing social position, particularly their 'de-domestication', would have profound consequences for the ability of families to support each other. They found, however, that support was widely exchanged, and our findings, more than 40 years later, paint a very similar picture.

Interviewees spoke about a range of different ways in which they supported each other, from simply 'being there' to caring for a child or older person on a daily basis or providing a deposit on a house. Often support was intertwined with daily interaction and not recognised as support. Indeed, much contact revolved around support rather than simply visiting for the sake of visiting. Thus, one woman spoke about the support she gave to her parents:

> But yes, if there is anything, if there's a problem, I would do anything for them. And I think they would do anything for me as well.... I don't think of it as support, it's just something I do, and I wouldn't think of doing anything else. I mean if my mum was worried about anything, well we'll try and sort it out.... I don't think of myself as supporting my mum, or helping my mum, I just do it, that's what, if I can make anything easier for her or my dad then I will do it. And my sister thinks exactly the same. (Female, 50s, Fairview)

Many described patterns of daily interaction with family members living in different households. Women would go shopping with their mothers or take their parents to the supermarket once a week, sisters organised weekly outings with each other, and men would paint and decorate for mothers, grandmothers and sisters-in-law who lived on their own. Sons often dropped by in the course of their work. One young man who had been brought up by his grandmother called in to see her every day. He decorated her flat for her and she provided him with a meal when he visited. Her sons also called in on a regular basis. These ways of supporting family members are so much part of the daily fabric of people's lives that they do not see them as support; it's 'just something they do', it's part of 'doing' family. However, such support is often what makes it possible for women to go out to work even when they have young children and for older people to retain their independence in their own homes even when they are no longer able to manage daily living without help.

Being there

Support takes place within networks of kin and often others, neighbours and/or friends, but, for the majority, family members are the first to be relied upon for support. Indeed 'being there', as well as indicating that families provide support, defines who is family. In response to a question asking what makes somebody family, one of our interviewees replied:

> They are just always there for me, I can always talk to them if I need like money or anything, they are all just always there to ask and give support, give me support. A lot of support. (Female, 19, Pen-cwm)

The same question elicits a similar response from two women interviewed together; the mother of one of them was also present.

> *1st interviewee*: I don't know, I suppose it's just being there isn't it.
>
> *2nd interviewee's mother*: And it's somebody to borrow off when you need to and somebody to look after the kids when you need them to, the truth be known. In that order.
>
> *2nd interviewee*: Somebody that if you need help they are there to help you.
>
> *1st interviewee*: Or just there, there all the time in the background, do you know what I mean. (Female, 31 and Female, 29, Pen-cwm)

Those who fail to 'be there' somehow disqualify themselves from family membership.

The fact that support takes place within networks of kin is apparent in the account of one of our younger interviewees whom we shall call Sharon and who lives in Pen-cwm. Her opening gambit was, 'I'm nineteen, I'm a single mother so I can't really work because I've got nobody to look after the baby, and that's about it'. We interviewed her at her mother's house, where she grew up and now spends most of her days. She has two older half-sisters, who live close by with their children, and a younger brother, who still lives at home with her mother. One of her sisters is also a lone mother and the other became a mother at 18 while still living with her own mother. Sharon sees not only her mother and brother but also her half-sisters and their children daily because they all congregate at her mother's house. Her mother looks after some of the children to enable Sharon's half-sisters to work. Sharon's parents separated when she was a child but they maintained a good relationship throughout and she has always been in contact with her father. Indeed, her mother surprisingly gave birth to her brother some time after she and Sharon's father had separated. Sharon sees her father most days when he visits her mother's house to see her younger brother (his son). Her older sisters have a different father. She also sees her aunts, uncles and cousins regularly. Her father lives with her paternal grandmother, and when she goes to see this grandmother she also meets her aunts and uncles from her father's side. When asked what sort of help and support she gets from members of her family she replies:

> Gosh, loads. Well everything I need or anything that is troubling me they try their best to sort it out for me, help me, I'm really lucky. [*Could you give me some examples, what for example?*] If I need a babysitter, they are always there, if I need to lend money they are always there, if something goes wrong in my house they are like, say my fire, catches fire or something, they comes over and wait with me for somebody to come out and see to it, which is very, all of them are very supportive in everything. [*Yeah so like with the baby your mother would look after him, or....*] Yeah, not that I leaves him because I don't like leaving I misses him too much. [*Oh*] But if I need a babysitter she will, yeah. [*So if you have to go somewhere....*] Yeah, like doctor's then my mother'll have him or my sisters. [*And what sort of support do you give to the other people in your family?*] Well I babysit my nieces and nephews, and my brother, and I'm always there if they have any problems, sometimes I help them out with money if I've got some. I try. I try to help them as much as I can, they help me, so. [*Yeah. So like your brother, you would then stay here to sort of look after your brother?*] Oh he likes to sleep over my house, or my nieces, sometimes they just sleep over there anyway, because they want to. So I've always got kids there. (Female, 19, Pen-cwm)

Such extensive and daily exchange of help and support with childcare, advice and money is typical for many kinship networks and shows that support is part of the way in which people 'do' family. This female-centred, extended family network was in our deprived, working-class area which is characterised by high levels of unemployment and lone parenthood; Sharon's description was echoed by many living in Pen-cwm. We return to Pen-cwm later in the chapter, first, however, we explore the types of support that are exchanged between households and, sometimes, within households, drawing out their gendered nature and the way they vary with class and cultural identity.

Financial and practical support

Setting up home

Many parents helped their children with setting up home, either with money for a deposit on a mortgage or by buying household items such as fridges, washing machines and even kitchens for them. One of our working-class interviewees told us that when she and her husband were doing up their house they had stayed with her parents and her parents had helped financially by paying for the kitchen. She said that they would never have been able to afford to do up the house without this help. One of our middle-class interviewees reported that he had had help from his parents with a deposit on a house and that they had also given him and his partner things like fridges and washing machines. A couple reported that his mother often made them gifts of useful household items and another told us that her father had put a considerable sum of money away for each of his children to serve as a deposit on a house. One of our older interviewees told us how he helped his daughters by doing renovation work for them on their houses. He did this rather than providing them with financial help as he thought it important for them to be independent.

> My eldest daughter I saw yesterday. I was up in [city] yesterday working on her house.... I do certain things with woodwork and what, you know, I make grates and things like that and I done the same for her and skirtings and plaster boarding and ceilings.... [Later, when asked whether he had helped them out with buying houses] No, it's always been in a support rather than [*Practical support?*] rather than financial. Well, I don't know. If it were me, I'd have preferred the cash. But then I'm biased. But no, when

it comes to buying houses, how can I put it? I think that very often you appreciate more what you buy and struggle for yourself. (Male, 59, Parkfields)

These examples illustrate class differences in the type of support that can be given by parents to children in setting up home, with middle-class parents being more likely to be able to assist their children to get a foot on the housing ladder. This is something that has been found in other studies (see for example Bradley et al, 2005). They also show that it is men who are generally involved in financial and practical support such as DIY and home renovations.

Education

Another major way in which parents support children is by helping them through higher education; this was much more evident in our middle-class areas. One of the men, when asked about support, said,

Financial, I mean, with three of them, between them they've gone – we've supported them through university for fourteen years… Gillian did six training to be a doctor, Angharad did four… Geraint's done three. Fourteen years of university. (Male, 59, Treforgan)

One of our Bangladeshi interviewees told us about the importance of a good education for his children.

I'll try my best to get them good educations. You see? That's why I'm send them in boarding school and do very hard work. It cost me a lot of money to support them. But I don't mind,…. what money you earn will be for them. So if you can support them and get them better education then they can earn the good money and have a good life as well. (Male, 45, Parkfields)

Many of those whose children had gone to university told us that their children were now working, with good jobs, but often living quite some distance away. The pressure of work meant that they did not see them very often. Children's participation in higher education clearly contributes to the greater dispersion of middle-class families. This is returned to in Chapter 7.

Language

Financial help was intertwined with other forms of practical support; it was often disguised as help in kind and usually flowed down the generations. However, our minority ethnic interviewees talked about financial and practical help that flowed upwards as well as downwards. For instance children could provide support for their parents with language, something that was a common experience for our minority ethnic interviewees.

> Most support actually goes towards the parents because their English is quite poor. And they can't read the language. So most of it goes towards the parents more than anything. Because we are quite independent really. [*In what way?*] We are independent because we can speak the language and read it, so we don't have to ask people to translate for us and go to doctors or go to solicitor, you know. Anything that's complicated they would need someone to translate for them. (Female, 31, Parkfields)

Children's greater familiarity with the languages and culture of Swansea can lead to their providing considerable support to their parents.

Bangladeshi households

In Bangladeshi households it was expected that adult sons would support parents and any unmarried sisters, thereby taking over the provider role previously played by their fathers. In these cases the support was either inter- or intra-household as some of our Bangladeshi interviewees lived in three-generation, extended-family households while others had set up separate households with their spouses and children. One of our interviewees described the situation in her parents' home, which was shared by her brothers and their wives.

> My father is still the man in control. Like he hasn't handed everything over to my brothers yet, he's still the one. And he has all the say in that still.... Like all the money. Like my brothers would work and give all the money to him and then he, you know, pays all the bills and although he's not working he still, they'll give him the money, he'll pay all the bills and anything, all the shopping. He'll do all the shopping. He'll look after the house, anything that needs

to be done, he'll do all that. It's like my brothers are just working, is their responsibility. (Female, 28, Parkfields)

She herself lived with her husband, his parents and brothers and their wives and children. In this household her father-in-law had handed over responsibility to one of his sons who was now responsible for supporting his parents and the other members of his family along with his brothers.

> My husband does most of the bills and, you know, all the household bills and the mortgage, he's responsible for that. All the food and everything is my brother-in-law is responsible for that. (Female, 28, Parkfields)

Another told us how she did not have to pay towards her own upkeep, this was taken care of by her brothers as her father had died several years previously. She explained,

> Culturally you don't take from your daughter's earnings. Your sons have to look after you. Because inheritance-wise my brothers get more than me. Because their duty is to look after me after my father. Their duty is to shelter, food, clothe me. That's their duty. So inheritance-wise they get more than me. I get half of what they get. Because of their responsibility towards me. And to be honest they are doing that. [*So your brothers support you?*] Yes. For me I don't need to work actually at all. I don't need to work for money at all. (Female, 25, Parkfields)

And one of our male Bangladeshi interviewees told us a similar story.

> Like, as I say, my father died in [year], at that time, I sort of relied on my elder brothers. They could have asked me, 'Look, we cannot pay your tuition fees, go and look for a job yourself. Or do something to make your own living.' ... It makes me think, although they are my brother, they were my closest friend. They have taken on the responsibility of my father. Though my father really brought me up, I think my brothers, they did exactly the same thing. (Male, 39, Parkfields)

Employment or labour

Family businesses

Many of our minority ethnic interviewees were involved in the catering trade, working in restaurants and takeaways which were often family businesses. These both provided employment for family members and relied on family labour for their continued existence (Phizacklea and Wolkowitz, 1995; Song, 1999). One of our Chinese interviewees, for instance, spoke about how she had chosen to sacrifice her career in order to be able to do her duty to her family and support her parents in their family business.

> With our culture we have to respect and obey but – obey the parents. Otherwise I would have had a different career after college or university. I would have gone on to university or something rather than give up the study to work with my parents. (Female, 31, Parkfields)

The support that adult children gave their parents was sometimes at their own expense even though, in this case, her father had bought her a car in recognition of her help in the takeaway.

Others spoke about how employment was provided for male family members, including those who had recently arrived from Bangladesh. Indeed the availability of work in family-run restaurants was often what had made it possible for men to come over to Britain in the first place. It also meant that children were expected to provide labour for the family business, often without remuneration. Thus, family businesses supported male family members by providing them with employment but were also supported through the availability of family labour. In the Bangladeshi community it was usually (though not always) the men who worked in the family businesses but among the Chinese it was daughters as well as sons. One of our Bangladeshi interviewees described this process.

> So what happened was when people heard we were in Swansea, like relatives and uncles, like my dad's cousins, they all decided to come. And because we had family businesses then we were employing cousins. Like my dad was employing cousins, brothers-in-laws, this that. (Female, 25, Parkfields)

Family businesses were not confined to our minority ethnic interviewees although they were more widespread among them than among our majority ethnic interviewees. A man in his early thirties worked in the family business with his parents and his grandparents who were in their nineties. His grandmother provided lunch every day for all five of them. He saw his employment in the family business as part of the way his parents provided him with financial support.

In these accounts there is little support for the idea that processes of individualisation have penetrated to the heart of the family. On the contrary, there is much evidence that people frequently put their own individual aspirations aside in order to fulfil family obligations and, as other research has shown, are actively engaged in balancing their own needs with those of others who are close to them.

Emotional support

Emotional support was something that was often the bedrock of kin relationships but did not always follow the intergenerational pattern of other types of support. Many interviewees reported being particularly close to their mothers, but others talked about their siblings, or one sibling in particular. One of our interviewees told us about the support she got from her sister, again using the language of 'being there'.

> She is always there for me, that's all, she doesn't babysit or things like that because she can't cope with my two kids and her daughter, like they drives her up the wall. But she is always there, if I got a problem she'll always help me out like.... But it's like, I don't know, she is just always there for me really. (Female, 25, Pen-cwm)

Mothers often talked of 'being there' for their children.

> So we are close knit. We are quite united in that way. And if you sense somebody is upset, I say, 'Are you alright? You are quiet.' We try and help each other by talking, by being there, showing the person, I'm here if there's anything. (Female, 52, Parkfields)

Interviewees sometimes preferred to share their problems with their siblings rather than with their parents.

I'm close to my brothers and sisters. I talk to them. Any problems, I talk to them. [*So you are closer to them than you are to your mother and father?*] Oh yes, yes. Because with your mother and father, I don't really tell them all my problems because they are going to worry. And they've got angina and I don't want them to worry. So they think I'm in a perfect world, living happily. But I don't talk to them. Not all my problems I will tell them, only my little things. But my brothers and sisters, I do talk to them. (Female, 28, Parkfields)

Women often said that their children rather than their male partners gave them support. One woman told us that her son was more supportive than her husband who was 'not understanding as much as I hoped he would'. She went on to say,

My son, he's always, from young, we are very, very close. We seem to know each other a lot. Understand. He will let me speak and hear…. Whereas with my husband, if I tell him, he will get annoyed first…. So I feel that sometimes I don't want to relate to him because he only get annoyed. (Female, 52, Parkfields)

Men, in contrast, often reported that their wives were their main source of support or said that they neither needed nor received this sort of support from anyone.

Support with strings

Emotional support, however, as with other types of support, is conditional despite the frequent resort to the notion that to be family meant 'being there' unconditionally. One of our interviewees, for instance, had helped his two younger brothers over the years when they were in trouble. More recently he had changed his attitude and now wants to restrict contact with them because he thinks that, despite his support, they have not changed. This account underlines the fact that support is not unconditional; if it is not reciprocated – even by something as intangible as attempting to change behaviour – then it may be withdrawn.

I've tried to help them over the years, and I'm ashamed to admit really that I've sort of given up on them in a sense.

Because I can't see, I certainly can't change them or make their lives any better.... You know, they, I've had lots of talks with Alan for instance, and James has gone way past it, because he is the registered alcoholic, and he probably will die within the next few years in any case.... but my other brother I've spoken to him many, many times, and he'll be the first to admit that his life is a shambles, and you know he just don't seem to have the will to get out of that. He's certainly had help and support, but he just, perhaps he don't really, it's either that he don't want to do it or he thinks it's too difficult to do. (Male, 40, Fairview)

Another interviewee, who was from a minority ethnic background, put it quite succinctly:

So as long as you do what, you know, the grandmother or the great grandfather has expected of his descendants, that sort of thing, you are entitled to this support.... you have to keep the family image. Or you have to keep the image and do what is expected with you. (Female, 29, Parkfields)

This alludes to the importance of maintaining the family's reputation (she talks of image); as long as you do this you are entitled to support.

Others spoke about a lack of support. One of our male interviewees told us that he did not get any support from his mother and siblings when he was homeless. As a result he no longer classes his brothers and sisters as family and, when asked what makes somebody family, he explained:

Good question. You don't even have to get on with them, it's just, family help each other. And they are there, what I look at as family anyway, is people who are there don't matter what, to help. Not just to take, are you with me, instead of being a taker, if you need to give, they are there to give as well. Which, with me, like as I said I was, you could call it down and out for nearly four years, didn't have really any home, I could call my home.... My family if I turned up just to wash all my clothes and have a decent meal, they shut the door. And to me families don't shut doors, they you know, they look after each other, and it wasn't working that way. So I got to be honest, that's what I would call family, family are there don't matter what. They don't just shut you out just because you're down and out. (Male, 41, Pen–cwm)

In his view his family had failed to 'be there' for him and, as a result, he no longer regarded them as family. A woman told us about her relationship with her mother.

> It's difficult to say about my mother. When I was doing this BA she was not at all supportive. Not interested, took her two years to ask me what I was actually studying, why was I doing it, why didn't I go out and get a proper job. But I called her bluff on that, because when I graduated I was actually offered a [job].… Which I decided not to take.… And I said to her, 'Oh you know you are always telling me to get a job, well I've got one.' 'Oh.' I said, 'Yes, it's in London for three years and then overseas.' She said, 'Oh well, you know when I said get a job I didn't mean a proper job, I meant around here.' What's going to happen to me, is what she meant. So I get sort of support from my mother. You know if I was ill I'd get support from her, but, I, not a lot of other sort of support. In a way she doesn't understand me. We are very different. She doesn't know what I'm doing and why I'm doing it, and so on. So we relate very much at one level and we leave it at that. There is no bad blood or anything, although she has been horrible in the past. But I, if you would say is your mother a supportive person, I would have to say no. (Female, 49, Fairview)

These accounts point to the way in which support can be used in order to shape behaviour: it can be conditional on the family member behaving in ways which are acceptable or can be used as a way of manipulating behaviour to create conformity to what are often unspoken rules. In some cultural contexts this is more explicit than in others; however, we suggest that although family support is, according to family ideology, unconditional, the conditions or rules which govern its availability often become apparent when someone fails to abide by them.

There is little evidence here to support the idea of individualisation processes having taken hold to such an extent that people pursue their own interests without considering their connectedness to and responsibilities towards others. Indeed the range of support offered by kin to each other across the social spectrum and between generations, and its embeddedness in kinship networks and patterns of daily interaction, suggest that despite increasing occupational, cultural and geographic differentiation, families are still a source of support for their members. The nature of the support provided does, however, vary between classes, a variation that was apparent in the differences between our ethnographic areas. In particular Pen-cwm, with its high levels of unemployment, stood out from the other areas. A discussion of the ways in which kin supported each other in Pen-cwm therefore gives us an indication of the effects of unemployment on the ways in which members of extended kinship networks support each other and illuminates how such support relates to social exclusion.

Unemployment

Unemployment, as we have seen, is associated – in policy discourse – with social exclusion and the solution to social exclusion is seen as integration into the workforce. This, however, does not take into account how families actually behave and the ways in which they support and care for each other, often in conditions which are extremely difficult. In the survey we asked whether respondents had experienced a period of unemployment longer than 6 months in the past 10 years. One hundred and thirty respondents (13.6%) had, with the majority of those (89, or 72%) having experienced such lengthy unemployment only once. Of these 130, 63 were women and 67 men, indicating little gender difference in the distribution of unemployment amongst our respondents. There was, however, a class difference with 81% of the men and 63% of the women being working class (n=107). Only 18 of those who had experienced 6 months or more of unemployment reported that their parents had also experienced periods of unemployment longer than 6 months before the respondent reached the age of 18. There is therefore little evidence here to support the idea that unemployment is passed down the generations as a way of life although it is clearly more likely to be experienced if you are working class. The survey figures are too small for us to be able to conduct any meaningful analysis of the ways in which unemployment affects patterns of contact and residence; we therefore explore the ways in which unemployment affects support within kinship networks by discussing our ethnographic data.

Pen-cwm

Pen-cwm, as we have seen (Chapter 2), experiences high levels of unemployment. It was also known for its high levels of crime and many of our interviewees talked about this when we asked them about whether they liked living in the area. A woman who had lived there since she was two, in the same street as her mother, told us that the area was going downhill.

> I mean, I would, people knock Pen-cwm and I've never, ever, ever said that there is anything wrong with Pen-cwm, but for about the last two years it hasn't been as nice living here as it used to be. Troubles has got worse, people have got nastier. Some of the kids around here are just, you know, they make it their mission in life to make your life hell. And it has got, our street must be one of the worst streets in Pen-cwm at the moment. You know the vandalism, and you know they just go out to annoy. So I mean other than that yeah, I've loved living here. (Female, 45, Pen-cwm)

Others spoke about the problems of living there, the dangers of going out at night and their worries about their children, particularly boys, becoming involved in drugs, joyriding and petty criminal activity. There was also far more talk of violence in these interviews, both violence on the streets and in the home, and several of our interviewees spoke of abusive relationships. There were also accounts of family members being murdered.

> Life is hard up here, very hard on this estate. That's what the boys say, dog eat dog. It's like scrambling for the last piece of meat, and there's a pack out there of wolves, and the weakest link goes. There is a lot of young boys have died up here, drug overdoses, there was two murders up here back two years ago, there was a lot of young soldiers have died from up here. (Female, 41, Pen-cwm)

In the context of this deprivation, many extended family networks provided substantial support to their members on a daily basis. Indeed people's accounts of the ways in which they shared domestic labour echo those in the original study. What comes across very strongly in the interviews is that these networks are based on different generations of women. Thus, as we have seen in the case of Sharon, she, her mother and her sisters see each other on a daily basis, giving each other practical support of many different kinds. Men are marginal; this does not mean that they are totally absent, though in many cases they are, but they are not central to the daily activities and support networks of the women.

> The men, up here it's mainly the women rule, let me tell you. It is, up here it's the women that are the heart and the soul of the family that keeps the family together, not the men. (Female, 41, Pen-cwm)

Women significantly outnumber men in Pen-cwm (the female-to-male sex ratio was 1.2 to 1 compared with 1.06 to 1 for Swansea) and, of our 56 interviewees, 36 were women and 37 were under 50 years of age. Despite their low profile, however, there were some men who were spoken about very fondly as providing considerable support. One woman who was a lone parent told us about her closeness to her father and how he gave her practical support.

> My father is very good. He takes my son to work, I don't drive, he drops my daughter, Suzanne, she is nine, to gymnastics, we go shopping together, me and my father are very close you know, good friends. I get on well with my father. (Female, 36, Pen-cwm)

Men who were unemployed were also able to provide considerable practical support to members of their families. One, for instance, had helped his mother-in-law move and decorate twice, something he would have found more difficult had he been in employment. His mother-in-law, however, was ambivalent about his lack of work.

> Well what I find strange about their household is that he doesn't work. [*Yeah that's different*] And I don't think it's a very good reflection for the kids growing up, I don't, but I mean she keeps telling me it's a different age, people are different nowadays, but I can't see how that changes that a man goes out to work to keep his children. That's the one thing I have against him, and that is that he doesn't work.... But it seems to be through choice really, it's not that he can't get a job. If he does take a job it's only for a few weeks. (Female, 59, Pen-cwm)

Our interviewees in Pen-cwm were overwhelmingly women (36 out of 56) and it may be that we were able to tap into the women's networks because we were talking to people about families. Indeed, one of the women told us that we would never be able to get men to talk to us on this topic. This suggests that the networks, as in Bott's study, are gendered and that women's and men's social worlds are distinct (Bott, 1957).

As well as close-knit networks there was also a lot of falling out with family members and inter-family conflict featured strongly in many of the Pen-cwm interviews (cf Gillies and Edwards, 2006). Thus, family members spent months and sometimes years not talking to each other and there were reports of whole swathes of relatives never speaking due to some feud that had taken place years ago. There was also an intense negativity expressed about families by some of our interviewees who saw them as always expecting support without giving anything in return. One of our male interviewees voiced this particularly strongly.

> My mother and father died and the family just fragmented then and we weren't a very close family anyway. I was always fighting with my brothers, both at the same time normally. [He says later] I'm more or less a loner. People can rely on me more than I can rely on them. I learnt a long, long time ago, not to rely on other people. [He supports his sister financially but says] She's a pain. She's a drain on my resources.... She's unemployed and she's got four kids. And I said to her, 'Get off your backside now and go out and get a job.' Because with working credit now, she'd have a proper little earner.... But she doesn't want to work..... It's normally us giving to everybody else. We're not at the receiving end. (Male, 49, Pen-cwm)

The social circumstances of many of those we interviewed led them to talk about constant hardship and the struggle to survive. It is in this context that kinship networks become indispensable to survival; many of those we spoke to said that they would not be able to manage without the support of their families, and by this they literally meant support with daily survival in very reduced circumstances. People give each other financial support, but this takes the form of borrowing money until the next pay day or until the Social Security payment arrives. Scarce material resources are shared when they are available, and the willingness to share is what constitutes family. Such generalised reciprocity can be seen as a survival strategy when resources are scarce (cf. Sahlins, 1972; Pahl, 1984; Gillies and Edwards, 2006).

Clearly, Pen-cwm is an area that is characterised by social exclusion, if social exclusion is taken to mean poverty and deprivation, but it is also characterised by high levels of support within kinship networks. This support coexists with conflict and suspicion of outsiders – because they might turn out to be representatives of the state. Some of our interviewees were reluctant to give us too much information in case we 'grassed on' them to 'the social', and indeed one or two of them told us that they had been 'grassed on' by members of their own family.

Discussion

In the context of debates about social capital and social exclusion, the support exchanged in Pen-cwm, in conditions of severe deprivation, and the networks of which it is part, could be described in terms of bonding social capital. It is support that enables people to get by rather than to get on (see also Pahl, 1984). It can also be seen as exclusionary insofar as it creates close-knit networks that are resistant to the involvement of outsiders (cf Li et al, 2003). Furthermore, in conditions of high unemployment, women are at the heart of locality-based networks with men often having a marginal position within families and kin groups. This, together with the importance women attach to 'being there' for their families and, particularly, their children, suggests that social exclusion may more accurately reflect men's rather than women's experience of unemployment. It is possible that unemployment leads to men being socially excluded because they cannot fulfil the provider role, which is still valued in Swansea, and this means that they are not only excluded from the labour market but are also marginal to the women's networks which are at the heart of extended families. For women, unemployment does not necessarily have this effect because they are fulfilling their role as mothers, daughters and kin keepers whether they are in employment or not. Social exclusion therefore seems to be a gendered concept which is derived from the effects of unemployment on men and men's experiences of it rather than women's. This limits its usefulness when considering the effect of unemployment on families' ability to support each other for two reasons. The first is that it fails to describe the poverty and deprivation in which women's social networks manage to hold families together and create a sense of inclusion and belonging, that is, women's centrality to the creation of social capital. The second is that it fails to recognise that women, unlike men, have a socially sanctioned role outside the workforce, 'being there' for their families, and that as a result the impact on them of unemployment may be different. This does not mean to say that its impact is unimportant but simply that social exclusion may not be the best way of conceptualising it.

Overall there are clearly gendered moral values underpinning these patterns of support; this is particularly evident in discussions of 'being there' and in the importance attached to men's ability to provide. This chapter also shows that the idea of individualisation does not adequately capture the ways in which family members relate to each other. Thus, people provide support for kin even when it means modifying their own aspirations and putting their sense of duty and obligation above what might be seen as their individual interests. And similarly, although Pen-cwm has a higher proportion of what could be seen as 'non-traditional families' than the other areas, there is little evidence that this is a result of processes of individualisation. On the contrary, these families are deeply embedded in networks of mainly female kin which link them into dense, locally based social networks with high levels of social capital (cf Gillies and Edwards, 2006). Similarly, there is little diminution in the moral purchase of ascribed roles even though they cannot necessarily be achieved. In the next chapter we turn our attention to the care that is exchanged within extended family networks, showing that it continues to be gendered and that there are important class differences in care and support; these variations are evident in the different patterns of family formation and kinship networks characterising our ethnographic areas.

SIX

Caring families

In the last chapter we explored the ways in which extended family networks support their members, focusing particularly on circumstances where unemployment is high and resources are scarce. In this chapter we investigate how people care for children, older people and those who are unable to care for themselves, whether temporarily, due to illness, or on a more permanent basis. We also discuss how the connectedness of kin networks varies and how this relates to class and patterns of women's and men's employment.

Much research into the care that takes place within families looks at divisions of labour within nuclear-family households, usually focusing on the gendering of care work and the implications of this in terms of women's and men's participation in the workforce. The authors of the original study focused on how care and other domestic services were shared between kin living in different households. They found an extensive reliance on kin, particularly mothers of daughters, for help with domestic labour and childcare and hypothesised that, with increasing differentiation within kinship networks, the ability to provide such care would diminish. Recent research, however, carried out in what might be seen as the home of individualisation, California, as well as in Britain, shows that women rely on their extended kin networks for help with childcare (Wheelock and Jones, 2002; Gray, 2005; Hansen, 2005). Furthermore, there are class differences in this reliance with women in middle-class, professional families making 'family needs contingent on work' while 'working-class and upper-class women demand that their employment accommodate their care-giving needs' (Hansen, 2005, 213). This suggests that the value attached to 'being there' for your children is related to class, although not in any simple way, and that it is influenced by the value attached to paid work (Duncan et al, 2003). In this context it is significant that women's paid employment, particularly if it is full time, reduces their availability to 'be there' for kin and to participate in kinship networks. And if 'being there' is highly valued, which it is among our interviewees, then it is likely that women will not be inclined to participate in full-time employment, at least while their children are small or if they have other caring responsibilities. In what follows we explore the care that is exchanged within kinship networks, drawing out its class and gender dimensions and the way it is affected by women's employment.

Caring for children

As we have already seen (Chapter 3) contact between adult children and parents is higher for those who have children than for those who do not and it seems that having children draws parents and adult children closer together. This is easily explained insofar as much contact between family members revolves around doing things with and for each other and, with the birth of a baby, the need for help in practical matters increases dramatically. This is apparent from the moment a baby is born. Thus, one of our interviewees told us how all her female relatives had descended to help her on the birth of her first child.

> I was surprised, it hit me after having Coral, people were coming down and helping me around the house because I've been independent, you know. Because I had this baby now and like [sister] came down and was helping my mother-in-law clean and [other sister] was doing the ironing and I couldn't believe how quickly everybody was, it just shocked me, it just, you know. Everybody just rallied around me because I was like, I used to do for them and all of a sudden now, I suppose it was my turn. (Female, 33, Parkfields)

This sort of response to the birth of a child is commonly reported in oral histories and is unremarkable, although in this case our interviewee was surprised by the level of support.

While the need for childcare might increase contact between adult children and their parents, contact between women in full-time employment and kin is lower than contact for other women. Our study shows that women who are in full-time employment see all categories of kin less frequently than do those in part-time employment, with the exception of child and partner's mother (Table 6.1). In particular, 9.4% fewer women in full-time employment saw their mother in the past week than did women in part-time employment (74.3% as compared with 83.7%). Men in full-time employment were less likely to have seen their own parents in the past week than were women in full-time employment (65.9% of men had seen their mother in the past week as compared to 74.3% of women). And, as we would expect, given the uxorilocality of patterns of residence, they were more likely

Table 6.1: Contact within the last week with family members not living in household, women and men in employment 2002 (%)

	Women		Men
Employment	Full-time	Part-time	Full-time
Child (most recently seen)	76.5	73.1	83.3
Father	70.2	76.6	60.5
Mother	74.3	83.7	65.9
Spouse's/partner's father	47.2	59.4	67.2
Spouse's/partner's mother	57.1	57.1	68.6
Sibling (most recently seen)	59.1	63.8	43.6

to see their spouse's parents than were women. The numbers of men working part time and both men and women who are unemployed are too small for us to be able to draw any meaningful conclusions about the effect of unemployment and men's part-time working on frequency of contact.

The way employment affects contact between kin was commented on by one of our interviewees whose daughter combines paid employment with mothering two small children.

> I'd say [daughter], now, the daughter that's married, they are a unit on their own, then. Whereas when I married and had the children, I was back and forth to my parents. My brother and sister-in-law, their children were always there, you know. [Daughter], I know she loves us to bits, but circumstances are such that she can't be back and forth all the time. You know, so in that way I suppose, because job-wise there is a lot of pressures on young families today, pressures on time, and so much more that the children do, and need, that we didn't need and we didn't do. And so there isn't the time then to spend with them as we would like. (Female, 60, Fairview)

These comments underline the pressures on time experienced by families which this woman links to her daughter's employment and to the fact that children are engaged in so many more activities now than they were in the past (Hochschild, 1997). This reduces kin contact between households and leads to a situation where heterosexual couples have, of necessity, to be more self-reliant (cf Hansen, 2005). Another of our interviewees spoke about the contact she has with her parents and parents-in-law and how this is affected by both geographical proximity and work commitments.

> My parents ... are retiring on Saturday.... But they live that little bit further away. And they work. Whereas my husband's parents are both retired. So, and they are that much closer. But I would see them, my mum and I are very close. So I would see them a lot more, and I probably will, when the baby comes I think my mum's moving in. (Female, 34, Fairview)

Her comments underline the fact that it is not only the work commitments of parents of young children which can reduce the time available for contact with kin, but also the work commitments of grandparents, particularly grandmothers (Gray, 2005).

Despite the demands of paid employment, the frequency of contact between women and their kin remains quite high even for those in full-time employment. This may to some degree be a consequence of arrangements for childcare. The survey showed that 39.5% of women in full-time employment and 30.2% of those in part-time employment required some arrangements for childcare. Of these, 70.6% in full-time employment and 75% in part-time employment relied on either their parents or the parents of their partner. However, whereas women in part-time employment were equally divided in their reliance on these two categories, women in full-time employment relied much more heavily on their own parents (58.5%) rather than on their partner's parents (11.8%). This reinforces our findings that women are closer to their own parents than to those of their partner. It also highlights the importance of grandparents in providing childcare, something that has been observed in other research (Strangleman, 2001; Wheelock and Jones, 2002; Gray, 2005).

In Britain as a whole, for instance, 55% of women and 38% of men aged between 25 and 34 years report that they receive help with childcare from their parents. Conversely, 70% of women and 50% of men aged between 55 and 64 report looking after their grandchildren (Nolan and Scott, 2006). We cannot provide comparable figures from our study, but just under a quarter of survey respondents who had children reported needing childcare in order to work in paid employment and 58% reported receiving help with minding the children. Of those needing to make childcare arrangements in order to work, most relied on their own or their partner's parents (50% of women and 25% of men relied on their own parents and 25% of women and 25% of men relied on their partner's parents). The preference for 'babysitting' was similarly for own or partner's parents, with 51.5% of women and 32% of men relying on their own parents and 17.2% of women and 34 % of men relying on their partner's parents. In the US 'other relatives' most often care for children whose mothers are in employment. In 1999, kin 'cared for 40.6 per cent of school-age children whose mothers worked full time' (Hansen, 2005, 9; for Britain see Wheelock and Jones, 2002; Gray, 2005).

These figures suggest that parents' first port of call for help with childcare, whether to enable them to engage in paid employment or simply to go out for an evening, is their own or their partner's parents. In what follows we explore the involvement of kin, especially grandparents, in caring for children and the ways in which older family members are cared for. We also investigate the impact of relationship breakdown on contact between parents, particularly fathers, and children, and the ways in which care is gendered. Finally we explore the relation between patterns of employment and kinship networks, drawing out class differences in the exchange of care.

Grandparents caring for grandchildren

Our suggestion that the decline in contact between women and their parents because of paid employment may be mitigated by the need for help with childcare is supported by data from our ethnographic studies. One of the women we spoke to was running a playgroup and commented that nowadays, because mothers are in paid employment, grandparents are much more involved in caring for their grandchildren.

> I think there are a lot more grandparents looking after children nowadays than there were years ago.... When I see them coming into playgroup, the amount that have grandparents bringing them in now is, is a lot more than even when we started. A lot more grandparents are taking on the childcare. (Female, 53, Fairview)

Some grandparents cared for children because they shared a home with them. One of our interviewees lived with his wife, his son and his son's daughter subsequent to his son's divorce. As a result, he and his wife provided considerable care to their granddaughter who lives with them 'part time'.

> She's here every day. She sleeps three nights one week and two the next. But every day she'll come home from school here and she has dinner here most days. She's not here on a Wednesday and alternate Saturdays she's not here. Otherwise she comes here some time every day. (Male, 68, Treforgan)

However, living in an extended family household did not always mean that help with childcare was available. One of our Bangladeshi interviewees told us that she had had to give up her job because her husband's hours of work did not allow him to look after their children while she was working.

> With my husband's brothers' wives, yes, they are OK. I can go out and say, 'Can you look after him?' or that when I'm not there, they'll look after him. But my husband's direct family, brothers and sisters, can't rely on them.... That's the whole reason I had to give up [work].... Some weeks it would have to be the whole two days that they'd have to look after them. So I can't do that. (Female, 28, Parkfields)

The involvement of grandparents in looking after grandchildren was highly valued by grandparents and parents alike – sometimes, however, there were differences of opinion as to how a child should be treated. One young mother, for example, said:

> I'd say I have most clashes with my Mum. It's not that I don't get on with her, it's just differences of opinion. I guess she is of one particular way of upbringing and culture, and I'm trying to tell her, 'Look, your children are with two cultures and this is their way'. So sometimes it clashes.... Again, now that she's looking after my daughter I don't want her to do certain things with my daughter, that she will do.... For example, I mean, things to eat. Certain things that I do not want my daughter to taste chocolate until at a later, later day. But my Mum will be stuffing little bits of chocolate. Or Coke.... But, you know, this is something I have to live with because I do need to have someone with her. (Female, 28, Parkfields)

Although there were some exceptions, especially where grandmothers were incapacitated, it was usually grandmothers who were involved in providing regular childcare for their adult children. This often meant that children also saw their grandfathers and that grandfathers were also involved in their care. The availability of grandparents to look after children was important to enable younger women to return to work or continue with employment after maternity leave. Some told us that the fact that their mothers were unable to look after their children meant that they could not consider paid employment until their children were at school.

> My mum fell ill a few years back, just before I had Ellie, and she's not really up to minding her, on a regular basis then. So I just have to wait until she goes to full-time school really. And get something then. (Female, 30, Parkfields)

The care provided by grandparents varied. Sometimes they provided care on a daily basis and sometimes grandchildren stayed with them at half term and for periods of time during the school holidays. The nature of care often depended on how far away grandparents lived. Several of our interviewees reported that they had moved to be closer to their adult children and this often enabled them to care for grandchildren. This was the case for one of our interviewees who had moved to Swansea to be closer to her daughter after her husband died. She saw her daughter every day and regularly looked after her grandchildren.

> We are very close. [*So you go over there.*] I just walk over, I mean they are not long gone actually, that's how, the floor always has crisps on it, the children, crisps and biscuits, and I'll see them probably at seven o'clock again this afternoon. Oh yeah, I see her a few times, I could see her twice a day, although definitely once a day every day, it's very rare for me not to see her once a day, and if I don't, the only time I don't see her really is when I'm on holiday. (Female, 59, Pen-cwm)

And some, because of geographical distance, had grandchildren to stay during school holidays.

> So I don't see them as often as I would like, because they are both working, the children are in school obviously, but I did have the children for must have been about three,

over three weeks in the summer, so you know they stayed here. Because Helen had just started a new job and didn't, ... she'd just started so she didn't want to ask for holidays ... so they came to me, and we had a whale of a time. It was really nice, because you know as I say, we don't see that much of them. Sort of high days and holidays. (Female, 60, Fairview)

In the eyes of one of our interviewees, there was now a better relationship between grandparents and grandchildren. The following exchange took place between two sisters.

First sister. Mind, I think grandchildren now have got a better relationship with their grandparents.

Second sister: Because they are the ones looking after them.

First sister. I think so. I think I've got a better relationship with my grandchildren than I had with my grandparents. (Female, 63, Parkfields; Female, 62, Parkfields)

Some grandchildren chose to move in with their grandparents, often when their custodial parent began a new relationship. One woman's grandson had recently moved in with her and her husband when his mother had repartnered. Another of our interviewees told us that when his daughter had divorced his ex-son-in-law several years ago, his ex-son-in-law had returned to live with his parents and one of our interviewees' granddaughters had gone with him. She had remained with them after his ex-son-in-law's death and was still there, even though his daughter was now living away from Swansea with a new partner. As well as showing the importance of grandparents in their grandchildren's lives, this also illustrates the practical support that parents provide for adult children by allowing them to return to the parental home when marriages fail.

Grandparents looking after grandchildren sometimes met with disapproval. A woman in her seventies and living in a flat in a sheltered housing complex looked after her 4-year-old grandson several days a week. He is her son's child.

Lots of people here say to me, 'Oh what are you doing that for, why do you have him every day? You're getting older now, your patience is gone and all this, and it's too much for you.' Well I don't think it is.... I say they've got to work. 'Oh my daughter wouldn't work and leave me to mind her children.' But I don't mind it.... They are always telling me, 'You shouldn't be doing it, she shouldn't be working now.' But that's me. [*If you enjoy it then that's great, isn't it.*] I do enjoy it, that's me. They are my life, my children and my grandchildren are my life.... And I'm quite happy to be doing it, all I can to help them, they've helped me and if I can do anything to help them I will. (Female, 71, Pen–cwm)

The disapproval expressed is for the daughter–in–law choosing to work thereby making herself unavailable to care for her child and placing demands on the child's grandmother. The grandmother, however, emphasises that her children and grandchildren are her life, she is not simply caring *for* them but also caring *about* them in a very fundamental way. This care is reciprocated and demonstrates that, although conceptually we can separate caring for children and older people, in reality they are different aspects of the same relationship and cement the kin network. Care is embedded in these networks. This interviewee had looked after her daughter's children when her daughter was a single parent so that she was able to go out to work; she had also helped look after her son's stepchild. Before moving into the sheltered housing complex she had lived a few doors away from her daughter. Now she has very supportive relationships with her daughter, her son and her son's partner. She often stays the weekend with her daughter, who works as a warden in a sheltered housing complex similar to the one where she lives. While there she helps her daughter with the washing. Her children supported her recently when she moved from one flat to another in the sheltered housing complex. They decorated for her and moved her furniture and also paid for a new carpet. Her children and her son's partner care for her when she is ill. She also mentions that her daughter and her son's partner often pay for her shopping or invite her along for shows and outings which they pay for.

This example shows the reciprocal nature of care within kinship networks. Outsiders see someone in her seventies, who is clearly in need of support herself, providing it for her son's partner as, in their eyes, it is clearly the son's partner rather than the son who is responsible for childcare. They view this as inappropriate. What they do not see, however, is the complex web of caring of which she is part and which enables her to both give and receive care and support. This is the 'tangled web of reciprocity' that characterises kin networks and that holds them together (Hansen, 2005).

Caring for grandchildren after separation or divorce

The contact between grandparents and grandchildren was often maintained despite the grandchildren's parents having separated. This was described by one of the men who had grown up in a single-parent household headed by his mother.

> I think, well, for me it's strange because in our house when I was a child there was my mother, myself and my brother who was disabled, and then living just up the road, a couple of doors up were my dad's parents. And even though we weren't in touch with my dad, his parents were still extremely influential in the way I was brought up, they were, they were just so close, they were – I don't think a day went past that we didn't see them. (Male, 29, Pen-cwm)

Caring arrangements could, however, give rise to tensions, especially when adult children had repartnered and existing care arrangements involved grandparents maintaining a relationship with an adult child's ex-partner. One woman in her sixties told us how she had given up her job in order to look after her grandchild for her son and his first wife and that she continued with this arrangement after their marriage ended. This meant that she saw her ex-daughter-in-law on a daily basis and her son much more seldom, a situation which did not meet with the approval of her son.

> [My son] says that I see more of her than him which I do … but he thinks it's odd that I'm still in touch with her. But it was only because of [grandson].... Had there been no children I may never have seen her again. It's just that we get a little bit of aggro [*He's not too happy about it then?*] No, it's only recently. Up until now he's not bothered you know. But now, whether it's his new partner or – (Female, 66, Parkfields)

Another of our interviewees described the way her father and her ex-parents-in-law helped with childcare. She told us that sometimes she sees her parents 'about four, five times a week',

> Yes, because sometimes my father will pick up Coral or
> Gavin from school. If I'm finishing at four because of flexi,
> and then my father will pick them up at twenty past three
> and I'm around their house by ten past, five past four....
> And they babysit for me. (Female, 33, Parkfields)

Her mother is unable to help her with childcare now because of her crippling arthritis, though when she first returned to work her mother looked after the children for her. She also gets help from her ex-parents-in-law, who have the children for half terms and during school holidays; she feels particularly close to her ex-mother-in-law and values the way that they entertain her children rather than 'just buying them things.'

These examples show how adult children's need for help and support once they have children, as well as bringing parents and their adult children closer together, can, in some circumstances, help to maintain relations with ex-in-laws.

Relationship breakdown

Relationship breakdown, however, even though contact with ex-parents-in-law might be maintained, often involved a loss of contact with children. As we have seen, all contact (apart from that between wives' and husbands' parents) is greater among the working class than the middle class and many working-class families have close and extensive kinship networks. Working-class men's contact with their fathers, however, has fallen between 1960 and 2002 and is now lower than contact between middle-class men and their fathers (see Table 3.9). This fall may be due partly to the increase in lone-parent families and partly to the increase in divorce between the two surveys. One of our interviewees told us that her parents divorced when she was 16. When asked whether she was still in touch with her father, she said, 'No I don't talk to him, I haven't spoken to him for seven years' (Female, 31, Pen-cwm). Of two other women whose parents divorced when they were teenagers one had occasional contact with her father (to remind him of her children's birthdays) while the other had no contact.

These accounts suggest that loss of contact is due both to fathers living in different households and to conflicts surrounding the divorce or separation or any new relationship fathers may have started. In some rare instances there were conflicts with mothers after a relationship breakdown, with children developing closer relationships with fathers, but this was only mentioned occasionally. For instance, one of our interviewees maintained contact with her father after he and her mother had divorced and even went to live with him for a while. She no longer considers him her father, however, because, in her eyes, he does not meet his paternal obligations.

It was not only adult children who spoke of reduced contact with fathers subsequent to divorce but also fathers who spoke about a lack of contact with their children. A man who was divorced told us that he never saw his children, one of whom was now 30 and the other in his late twenties. He was clearly upset about the circumstances while talking to us.

> I saw them about, before she [his wife] got − it's very difficult to talk about because she married a guy and they either encourage you to be with your children or they're the opposite. Unfortunately they were the opposite and I saw my daughter when she was fifteen, that was the last time. So it was a long time ago. [*How old were they when you got a divorce?*] Eight, my daughter was eight and my boy was four, so my boy probably don't remember me anyway, you know. (Male, 61, Treforgan)

The lack of contact was not always because of conflicts, sometimes it arose because contact was seen as disturbing a new family set-up and fathers might feel they had no right to see their children.

> Well you know, when I went to London, you know technically I was, I was the one that left. And you can't expect really to split up and leave a wife or a daughter and then think you can just come back two, three, four, five years later and carry on from there. So obviously the bitterness was there. (Male, 55, Pen-cwm)

These accounts illustrate the difficulties that relationship breakdown can create for fathers' contact with children and also that, in some circumstances, fathers do not feel that they have a right to see their children. Such difficulties, together with the higher proportion of lone mothers in 2002 than in 1960, might go some way towards explaining the reduced contact between working-class men and their fathers between the two surveys.

Separation, however, does not always disrupt fathers' contact with their children. Thus, one young woman spoke positively both about her own father, who is separated from her mother, and her child's father, from whom she is separated. Her child's father visits his child, he supports her financially and also cares for their son.

> Yeah he takes him down to see his mother every Saturday or every Sunday or in the weekend. (Female, 19, Pen-cwm)

There is an interesting difference between Fairview and Pen-cwm in attitudes towards relationship breakdown. In Fairview, divorce and separation are seen as disrupting a stable family life, a stability which is aspired to. In Pen-cwm, however, as we have seen, relationships with men are central neither to kinship networks nor to the 'essence' of family life which means that divorce and separation are not so disruptive. We return to these differences later in the chapter.

Caring for parents

Caring for parents was quite widespread among our survey population, with 23% of men and 22% of women supporting someone outside their household, most usually their parents. Such care could consist of calling in on a daily basis to see if they were all right to helping them with shopping and providing more intimate care if they were unable to look after themselves. A woman in her fifties spoke about the way she supported her mother who had moved to Swansea to be closer to her. This was a pattern which was more common among our middle-class interviewees who had often moved some distance away from the parental home for work.

> I take her for hospital appointments, do things on the phone for her, arrange for someone to come and repair things, I go to the library for her, I make sure that she's got enough food in the house, she mostly eats these microwave meals now, so I get those, various different things, especially something new that I think she might like. Occasionally, if I make a Sunday dinner, I put one on a plate for her and take that up. I used to be there when she had a bath, but she can't bath at the moment because her arm is in plaster.... And if she falls over she calls me out to pick her up. (Female, 49, Fairview)

Sometimes elderly parents, particularly if their spouse had died, went to live with one of their children. More often, however, parents who were growing older lived close to their adult children rather than sharing their homes.

Maintaining independence

In the exchange of care it is important to ensure that independence is maintained. This need to maintain independence was found in the original study and is a common theme when exploring kin contact and care for older people (see, for example, Finch and Mason, 1993; Phillipson et al, 1998). One of the men we spoke to, who was in his late sixties with two sons living nearby, talked about the need to maintain independence.

> It's great, they are near enough to walk to see each other, but we don't live in each other's pockets, we all lead our own lives. But you know, we all, if you like, if I want anything, or he wants anything, or they want anything, then they can ask you know. And we'll help each other.... but as I say we don't live in each other's pockets. (Male, 69, Fairview)

He contrasts this with a situation where an unwelcome dependence was created between himself and his mother.

> When my mother lived in town after my father had died, I used to pass my mother's door ... every day, going back to town. And I begun to call to stop every day to see her, and I found it wasn't the best, because if I was unable to call one day, she was vexed because I didn't call. She was vexed until the next day she saw me. And she would say, where was I yesterday. Forgetting the fact that I had been in every day anyway. You know, her concern then was where was I yesterday. And I realised then that the one thing you shouldn't be is regular about anything with relationships, is that people focus on the wrong bit of it. You know they focus on the bit when you are not there rather than on the bit when you are. So I stopped calling regularly on my mother, on a daily basis, but I called regularly on an ad hoc basis. And of course the result of that was that every time she saw me she was pleased to see me. And when she didn't see me, she didn't worry about it. (Male, 69, Fairview)

This had led him to conclude that it was more important that contact be enjoyable and spontaneous rather than regular and formal. This is fine if all parties are able to be independent; dependency, however, due to ill-health or frailty, both requires regularity and threatens independence.

One of our older interviewees talked about the need to maintain independence and not rely too much on her daughters in light of her own experience with her mother.

> My mother was a very needy person. She was a very good mother to me and was marvellous to my children. But she needed me more than she did anyone when my father died and I think that was a big strain.... So I always said I would never, ever impose that on my children, if I can help it. (Female, 67, Fairview)

She achieves this by calling on a range of people to help her and her invalid husband, for whom she cares, rather than always relying on her daughters.

These comments indicate the importance of maintaining independence, not only for those who are in need of support but also to protect those who might be expected to provide it. This is a balance which was noted in the earlier study (Rosser and Harris, 1965) and underlines the importance of reciprocity in the giving and receiving of care (Finch and Mason, 1993; Hansen, 2005).

Grandchildren caring for grandparents

Grandchildren, as well as being cared for by grandparents, were involved in caring for them in turn. One of our younger interviewees who, as a student, was living away from her parental home during term time, was close to her grandparents and helped her grandmother to look after her grandfather when she was at home.

> If my grandparents are ill then I'll go home and help out, but I talk to them on the phone a lot, I speak with mum usually three times a week, my grandparents at least once or twice a week. Try at least once. And we don't usually write or anything, just usually speak on the phone to keep in touch. (Female, 19, Fairview)

Ill-health and bereavement

Kin also need to be cared for if they are ill or bereaved. One of our older interviewees, who was in her eighties and one of nine siblings, had lived in Fairview all her life. After her mother died, her sister had become ill. Our interviewee had looked after her and later helped her to sell her mother's house, which, being the only unmarried sibling and having lived with her mother until she died, her sister had inherited; she subsequently helped her sister find another house. On another occasion she had looked after the same sister when she had been ill and spoke of her as the closest of all her siblings.

> So I used to take her for her treatment. So this is why she is the one I'm closer to. Than, I'm close enough with all of them, but there is a different relationship. And as I say she is ten years younger than I am. And so that happened. (Female, 80, Fairview)

The support and care she gave to her sister reinforced the closeness of their relationship. It was common to talk about the development of especially close relationships with family members or friends when people needed care in this way. Another woman cared for one of her cousins.

> But again I'm very involved with her. Because she is housebound. Even though she's got five boys I'm the only sort of female cousin that's there.... I think she relies on me because I'm the only sort of female cousin she's got left. So I'm very close to her. And she is nineteen years older than me, twenty-one years older than me. So she brought me up a great deal of the time. My mother was involved in the business, and she used to take me off you know for weeks at a time. So she is like a surrogate mother in a way. (Female, 67, Fairview)

These comments emphasise both the association of care with women and the ways in which kinship relations are constructed. One of the reasons she looks after her cousin is because she is the only female relative, the other is that her cousin was 'like a surrogate mother'. In the previous example also, there was a ten-year age gap between the two sisters, which made the relationship 'different'. Both these relationships are constructed as being like that between mother and daughter, and this is offered as explanation of both the caring and the closeness of the relationship.

Several adult children who lived a long way away from their parents reported returning to be with them in case of illness or hospitalisation. This was true even when parents were living on another continent. One son, for instance, had returned to Bangladesh to be with his mother when she had broken her wrist and needed hospital treatment.

> I was there, physically I was there when the operation was carried out. And she needed blood so I had to give her, well I insisted, the doctor to take blood from me. So of three of our brothers, we all donated our own blood. Yes, it is a responsibility. Like, same thing, when my father-in-law was here, unfortunately he died last year. And I used to visit him almost every day. He was suffering from diabetes and he had renal problems. I used to visit him every day to find out how he is, does he need any help, this and that. (Male, 39, Parkfields)

This interviewee spoke about the moral responsibility he has for his mother and other relatives who are in need of care and support. Another man told us about how he cared for his dying sister.

> It's like, Mary was ill for what, she was ill six months, and I took it upon myself to help my sister for good reasons … And I spent a lot of time with my sister when she was extremely ill … my sister passed away then. ….You know there is very few of my family I can think that wouldn't do what I'd done there. (Male, 48, Pen-cwm)

Although he says that other members of his family would have done the same, he has clearly developed a special ability to care for very ill people that is drawn on by his family; it is part of the 'kinscript' (Stack and Burton, 1993). At the time of the interview he was supporting another sister who had recently lost her husband and was suffering from depression. Most men, however, were not involved in caring so closely for those who were ill or dying.

Conflict and resentment between adult children could and did emerge when parents became frail and in need of care, often revealing the expectations surrounding its provision. A man whom we interviewed, for instance, told us about how he had had to shoulder the main burden of caring for his mother.

> There was my sister, unfortunately. I don't, I cannot stand
> her. I shouldn't say that really ... I don't get on with my
> sister, my brother doesn't get on with my sister at all.... I had
> my mother living with me when she was dying for a year
> ... and her participation, because I was working, looking
> after her, it was terrible. And she was the same when she
> died.... So we don't get on.... I was a little disappointed in,
> in that the family could have done a lot more. You know?
> I had people opposite when I was working who were in
> their seventies, while I was working keeping an eye on
> her, you know? I mean, my brother and my sister, it's only
> expected they should take their share. [He said later] My
> sister didn't have the temperament to deal with it. (Male,
> 61, Treforgan)

Neither his brother nor his sister had pulled their weight when his
mother was dying but in his comments it is his sister who bears the
brunt of his opprobrium.

The gendering of care

This sort of care and support is clearly gendered as are the expectations
surrounding it. This is clear from the experience of the grandmother
who is caring for her grandson and the disapproval that it elicits from
her friends, and in the comments from the man about his sister's failure
to help care for their dying mother. The expectations are that women
generally look after children and older people while men provide the
more practical support such as decorating, driving people around or
fixing gadgets. These gender differences do not mean that men are not
involved in caring at all. Some are, as we have seen, and a few of our
interviewees thought that men's involvement in caring had changed.
One woman told us how her husband had become more helpful
round the house.

> Yeah he's got more sort of helpful the older he is getting.
> Like before he wouldn't watch the kids for me to go to
> Tesco's or nothing, I drag them all down with me and I
> didn't have a car then, I used to drag them all the way
> down to Tesco's and back and whatever, but like now he
> will just watch the kids while we go down. (Female, 47,
> Pen-cwm)

And another woman told us that one of the most significant changes in her family is that her son-in-law does not work, in contrast to her father, her husband and her brothers who had always been in paid employment. On the other hand her son-in-law did a lot of housework and cooking. In the following exchange her daughter and son-in-law, talk about this.

> *Him*: You never seen a husband in the house cleaning or looking after the kids would you in the sixties.
>
> *Her*: There were men that have done it then, but it just wasn't promoted the way it is now.... My grandfather used to help my nan, you know.... It just wasn't promoted.
>
> *Him*: But they wouldn't, like you said, they wouldn't shout about it, like you see them on the telly.
>
> *Her*: It's just the modern times.
>
> *Him*: But it's all, oh my husband say look I'm out now, I'm out shopping with my friends. Oh where is the kids? Oh my husband's got them. And I mean you say that. (Female, 31, Male, 39, Pen-cwm)

Despite such changes, caring was generally seen as something that women were better at than men. This was clearly expressed by an older couple who were interviewed together. He had suffered a heart attack several years previously and praised his daughters for the way that they had looked after him at the time and subsequently. His wife echoed his praise, comparing their own luck in having daughters with that of her husband Jim's brother, who has sons.

> I've got two wonderful daughters and Jim's so lucky because his brother's got two sons, his wife is ill, one lives in London and the other is working away a lot. And his wife is ill and he's on his own really with her, looking after her. (Female, 70, Parkfields)

The implications of this are that sons cannot be relied upon like daughters. They move for work or to live closer to their partner's parents whereas daughters are more likely to stay close (Leonard, 1980). This couple's daughters were in and out of their house on a daily basis even though they both worked full time. Indeed our interviewee had looked after both daughters' children so that they were able to continue in employment. They were very proud of how well their daughters had done; their broken marriages were sad but had not changed the close and supportive relationship they had with them.

Others also spoke about gender differences in caring.

> I find males very selfish. 'I'm okay, don't worry about anybody else.' I mean don't get me wrong, my brothers, if one of them is in trouble, then the others will go to see if they can help. But they only think of themselves, they don't think of the rest of us as a family.... you know if I phoned up and said 'oh Heather is in hospital', they wouldn't say 'oh you know I'll come and visit Heather in hospital with you', because they wouldn't go if somebody else was in. You know whereas the females of the family, I would go to visit Heather, Heather's children would go to visit my mother. But the males, no. That's why I think males are selfish. (Female, 37, Pen-cwm)

Not all men behaved like this, however, as we have seen. And there are also cultural differences in the gendering of care. Among Bangladeshi families, for instance, it was sons rather than daughters who had a moral responsibility to ensure that their parents were cared for and it was the norm for sons rather than daughters to live with or close to their parents. This does not mean that they were involved with the daily work of caring, but there are clearly different cultural expectations as to who should be responsible for the provision of care which affect the way women and men behave.

Class, kinship networks and care

At the beginning of this chapter we discussed the ways in which employment, particularly when it is full time, reduces the amount of time for interacting with kin. This is often seen as a problem arising from women's employment but it is important to remember that men's employment has the same effect. This lack of time can lead to a greater 'isolation' of heterosexual-couple households from their extended kin and be associated with looser-knit kinship networks (cf Gillies and Edwards, 2006). Here we explore the relation between relatively high levels of employment, the provision of care, and the nature of kinship networks in our different ethnographic areas.

As we have seen, women who are in full-time employment have lower rates of contact with kin than do those in part-time employment, a pattern which is reflected in national figures (McGlone, Park and Roberts, 1999). Our survey data show that there is a link between patterns of employment and class, such that 36.5% of women in Rosser and Harris's 'middle' and 'intermediate middle' social classes were in full-time employment, as compared to 20.3% of women in 'working' and 'intermediate working' social classes. Similarly, in our two more middle-class ethnographic areas, women's and men's economic activity rates were significantly higher than in our inner-city and working-class areas. Indeed, in Fairview, among 25- to 34-year-olds, men's economic activity rates were 90.2% and women's were 78.9%. Economic activity rates were slightly lower in Treforgan and considerably lower in Pen-cwm and Parkfields (Table 6.2).

We have already seen that there are class differences in the types of support that parents are able to offer their adult children which are clearly related to employment. Thus, in Pen-cwm help with housing consists of identifying a council house that is empty and close and subsequently providing practical help with decorating and furnishing, while some of our middle-class interviewees talked about providing the finances for a down-payment on a house. Frequency of contact is also greater among our working-class respondents which suggests that practical and daily support is also likely to be greater. This certainly seems to be the case. Thus, in Pen-cwm, intergenerational care and support was embedded in extended, inter-household networks of mostly female kin (see Chapter 5). In Fairview, in contrast, family households generally consisted of a heterosexual couple where the man was the main provider and the woman the main carer. High levels of employment meant that men were able to give what was often significant financial support to adult children and that there was less time for kin contact. As a result, nuclear-family households appeared to be more self-sufficient than was the case in Pen-cwm and there was less intense *daily* interaction with members of the extended family.

Table 6.2: Economic activity rates by age and sex

Age (years)	Pen-cwm		Parkfields		Treforgan		Fairview	
	Male	Female	Male	Female	Male	Female	Male	Female
20-24	68.0	40.0	38.0	37.0	86.0	69.7	61.3	56.9
25-34	74.0	40.0	69.0	65.0	87.5	72.2	90.2	78.9
35-54	61.0	48.0	59.0	65.0	84.5	73.9	90.1	74.1
55-59	42.0	27.5	49.0	40.0	64.7	51.5	81.4	48.5
60-64	15.0	7.0	32.0	13.0	33.2	23.5	38.5	49.5
65-74	0.0	4.0	2.0	4.0	7.6	5.2	10.1	6.7

One of our middle-class interviewees living in Treforgan commented on this.

> I think we're very much a small nuclear family, really, now. Although we came from families that were extremely large. I mean, you know, my mother's side were about sixteen children. (Male, 59, Treforgan)

Another, from Fairview, told us that he and his wife 'felt very self-contained, and it wasn't that important to us whether the rest of the family were close or not.' He went on to say,

> And my wife and I used to sort of find it funny that a lot of her friends, there'd be a real big sort of mother–daughter thing, you know, in the East End [of London] mothers and daughters would always be in and out of each other's houses, and we never did that sort of thing, you know, we always wanted a little bit of distance between ourselves and our parents.... My wife and I are the primary deal and the rest is ancillary to that. (Male, 46, Fairview)

These comments support our contention that when both parents are in paid employment, nuclear-family households tend to be more self-sufficient and, possibly, isolated. This was particularly apparent in Fairview, where priority was given to nuclear rather than extended family networks, and people commented on families being more of 'a unit on their own'. In Treforgan, however, where there was also a substantial middle-class population, there was more evidence of the continued existence of extended kinship networks. This difference can, we suggest, be related to the cultural differences between Treforgan and Fairview, with the former being more 'Welsh' than the latter.

There was also an impression in Fairview that kinship networks were less close knit nowadays and this was linked by some to changes in women's employment. A retired teacher told us that in the past,

> Mothers didn't work, I think that was a point of your question, mothers didn't work, they were family mothers. Very interestingly a lot of the one-parent family mothers didn't work in my old, in my school. They were, the state provided for them, extra allowance, because they were one-parent families. (Male, 74, Fairview)

These comments reflect the fact that women's employment rates have increased and are higher in Fairview and Treforgan than in our other two areas. This, together with our survey findings that middle-class respondents lived further away from their parents than their working-class counterparts, suggests that kin networks in middle-class areas are less dense and less likely to be available to provide care and support for children (see also Gray, 2005). This may not only be because of a lack of proximity of kin but may also relate to the demands of middle-class careers which make it difficult to engage in the reciprocity necessary to sustain the kin networks which can be mobilised to provide childcare. In these circumstances our interviewees turned to more formal childcare provision, either childminders or day nurseries. We are unable to provide data on how class influences the use of formal childcare, but recent research in the US found that professional middle- and upper-class families were more likely to rely on formal childcare, while working-class and middle-class families were more likely to rely on informal care provided by kin (Hansen, 2005). Similar patterns are reported for Britain (La Valle et al, 2000; Gray, 2005).

These findings tie in with other research into extended family networks and suggest that kin networks in middle-class areas are less dense than those characteristic of working-class areas. Moreover, a reduction in social capital in the form of close-knit, informal networks based on kin may be a middle-class phenomenon arising from different patterns of paid employment and greater geographical mobility. Thus, greater differentiation within family households and kinship networks does indeed lead to a lessening of kin support, as was predicted by the original study, and is most apparent in Fairview, our most middle-class area, as well as among our more middle-class professional interviewees in Parkfields.

Discussion

Taken together, this and the last chapter demonstrate an intricate set of norms and beliefs regarding support. Thus, expectations of support are age and gender specific and people over a certain age or who are not in good health are not expected to provide support. Exceptions often help to illustrate these norms because of the way that interviewees justify or verbalise expectations that are otherwise only implicit. There is an expectation of reciprocity in the provision of care and support; this does not necessarily mean exchanging the same or similar sorts of care and support but can often be a more symbolic gesture which expresses appreciation. Reciprocity is also often delayed and can take the form of generalised reciprocity.

Reciprocity in the provision of support is also closely linked to the balance of independence and dependence. If interviewees feel they can offer something in return for support this means that they are not totally dependent and this is an important consideration for those who are recipients of care (cf Gillies and Edwards, 2006). These expectations of reciprocity, together with the need to maintain a balance between dependence and independence, link kin in a 'web of reciprocity' (Hansen, 2005).

Our findings also show that support between households continues to be part of the fabric of family life and is still gendered. Even though kinship networks and the way care is provided vary in our different ethnographic areas, we found hardly any really insular families or individuals. Expectations of support between family members, such as being there for one another and helping in times of crisis, are generally held even if they are not realised in practice. This remains the case, notwithstanding the considerable changes in patterns of family formation and, particularly, women's increasing employment and rates of marital breakdown. Indeed, women's employment is one of the things that bring together women of different generations in the provision of childcare.

There are, however, significant differences between our ethnographic areas in the density of kinship networks and the care and support exchanged. These are related to differences in employment patterns and geographical mobility, both of which are associated with class and cultural differences.

SEVEN

Dispersed kin

As we saw in Chapter 3, there are high levels of geographical stability among the survey population, with relatively few respondents having lived for substantial periods of time outside Swansea, let alone outside Wales or the UK. However, there has been a small but significant increase in geographical mobility between 1960 and 2002 which is greater among our middle-class respondents. This, together with class-related patterns of employment, is reflected in the variation in the kin-connectedness of our different ethnographic areas with Fairview, our most middle-class, culturally 'English' area, being characterised by less dense kinship networks than our more working-class and culturally Welsh areas. In this chapter our focus is on those who have experienced geographical mobility and whose kin are dispersed. We explore how kinship networks are maintained over distance, how technology facilitates this maintenance, the significance of ritual in cementing relations between kin, and the meaning of place in connection with family and kinship.

First, however, we look briefly at findings from other research into geographical mobility and its effect on support and contact between kin. As we have already seen (Chapter 3), studies suggest that, within the UK, most family members live within relatively easy travelling distance of each other (McGlone, Park and Roberts, 1999; Nolan and Scott, 2006). Living at a distance, however, limits the ability to engage in 'the kinds of daily tasks involved in caring for someone such as transport, household assistance, meal preparation and shopping' (Ackers and Stalford, 2004, 136) and, as we have seen, informal childcare. This does not mean that support and care are not exchanged, simply that they take a different form from that which we have discussed so far. Thus, research into families of Pakistani origin in Yorkshire found that communication between kin living on different continents is frequent and that kin relations are maintained by regular visits which often coincide with important family occasions such as weddings; 'being there at key moments' is an important part of kin-keeping (Mason, 2004, 425) as is 'co-presence with and in a place' (Mason, 2004, 427). In studies of Caribbean and Italian families kin-keeping took various forms ranging from 'providing small favours and money loans, to telephone calls to family members to give advice, support or just merely "checking in'" (Zontini and Reynolds, 2007, 263). It also involved regular visits home, coming together for family events and celebrations, organising family meals, giving gifts and having kin to stay in the UK (Zontini and Reynolds, 2007). These ways of ensuring that kin networks endure are not peculiar to those who have travelled across continents and suggest that geographical mobility does not necessarily weaken kin networks, although it may change the forms taken by contact and support. And although caring for someone in the sense of looking after them is difficult when kin live at great distances from each other, there is evidence of such caring taking place across continents as well as over distances of hundreds of miles within the UK (Mason, 1999; Zontini and Reynolds, 2007; Baldassar et al, 2007). These findings run counter to the argument that distance attenuates networks of kin and the support they are able to provide for each other, and suggests that long-distance kinship networks are not necessarily associated with a decline in social capital (Zontini and Reynolds, 2007). And although these kinship networks may be disembedded, this does not mean that the local social relations constituting place are no longer significant.

Geographical mobility

Our survey results show that there are gender differences in geographical mobility. Thus, men are rather more likely than are women to have lived most of their lives outside Swansea and its surrounding area (22.3% of men as compared with 15.3% of women). Conversely, women are more likely to have spent all their lives in Swansea (82.7% as compared with 74.4% of men). And, as we have seen, there are gender differences in proximity to parents with women being more likely than men to live close to their parents. There are also class differences in geographical mobility with working-class respondents being more likely to have spent most of their lives in Swansea than their middle-class counterparts (see Table 7.1). This reflects national data which show that middle-class professionals and managers are more likely to be geographically mobile than is the working class (Fielding, 1995).

In all cases, women and men show similar class gradients, but geographical mobility is consistently higher among men than women. Thus, working-class women are the least geographically mobile (measured by these means) and middle-class men the most mobile, with 30.6% of middle-class men as compared with 6% of working-class women having spent most of their lives outside Swansea and its environs.

Table 7.1: Place where respondents have spent most of their lives by social class (%) (N=808)

	Middle class	Intermediate middle class	Intermediate working class	Working class	Total
This part of Swansea	44.9	53.3	69.9	68.2	60.1
Another part of Swansea	22.8	25.5	17.9	19.8	21.2
In region around Swansea	1.6	4.8	1.5	2.3	2.5
Another part of Wales	5.3	7.3	2.6	2.3	4.1
Another part of Britain (not Wales)	19.0	7.9	8.2	6.2	10.0
Outside Britain	4.8	1.2	0.0	1.2	1.7
N/A	1.6	0.0	0.0	0.0	0.4
Total	100	100	100	100	100

Similarly, it is among our middle-class respondents that the greatest dispersion of children is reported. For both first-mentioned and last-seen child, the proportion with children living outside Wales is greater for middle- than working-class respondents and this is the case even for last-seen child. This can be seen in Tables 7.2a and 7.2b.

This mobility of children of middle-class parents can, we suggest, partly be explained by children's participation in higher education. We discuss this further below.

Table 7.2a: Geographical dispersion of first-mentioned child (%)

	Middle class	Intermediate middle class	Intermediate working class	Working class	Total
This part of Swansea	18.0	29.6	23.6	32.4	26.4
Another part of Swansea	23.0	32.1	37.7	36.5	32.9
In region around Swansea	7.0	1.2	3.8	9.5	6.0
Another part of Wales	11.0	8.6	11.3	8.1	9.7
Another part of Britain (not Wales)	31.0	23.5	18.9	10.8	19.8
Outside Britain	10.0	4.9	4.7	2.7	5.3
Total	100	100	100	100	100

Table 7.2b: Geographical dispersion of last-seen child (%)

	Middle class	Intermediate middle class	Intermediate working class	Working class	Total
This part of Swansea	23.0	33.3	31.1	41.6	33.3
Another part of Swansea	24.0	33.3	44.3	36.2	34.9
In region around Swansea	8.0	1.2	5.7	7.4	6.0
Another part of Wales	10.0	7.4	6.6	6.7	7.6
Another part of Britain (not Wales)	29.0	21.0	12.3	8.1	16.3
Outside Britain	6.0	3.7	0.0	0.0	2.1
Total	100	100	100	100	100

The extent of geographical mobility varies in our four ethnographic areas, reflecting their different cultural and socioeconomic characteristics. Thus, in Treforgan and Pen-cwm, 73% of our interviewees had never lived anywhere other than Swansea; indeed close to one-third of our Treforgan interviewees had lived in Treforgan all their lives. In Parkfields and Fairview, in contrast, the proportion of interviewees who had always lived in Swansea was lower, at 51% and 48% respectively. In Fairview this reflects its overwhelmingly middle-class composition and in Parkfields it reflects the fact that there are both a sizeable middle-class population and a sizeable migrant and student population. The places where incomers originate also differ between the areas. Thus, in Pen-cwm 'incomers' tended to come from other parts of Swansea or its surrounds, in Fairview and Treforgan, despite their differences in terms of class, Welshness and geographical mobility, 'incomers' had come from further afield and, in Parkfields, the substantial minority ethnic and student population meant that there were incomers who had originated on different continents. In addition, Parkfields was an area of transition for those wanting to better themselves by moving from Swansea East to Swansea West.

In what follows we look at the way geographical distance affects the sort of support that is exchanged between family members and the type of contact that they have with each other. We look first at those whose families are within Wales and the UK and then focus on those, mainly our minority ethnic interviewees, whose kinship networks stretch across continents.

Support at a distance

Geographical distance affects the form taken by support rather than eliminating it altogether. In the accounts given by interviewees, visits, the exchange of gifts, financial support and telephone contact were all emphasised as important ways in which kinship networks retained their vitality. One of our older interviewees, for instance, whose son lives in England with his wife and children, goes to visit him regularly and they come and stay with her. She gives her grandchildren pocket money and often buys them clothes. She buys presents for her son and his wife and, when her son set up his own business, she and her husband helped him financially. As with support when children live close by, its gendered nature is clear even at a distance. A woman spoke about the support she gets from her children, both of whom live an hour and a half's drive away. Her daughter always accompanies this woman and her husband to hospital when her husband has an appointment.

> She nips down and meets us there [hospital] so she can come in with me when we see the doctor. Because, I say, the more minds listening, especially with me, because I've got a butterfly mind coming, I know. To make sure we've got the points, and what to do for Stan. [*Yes. And then she brings you home?*] Brings us home, we have our lunch.... And then she goes back home, in time for her children to come back home from school. (Female, 76, Treforgan)

Her son, in contrast, on his father being diagnosed with a serious illness and because his father was the one who did the washing up, immediately went out and bought a dishwasher.

> So Andrew said,... 'You come along Mum. Come to Comet. Just have a look at these dishwashers.' I said, 'I'm not getting a dishwasher.' 'Just come and have a look at them.' Anyway, went, I did see them and we've got it in the kitchen now. It's in the kitchen. That's all right. But I never said I wanted it. Because I didn't. Because it's so small, our kitchen. (Female, 76, Treforgan)

The difference in support offered by this daughter and son reflects men's propensity to provide support by spending money on 'things' and women's inclination to spend time and 'be there' even when they live a considerable distance away. Another of our older interviewees told us how his sons visited rarely but gave him gifts such as a TV, DVD player and mobile phone. He said,

> But they are very good to me. They'll buy me anything I want. So I haven't got support in that sense but I think if I needed it they would be there. (Male, 82, Parkfields)

His sons lived away and were not therefore available to provide other support for which he relied on neighbours and friends.

Visits were an important part of maintaining kinship ties, thus emphasising the importance of co-presence (Mason, 2004). However, greater distances tended to make visits less frequent. One of our interviewees told us that now that his sister was living in Europe it was more difficult to see her.

> I see my brother quite a lot, well quite a lot, to put a figure on it, three or four times a year, my sister not so often. I went to [European city] last year to see her, and I suppose it must be about once or twice a year. It depends you know, I haven't seen her for a long time, but just before, up until about a year ago I saw her quite a lot in a short space of time because of family weddings and this sort of thing, you know, we saw each other a lot, but it's difficult, when your family is very spread out, it's difficult to see each other very often if you are all working and busy, it's not so easy. (Male, 41, Fairview)

He says that he is probably closer to his brother than his sister although he turns to her for advice about 'serious' things. He maintains contact with both of them between visits by regular phone and e-mail communication.

The sort of support that can be exchanged at a distance most often takes the form of talking frequently on the phone, particularly if someone is in need of advice or going through a sticky patch. And visits may be more frequent if someone is in need. Thus, one of our interviewees had experienced a marriage breakdown and because of this she, her brothers and their families had made the effort to go on holiday together.

Telephone contact, like other forms of communication, is gendered. One of the older women told us that she spoke to her daughter twice a week on the phone, whereas she only spoke to her son once a week. And men's paid employment provided a rationale for their telephone contact with kin being less frequent than that of their wives. One man spoke about contact with his son who was living in another Welsh city.

> He was here a fortnight ago because it was my birthday. He comes, he comes now and then and I've been up to see him. But we don't go long apart. [*Do you phone each other?*] The wife will phone a lot. And he will phone a lot. It's when and where I am because of the shifts....They can't work out my shifts. They just phone and hope. (Male, 50, Treforgan)

E-mail contact was not mentioned by many of our interviewees, although some spoke of using it to keep in touch; texting was only mentioned by one or two of our younger interviewees. Our survey results showed that over 68% of parents had had telephone contact with a child in the previous week compared with only 1.6% of older and 2.2% of younger parents who had used e-mail to contact a child. Indeed, interviews were often interrupted by phone calls between mothers and daughters, even when they lived in adjacent streets.

Caring at a distance

It was rare among those who had been geographically mobile to be caring for ailing parents, although the example of a daughter travelling to be able to attend her father's hospital appointments demonstrates that it does happen. It was more likely that parents moved to be close to their children or that there were other siblings who could take on these responsibilities.

If parents moved to be closer to their children this often happened on retirement. One woman whose daughters were working and studying in a nearby city told us that she was considering early retirement and moving to be nearer to them. And one of our male interviewees told us about his parents' move.

> We moved here in [year], and then two or three years later after my dad retired they moved as well. So it's a lovely place to live, so, and good for the children as well to be near their grandparents.... We are living in a mobile society now, it's good that they can see their grandparents when they want to. And help with babysitting of course and bringing them up, which is good. (Male, 34, Fairview)

His comments on the 'mobile society' reflect Rosser and Harris's characterisation of 1960s Swansea; the meaning here, however, is somewhat different. They also highlight another issue which arises when kin are geographically distant from each other which is that, as well as it being difficult to care for ailing parents, there is also little opportunity for help with childcare. We noted this in Chapter 6 and it was noticeable how frequently women lamented their distance from their own parents, even if they were close to their parents-in-law, as help from parents-in-law was not so forthcoming as they thought help from parents would have been.

Parents could, however, be reluctant to move. One of our Bangladeshi interviewees told us of her maternal grandmother's visit which had been sponsored by one of her brothers. Her grandmother had come over for a family wedding and could have remained with her daughter and her family permanently. Her account underlines the difficulties of caring for kin at a distance and the anguish that separation can cause.

> We did so much to keep her here. Because the problem is she's got no one back home. She's got two daughters, her sons are here as well. And my mother's brothers are here. So it's usually the sons who look after the mother.... And since my grandfather died it's really bad because she's gone really lonely and sad. And even despite that she'd rather be lonely and sad than live in this country.... But she just had this fear of dying here. She, 'don't want to die here', she said, 'whatever happens I don't want to die here'. (Female, 25, Parkfields)

The significance of class

As we have seen, participation in higher education could contribute to a greater dispersal of kin, particularly over the generations. Indeed, some of our interviewees had moved to Swansea as students and stayed and, as a result, were at some considerable distance from the rest of their families.

> Our family are all quite dispersed now.... the reason I came to Swansea was I came to university here, and like many people I just stayed you know and met a local lad and all the rest of it. So I just never moved away really. (Female, 46, Fairview)

Conversely, several of our older interviewees told us of their children's successful careers which had started with a university education and resulted in their moving away from Swansea. This raises an important question about the ways in which family responsibilities are negotiated and the sort of balance that is struck between individual life goals, often involving career, and the need or desire to stay close to family. We have already seen an example of a young Chinese woman giving up her aspirations for higher education to work in the family takeaway. In contrast, one of our older, middle-class, geographically mobile interviewees told us that she was prioritising her own need for self-development. She said that what made someone family was that,

> Everyone understands everyone else's sort of limitations and aspirations I think. And we all know that if, that whatever goals we have in life, everyone understands those, so if the goals in life sort of supersede sort of family contact for one reason or another, everyone is quite understanding, and we catch up with them later.... But it doesn't matter if you don't talk to them, maybe for a couple of weeks or a couple of days or something like that, they know oh I must be busy, and catch you later. (Female, 55, Fairview)

She was putting this philosophy into practice by living apart from her husband in order to pursue her educational goals. She went home every three weeks or so. She also lived a long way away from her mother, visiting her every few weeks, and told us that her mother had 'always been really independent'.

There seem to be class and cultural dimensions both to the relative valuing of individual 'careers' and family and to the balance between frequency of contact and independence. Thus our middle-class respondents, particularly those in the professions, tended to emphasise the pursuit of individual goals through education or paid employment. This contrasted with our working-class respondents who stressed the need for jobs to fit in with their families (cf Hansen, 2005), a view which was shared by some of our minority ethnic interviewees. Many of those who identified strongly as Welsh had clearly also made job choices that allowed them to stay in their home communities; one woman in Treforgan told us how her fiancé had accepted a teaching job in London because, at the time, there was nothing available locally. She had stayed in Swansea and he managed to return to the area two years later when they were married. This is reflected in the patterns of residence and contact among our Welsh respondents (see Chapter 3).

Similarly, expectations about frequency of contact were related to class. This comes across in one interviewee's account of the differences between his own and his father's expectations of family visits and those of his father's new wife.

> I have to go there from time to time, otherwise he thinks I've fallen out with him, so – actually his new wife does, he doesn't mind. I mean honestly he and I are on the same wavelength, but his wife is a [valleys town] person and her family has always been around her and a very close-knit family. And she finds it very strange that we are not always ringing each other up and always visiting and we are a little more distanced. I mean we are very close, but we don't feel the need to see each other all the time. And so I often pop in to make her feel happy really, because otherwise she feels there is something wrong with his family. (Male, 46, Fairview)

His account underlines the different family practices associated with class. His father's new wife embodies working-class expectations of regular and frequent contact while his own and his father's views are more characteristic of the middle class.

Both these things, valuing a 'career' and a lower frequency of contact with kin, went hand in hand with an emphasis on independence. It also changed parental expectations of what their children would do for them. One of our interviewees who was caring for her husband had a daughter living and working in England and a son in Swansea. She had herself been a nurse until her husband became ill. She said of her children,

> *Wife*: They've got their own lives, and they've got their own professions.

> *Husband*: They can't stop their jobs to come and help their mother with the old crock.

> *Wife*: So this is why when I'm old I've made provisions. And I'm going to go into a home. And I don't expect my children to cater for me, I wouldn't expect them to cater for me. I don't think it's fair, you know, in this day and age they have mortgages, and even if they have good jobs, they should carry on with their jobs. (Female, 63, Fairview)

This attitude is similar to that reported as being typical of Dutch parents of migrant children which reflects the 'cosmopolitan, individualistic' culture of the Netherlands. It is also associated with a high value being attached to independence (Baldassar et al, 2007, 50). Despite this emphasis on independence, several interviewees told us that they had moved back to Swansea to be closer to their parents as they aged and were more in need of support. And it was usually the case that even though some children might move away for work, others remained to do the necessary kin-work (Stack and Burton, 1993).

Independence and individualism

Geographical distance did not imply a lack of emotional closeness, although this was sometimes the case. One of our interviewees, when asked how important her family was to her, said,

> I wouldn't really say it's that important. Not, not now. I mean I've never depended on my father for anything. It's like, I'm always amazed when friends of mine, even at my age, they're sort of 'Oh, I'm going to have to ask my mother or whatever for some money or maybe they'll help me out with the tax for the car.' And I think, 'Oh my God,' you know, because I've been … staunchly independent, even when I was living at home. (Female, 45, Parkfields)

These views contrast quite markedly with the expectations and practices of support which characterise Pen-cwm, our working-class area, and other working-class neighbourhoods. This interviewee came from a middle-class background, had moved to Swansea as an adult and told us that she regarded her friends and neighbours as family as well as her 'genetic family'.

> I think the people you know are family. The people you generally know and get on with … particularly these days, yes. You can be closer to your neighbour than you are to your sister or whatever. (Female, 45, Parkfields)

Emotional distance, however, is not always reflected in physical distance. Another of our middle-class interviewees who had returned to Swansea after going away to university and whose family still lived in Swansea told us:

> Well we don't see each other as often as I think we would like. We are in touch by phone, but sometimes months can pass without us meeting. It's partly to do with the fact that I don't have a car. So I find it difficult to actually physically get to their place. I've got a bicycle, but my sister is too far away really for me to cycle, and my brother, again, he lives up a hill…. So my mother too, I don't see enough of her either, for the same reason really, that I don't have any transport…. But we get together for birthdays, family birthdays, we usually have a meal … and other special occasions we get together. (Male, 51, Fairview)

These comments underline the fact that even when kin hardly ever see each other in the daily course of their lives, getting together for important family occasions is a way of maintaining kinship ties. However, several of our middle-class interviewees told us that their friends were more important to them than their families. It was interesting that in these cases they were sometimes referred to as an 'elective' family and the same practices that kept families close were engaged in. Thus, communication by phone or e-mail was frequent, they visited each other and went to each other's weddings. If they lived close they provided each other with support. One told us that his relationships with friends were 'stronger than most family relationships I think'. He went on,

> We keep in touch, yeah, phone, e-mail…. And because there is often a wedding or something like this coming or a christening or something there is always a reason for a big reunion…. We come together on these occasions and you know just have a really good time. (Male, 41, Fairview)

He gets a 'feeling of permanence' from his group of friends, much as he does from his family.

> As you get older you suddenly realise there is this bunch of people you've known for all your life, you know. And there is a sort of permanency there which is – probably gives you some sort of secure, security, psychologically probably…. I think that's why they are important, because it gives you a little bit of permanency in your life, everything else might change. And they are always there, so there is a thread, continuity, continuation. (Male, 41, Fairview)

Thus, although support might be different when living at a distance, family remained important for people's sense of identity and belonging, and this was reinforced by coming together for important ritual occasions such as weddings and funerals.

It seems that among those interviewees who are geographically mobile there is more of a sense of independence and individualism. This may be what impels them to move away from kin in the first place and certainly differentiates our areas and our interviewees. Thus, as well as more of our interviewees in our middle-class, 'English' area (Fairview) living at a distance from kin than did those in our middle-class 'Welsh' area (Treforgan), there was also more emphasis on the importance of independence and being able to pursue individual life goals which were separate from the family. We suggest that there is both a class and cultural dimension to these differences.

Family occasions

However far away kin live from each other most of them talked about coming together for family events such as weddings, funerals and important birthday celebrations. Weddings and funerals are occasions when more distant kin such as cousins gather together (most of our interviewees regarded cousins as distant kin, although among Bangladeshis they were regarded as 'immediate' family (Becker and Charles, 2006)). Birthdays seem to be times when closer family members come together, unless they are significant birthdays. Thus, for a fiftieth or sixtieth birthday extended family networks gather together to have a special meal and celebration, but for birthdays marking later decades more distant kin, in both geographical and degrees of affinity terms, are invited to celebrate the achievement of a long life. Thus, one of our interviewees told us of his own fiftieth birthday celebrations and those of his mother when she reached eighty.

> Yes. All here. Brother, sister, his boy and his girlfriend who's going to be his wife now in August.... My three sons and their girlfriends were here. My sister, my wife's sisters, because she's got three sisters. Only one husband came though, the other two were away on a golf trip. And the reason they went is because, for my fiftieth it was planned we'd be abroad. (Male, 50, Treforgan)

Fifty people had attended this celebration. But for his mother's surprise eightieth party there were 100 people. A lot of close friends were included but also many cousins whom he and his mother would not normally see.

> Oh I'm trying to work out the cousins now, my first cousins, three, four, three boys and a girl from one family and their wives and kids. Then there's, one didn't come because the daughter was, no, their son had a bump, their Alan he'd had a bump. So my cousin didn't come but her daughter did. Because it was touch and go if they were going to come anyway because her daughter was due any time but she came.... She came and her husband. And of course we hadn't met her husband. And another two came. I'd have thought about 25, 30 came from up there [England]. [*And these are people you wouldn't have seen as a rule?*] Yes. As you say, they are first cousins, they are all my mother's nephews and nieces then. Because she's got no brothers and sisters left up there. (Male, 50, Treforgan)

These face-to-face events are important in maintaining kinship ties and bring together people who may not see each other at any other time.

It is important to remember, however, that those who are geographically mobile and who live at a distance from kin are in a small minority in our sample, as elsewhere in the UK, although the trend between the two surveys shows that their proportion has increased. It is still the case that overwhelmingly, in Swansea, kin live close to each other and are 'there' for each other and this is the predominant culture of the area.

Transnational kinship networks

Those who had transnational kinship networks differed from each other insofar as some shared many of the characteristics we have already discussed, albeit distances were greater, while others had dense networks of kin in Swansea as well as kinship networks stretching across continents. The latter was particularly the case for our Bangladeshi interviewees. Despite their being separated by large distances, communication between family members was frequent. It was most likely to be initiated by those who were in Swansea because of the expense of telephone calls. One of the Bangladeshi men said:

And you won't believe, like, every week, if I don't talk to my mum it makes me feel I haven't quite completed my week. Something is missing and that's my mum. [*So you talk to her.*] Every week, sometimes three or four times a week. (Male, 39, Parkfields)

Regular telephone contact with kin living at a distance is associated with support such as providing advice and being available to discuss problems; however, as one of our interviewees said, distance means that it is difficult to provide 'physical' support. Thus, a woman whose parents and siblings were living on the Indian subcontinent kept in touch by phone and letters. She said that she speaks to her parents regularly, possibly once a fortnight, more often than she speaks to her siblings. This contact is a source of support.

But just emotional probably, talking to them, you know, that sort of thing.... Discussing problems or if we've got a problem with the children or something, we talk about. That sort of thing. Rather than physical support that if we were in the same place, maybe things would have been different. (Female, 48, Parkfields)

However, as we saw in Chapter 6, kin may travel very long distances to provide support if someone is ill and in need of help. Thus, one of our Bangladeshi interviewees told us that his wife was currently in Bangladesh, providing childcare for relatives while they went on *Hajj* (pilgrimage).

Visits

Almost all our minority ethnic interviewees told us about regular visits back home to see their parents and other kin. As well as being important to maintain contact with kin, such visits were also a way of keeping the culture of home alive. Thus a son told us that he, his wife and children visit his mother once or twice a year.

I think it is so important for me to keep the culture. Otherwise, if I don't do it after, maybe, second or third generation, the culture will die a death.... So it is important for my mother to know them and for them to know my mother. They've got to know who their grandmother is, who their granddad is. Where they live. And the difference we've got between Great Britain and Bangladesh. Where they came from, what's the lifestyle out there. And that is my culture. They have to know this. I think it is part of education for my children. And I will always encourage them to keep Bengali as their language. (Male, 39, Parkfields)

Sometimes, however, visits home were less frequent than interviewees would have liked, because their children preferred to go on holiday to different places rather than always visiting family. And financial constraints could also reduce the frequency of visits or eliminate them altogether; this was, however, unusual among those we interviewed as most of them had the means to finance international travel.

Family was sometimes defined in terms of visiting, something that reveals the significance of the visit in maintaining kin ties.

I mean apart from being blood related, it's just that you know that some people really care about you, and keep regular effort to visit you, and you make an effort to visit them.... So when we are there they all take time out and they all spend time with you. It's like the whole world stops while you are there. So it makes you feel like, yes, this is my family, there is nobody in the world that will treat you like that you know. (Female, 28, Parkfields)

Visiting family also took place within Britain. Women who had moved away from their parents and siblings on marriage often returned home for extended visits during school holidays and most interviewees made regular visits to kin living in other parts of the country.

Visits carried kin obligations. For instance one Bangladeshi man told us that when he goes to Bangladesh he visits poor relatives as well as rich ones.

I've got, like, poor relatives back in Bangladesh and I've got rich relatives as well. So whenever I go to Bangladesh I make sure I visit my poor relatives before I visit my rich relatives.... Relatives are relatives. Poor, OK, probably I've got a little bit better lifestyle than them, but I could be one of them. If I didn't come to Great Britain or if I didn't have the education I would be living in exactly the same place where they are. So it is important for me to remember my background and all my relatives. (Male, 39, Parkfields)

Others, however, distanced themselves from some of the family practices they encountered in Bangladesh. One young woman, for instance, spoke about the inequalities and status hierarchies that she encountered when staying in her uncle's house, saying how she did not like to see the way servants in the homes of her kin in Bangladesh were treated. And another of our younger interviewees said,

> I've been back to Bangladesh for visits. But only for visits. This is a way of life for me in this country.... It's like going back a couple of centuries. They live life different, men dominate the women. The women are just, even if they have an education and they work, they go to school and stuff like that and they work before they get married, as soon as they are married, they are housewives.... Getting married and having children and looking after the children are a way of life. (Female, 28, Parkfields)

It is interesting to contrast these comments with those of another of our interviewees who said that her joint or extended family was much more traditional than were families in Bangladesh. Her cousin had recently arrived from Bangladesh.

> She's really shocked that we keep in touch with everybody, how we are together. She said, 'We never see anybody back home.' Because back home we still have relatives and she hardly sees any of them. It's very private, family have become very private. But we've kept the tradition going as much as we can. (Female, 25, Parkfields)

Of course these two women are talking about different aspects of tradition: the first is talking about gender relations and the second is talking about kin contact between members of extended families. However, what these comments reveal is that they both perceive there to be differences in family practices between Bangladesh and Swansea, and that such differences mean that Swansea, rather than, or perhaps as well as, Bangladesh, is regarded as home.

> We stayed 6 months, I tell you I was dying to come back. [*Were you?*] Yes. I mean I'd go there for a holiday. I don't think I could stay more than 6 months. Even 6 months really got to me, I just wanted to come back. I think I could stay there just for about 3 or 4 months but after that it just

gets to me, so you just feel homesick because all my family are here. Even though I've got my mother's side of the family over there, but do you know, do you know because you're not used to that…. It's a completely different life. I mean, the life out there is quite good obviously but I just felt homesick really. I just wanted to come back to Britain. (Female, 31, Parkfields)

These accounts, as well as underlining the importance of being together in a particular place for maintaining kin relations, also point to the significance of tradition in maintaining a sense of identity and belonging; and tradition is embedded in specific family practices.

Ritual occasions

Visits often took place for weddings and several of our Bangladeshi interviewees or their siblings had been married in Bangladesh.

My brother's wedding … was in Bangladesh…. [We all] went to Bangladesh, my mum's side, you know, my side of the family went. We all went to Bangladesh, he was married over there. But next week there's another wedding on my husband's side of the family, so that's the next wedding. (Female, 28, Parkfields)

Weddings of remoter relatives were also attended. One of our interviewees had attended the wedding of her father's brother's wife's brother in Bangladesh.

My auntie's brother. That was the last, well, a relative's wedding I went to…. My dad is thinking of getting my brother who is in university now, getting him married. If he agrees to it that is, if he agrees to it. Which I'm sure he will…. So we are all planning to go to that wedding together. [*And is that likely to be in Bangladesh?*] It's likely to be. Because everyone is out there, you see. So even if it's somebody from this country we'll go out there to Bangladesh and he'll get married out there. (Female, 28, Parkfields)

Weddings did not necessarily take place in Bangladesh but, if they did not, every effort was made to enable kin to travel to Britain for the occasion. One of our interviewees told us that when her brother got married he financed visits for his maternal kin.

> I mean, my brother's wedding, my brother got my nan here and my mum's older sister and her husband. Especially for his wedding so, yes, I mean, obviously you can't get everybody because you need the money as well. So, you can't get everybody but he afforded those three people so he brought them over for his wedding. (Female, 31, Parkfields)

And she also told us that all close relatives had to be invited to weddings. We asked who they were.

> In that sort of situation say like both, from his mum's side and his dad's side, he has to invite everybody. From his dad's side I mean, from anywhere, he needs to, all the brothers and sisters, cousin sisters, cousin brothers. From his mum's side as well, cousin brothers, cousin sisters, aunts, uncles. Not just close ones, far distant ones as well. (Female, 31, Parkfields)

Here she is talking about a much wider range of relatives than is usually mentioned by our majority ethnic interviewees. And she uses the terms 'cousin-brother' and 'cousin-sister'. As Shaw notes in her study of Pakistani migrants in Oxford, 'In large households, it may be difficult to tell exactly whose child is which, or whether siblings are "real" brothers and sisters or first cousins. Cousins will generally refer to each other as brother (*bhai*) or sister (*bahin*)' (Shaw, 2000, 95). This system of classification relates to the joint family system practised among both Pakistanis and Bangladeshis which is reflected linguistically. Thus the men tended to refer to each other as 'brother' while, according to the prevailing classification system in Swansea, they would be defined as first cousins. One of the Bangladeshi women was talking about her sister, and only some way into the interview did it become clear that she meant her first cousin, or cousin-sister. Interestingly, one of our Welsh interviewees also referred to a cousin whom he regarded as a brother by virtue of the fact that he saw him a lot and felt closer to him than to other members of his family. And several of our informants mentioned first cousins in their own or earlier generations who had been brought up as siblings.

The rituals of death

As we saw earlier, a Bangladeshi grandmother's reason for wanting to return to Bangladesh rather than stay with her sons was that she did not want to die in Britain. This wish to die or be buried at home was spoken about by several of our Bangladeshi interviewees who told us about kin dying in Britain but being buried in Bangladesh (see also Shaw, 2000; Gardner, 2002; Mason, 2004). One, whose father had died and been buried in Bangladesh, thought that she herself would probably want to be buried there with him. She said that bodies were often sent back to Bangladesh for burial because 'family back home would like to see them and they have their own grave' (Female, 31, Parkfields). Then she told us about her father-in-law.

> My mother-in-law, she was buried here but I don't understand. It's his wife obviously, he's put his wife in this country but then when it came to his brother, he told the sons to take him back. So, I mean nobody could understand that because they were surprised. I mean, you get your wife buried here but then you like to give your brother's body in Bangladesh. And even then he was saying, 'Send my body to Bangladesh if ever I pass away.' (Female, 31, Parkfields)

One of the men talked about the ritual sacrifices associated with burials in Bangladesh and how he had accompanied his brother-in-law's body to Bangladesh in order to ensure that sacrifices took place and meat was distributed to the patrilineage and the wider community.

> Everybody went to Bangladesh after my brother-in-law dead.... And they make some donations to the poor peoples, they sacrifice the cows and things and they come back. (Male, 47, Parkfields)

Apart from its religious significance (Gardner, 2002), the desire to be buried in Bangladesh indicates the importance attached to place. That is where people's roots are and that is where they wish to return when they die. It is also where those kin are who will visit and pray for you after death (Mason, 2004). We did not explore these issues with our other minority ethnic interviewees and so cannot say whether these sentiments were shared. Neither did we explore them with our majority ethnic interviewees. However, many spoke about the importance of funerals for bringing kin together and, in the Welsh tradition, attendance at funerals, particularly by men, is an important way of discharging kinship obligations. This may relate to the cultural significance of the chapel and nonconformism in Wales and was commented upon by one of our interviewees. He said that funerals are 'very important' and that he would think it strange if a family member did not attend. His mother, however,

> has got it into her head that women don't go to funerals. So she never goes, she would be present at the after-funeral event, the wake if you like, she will never actually go to a funeral. She didn't even go to her mother's funeral, which we thought was odd. (Male, 51, Fairview)

His mother was correct insofar as the public side of funerals in Wales used to be an all-male affair. This gendering of religious rituals may have been attenuated but it is still apparent in funeral rituals and is something which is common to both our Welsh and our Bangladeshi interviewees. Attendance at ritual occasions, such as weddings and funerals, is an important indication of belonging and, in some way, attendance symbolises the importance of kin in your life. Attendance can cement and keep alive kin relations, even if contact in between such events is sporadic and distances between kin are great, and, like visits, it provides an opportunity for reinforcing very dispersed kinship networks.

The significance of place

The fact that some of our Bangladeshi interviewees talked about a wish to return to Bangladesh to be buried indicates that place is important both to kinship and to ideas of home. Similarly, visiting kin 'back home' and the importance of being together in a particular place underlines the significance of place to the reproduction of kinship (Mason, 2004). Homesickness is another way of indicating the importance of place and suggests that for some of our minority ethnic interviewees Britain is more home than where they or their families originated. This feeling of home may also be related to their most important kin being in Britain rather than elsewhere. The link between family and place is clear in the following account.

> I am very glad that I consider myself to be a member of a family. In the sense that I can say, well I came from there and, you know, this great aunt is living there, and that aunt

is living there, and this one is there.... Actually seeing the people doesn't matter so much. But it's the sense of knowing that I come from this area. And I do like that. And that's one of the reasons we moved back here was so that Rose would have somewhere that she came from. (Female, 49, Fairview)

Many people talked about moving 'back' to Wales, emphasising the importance of place and family in their decision to return. People spoke in these terms even when they themselves had been born elsewhere and it was in fact their parents who had left Wales. One, for instance, said,

My father had to go to London to get work, and was a school teacher in London, and I was born and brought up there and came back to Swansea quite by accident really. (Male, 46, Fairview)

And another whose parents had moved to be near him and his family said,

Well my father is Welsh, my grandfather was Welsh, so it's a kind of coming home for them. (Male, 34, Fairview)

The significance of place is also clear in the way interviewees talked about the different parts of Swansea; places invoke subtle differences of class and culture as well as differences in the sorts of family and kinship relations that characterise them. Many interviewees, when talking about moving from or growing up in other parts of Swansea, spoke as if these places were miles away and totally different from where they currently lived. This has been termed local thinking (Mason, 1999). It also perhaps explains the common view of Swansea as being made up of distinct villages (Rosser and Harris, 1965). Indeed these 'villages' are often culturally and structurally distinct and this is one of the things that enabled us to select four areas within the city that were significantly different in terms of their socioeconomic and cultural make-up. Local thinking is also apparent in the fact that moving to a different part of Swansea can affect frequency of contact with family and friends.

In fact friends, if they move out of the vicinity of the flat and they go up the hill then I start to lose touch with them. I get them on the phone and they say, 'Helen, you never come up and visit.' And I say, 'Oh yes, but it's up the hill,' and they go 'Look at it this way, Helen, we come down to your place and then we have to crawl back up the hill whereas you just have to turn round quick.' 'Yeah, yeah.' It's like, it's a totally separate area. Swansea is very much made up of separate areas. (Female, 45, Parkfields)

These sorts of separations and differences and the nature of community in our four ethnographic areas are the topic of the next chapter.

Discussion

Living at a distance from kin makes the exchange of support and care more difficult, although considerable effort is put into maintaining contact, usually by phone, and regular visits. Kin also come together on ritual occasions, such as weddings and funerals, and special occasions, such as birthdays. It was our middle-class respondents and interviewees who were most likely to live some distance away from their families and, for many, this was associated with a particular valuing of work and family. They tended to see work in terms of individual fulfilment rather than something that provided the wherewithal to survive. Associated with this is the high value attached to independence. Thus, our middle-class interviewees, particularly those in Fairview, were more likely to have loose-knit kinship networks which were not so firmly based in a particular place (Bott, 1957; Pahl, 1970). However, for most of the rest of our interviewees, including those with transnational kinship networks, their networks were close knit and rooted in place. Our Bangladeshi interviewees, for instance, had kinship networks which, as well as stretching across continents, were very close knit and rooted in Swansea as well as in Bangladesh. Thus, place was experienced as an important aspect of kinship; kinship tied people to a place as well as to each other. In that sense Bangladeshi kinship networks show similarities to the close-knit, working-class, kin networks in the parts of Swansea where they live as well as to the kin networks of those who are culturally Welsh. There is little sense here of individualism threatening close-knit kinship networks and high levels of social capital are very much in evidence. These issues are explored more fully in the next chapter.

EIGHT

Families, friends and communities

This chapter considers the variety of living arrangements that are found in contemporary Swansea, contrasting them with the findings of the 1960 survey. We noted in Chapter 3 that there has been a striking increase in single-person households between 1960 and 2002 as well as a substantial increase in married or cohabiting heterosexual couples living alone. In this chapter we examine the nature of these categories in more detail and ask what these household types mean in terms of contact with kin. We do this in part to show that, although people may not live in so-called 'traditional' family households consisting of a heterosexual couple with dependent children, they continue to be embedded in kinship networks which are linked to their families of origin and/or to previous partnerships. They also often have other family-like ties with friends and/or neighbours and in what follows we consider the nature of these overlapping relational categories of family and friendship. Furthermore, even the ideal-typical 'traditional' family only assumes its defining form for one phase of the life cycle: there is usually a phase prior to the birth of the first child, as well as another after the departure of children, during which the household consists only of a heterosexual couple. These two phases form an increasingly longer segment of the life cycle as the birth of the first child tends to come later in the woman's reproductive years, numbers of children decline and life expectancies increase. There is also likely to be a phase where only one parent remains and, as we shall see, this type of household accounts for a sizeable proportion of single-person households.

We also explore the ways in which people talk about those who are closest to them, whether they include friends and/or neighbours in their definitions of family and, if so, how they perceive these family-like relationships. Some of our interviewees spoke about the way friends had come to replace family in their lives and this suggests that friendship networks can take on some of the characteristics of networks based on kin. Such developments have been understood as indicating the emergence of 'families of choice' (Weeks et al, 2001) or 'elective families' (Beck-Gernsheim, 1998) and as being 'pioneered' by gay men and lesbians but by no means confined to them (Giddens, 1992; Roseneil,

2005). Others, however, argue that although increased dispersion of kin has led to a decline in '"solidaristic" kinship networks', categorical distinctions between family and friends remain strong (Allan, 2005, 234). We therefore investigate how friends come to be 'like family', what distinguishes them from kin, and the extent to which family as well as friends are, in some senses, 'chosen' (Pahl and Spencer, 2004a; Allan, 2005).

Finally we look at people's ideas and experiences of neighbourhood and community, how they relate to family life and how they differ in our four ethnographic areas. Much contemporary research into family and community mobilises the concept of social capital distinguishing, as we have seen, between bonding and bridging social capital (Putnam, 2000). Thus, ties of family and friendship constitute people's social networks and are understood as having an impact on the resources available to them, whether these be material, practical or emotional. Social capital is also understood as an aspect of localities, whether neighbourhoods, cities or states, and as something which inheres in local social life at the level of associations, organisations and social networks. This leads to differences between localities in levels of social capital which have a bearing on both the ability of people to 'get on' and their vulnerability to social exclusion.

Household composition, 1960 and 2002

The baseline study developed a typology of household composition that contained nine categories, ranging from single-person households, through those with and without dependent children, to unrelated persons living together. When we reproduced this table on the basis of our data, perhaps the most significant general observation was the inappropriateness of most of the categories for Swansea in 2002, in that each of five of the original categories contained only 0.5% or less of our sample (see Table 3.2). The intention of these categories had been to measure the incidence of extended family households which, by 2002, had declined to such an extent as to be insignificant. Related to this is the very shallow generational depth of most households in 2002, with only 19 respondents (1.9%) living in a household with three or more generations, whereas in 1960, 15.5% of respondents were in such a household. Household size also fell between the two surveys: the median household size in 1960 was three, by 2002 it had fallen to two.[1]

The most prevalent household type in both 1960 and 2002 was that of parent(s) and unmarried child(ren); however, the percentage of this type of household fell from 49.2% to 43.2% over the period. Although comparative data are not available from the 1960 survey, it is important to note that 5% of our respondents in this category represented single-parent households, that is, 'single, widowed, divorced or separated' with at least one child under 16 still at home. Two other household types increased significantly over the period: single-person households, from 5.5% to 19.9%, and married or cohabiting heterosexual couples without dependent children, from 19% to 32%. The increase in the former is due partly to the delay of co-resident partnerships and partly to the larger number of older people continuing to live independently. As noted above, the increase in heterosexual–couple households without dependent children also reflects changes at both ends of the age spectrum: the deferment of child bearing and the rise in the age of partnering at one end and, at the other end, the longer period between a couple's last child leaving home and the death of one of the partners. Taken together these changes have resulted in a fall in the proportion of respondents who were living as heterosexual couples from 76% (all of whom were married) in 1960 to 59% (9% cohabiting) in 2002. With this fall in the percentage of heterosexual couples, there were corresponding increases in the proportion of both single persons in the sample, up 7.8% to 19.6%, and respondents who were divorced, up 6.8% to 7.6% (see Table 2.1). If this last figure seems surprisingly low it should be recalled that divorcees frequently re-partner. Like the unemployed, they are often between past and future statuses.

Looking more closely at the category 'single-person household', we see that nearly half (48%) of these are constituted by those who are widowed, with another 23% separated or divorced, which leaves 29% of this category who were single, in the sense of never married. Given that 7% of this category were under the age of 30, the proportion of single-person households made up of individuals who have never married and are fairly unlikely to do so is about 22%. The age of 30 is the lowest 'at which being partnered is the statistical norm' so living alone at younger ages is not unexpected and cannot be seen as indicating a trend away from partnering and parenting (Wasoff et al, 2005, 208). Similarly, when we consider the breakdown of the household composition category of 'married or cohabiting couples living alone', we find that 86% are aged 50 or over and just over half are aged 65 or over, again suggesting that many of these couples are living alone after the departure of children. At the other end of the family cycle, 7% of these couples are under 30 and may simply be delaying having children. We asked childless respondents whether they had chosen not to have children, and 117 responded positively; of these, 29% were either married or cohabiting, and quite a high percentage of the total (62%) were under 30, suggesting that this decision is not irrevocable and may well be reversed in a significant proportion of cases.

When we look at our ethnographic data, we find a similar complexity in the actual make-up of single-person households, as well as the family circumstances of heterosexual couples living alone. In three of our case study areas, all the interviewees living in single-person households were either widowed or divorced, with a ratio of widowed to divorced of 2 to 1 or higher. Similarly, the majority of heterosexual couples living alone had adult children, with only a small minority having never had children. This under-representation of single persons (in the sense of never partnered) and of heterosexual couples with no children was an artefact of our describing the research as being about families. Potential interviewees often thought that we would not want to talk to them if they did not have children. This in itself says something about dominant understandings of family and is something that other family researchers have also found.

The ethnographic data allow us to look more carefully at the complexity of family and family-like relationships to be found in these various categories. Turning initially to single-person households and heterosexual couples living alone, we found some examples of people who were very isolated and seemed to fit the stereotype of childless people or couples with few or no family contacts and virtually no other close relationships. For example, one 86-year-old widower, who had spent most of his adult life nursing his seriously disabled wife, said he had no family with whom he was in contact. This was in spite of the fact that they were both from very large families in areas near Treforgan which was where they had lived all their married life.

> [*Did [your wife] have family around here?*] Yes, she did, yes. Six, six or eight children. Eight sisters. Eight sisters, you see? Aye, aye. Oh yes. It was a very large family, see? [*Yes. Are you still in touch with them?*] Most of them passed away, my dear. She had a twin sister up in [village], top end of the valley, she never seen her. Never seen her twin sister. Top end of the valley. Never seen her. [*Didn't come down here?*] Oh, no, no. Very independent. Whole family altogether. Oh yes. Very independent family. The sisters kept themselves to themselves. That's the thing. [*So you didn't see a lot of them?*] No, no, no. [*At all?*] No, not at all. Oh no. Aye. It's been a hard life. (Male, 86, Treforgan)

In order to explore interviewees' social networks[2] we asked them to complete a diagram (following Phillipson et al, 2000). This consisted of three concentric circles, the innermost to include those people who were so close it would be impossible to imagine life without them and the outer two circles to include those of decreasing importance (see also Pahl and Spencer, 2004a, 2004b). This man had no one whom he would put in the innermost circle and only with some prompting did he agree to include in an outer circle a neighbour he had mentioned who called to see him occasionally:

> There's nobody left at all, see lovey? I've got nobody at all. I'm on my own. [*Yes. But you were talking about that friend.*] Friend. Well, now and again he comes. [*Would you put him there but a bit further away?*] ... Shall I put twice a week if they've got time? (Male, 86, Treforgan)

Another man in his 70s, who initially declined to be interviewed because, as he said , 'I've got no family,' was similarly isolated, having lived with his mother until her death and having only one friend with whom he seemed to have fairly regular contact. These two men were, however, atypical of our interviewees who were living alone, even of those whose circumstances as single, divorced or widowed might suggest comparatively sparse family networks. For example, a woman in her 30s who had recently moved to Swansea was living in lodgings and told us she was still quite upset about a relationship that had ended, nevertheless she had chosen to come to the area because she had cousins nearby.

> I mean I wouldn't have come to the area if they hadn't have been here,... And I wouldn't have come unless I felt really close to them. Because I'm from, like, a big sort of, like traditionally Irish family and my family is really, like, strong and that. It's like, I'd find it weird not to have family at all around. I really value that. The sense of connection that I have with family really. (Female, 31, Parkfields)

Thus we found that family circumstances and household type were not particularly good indicators of people's connectedness, whether to family or to friends. As a final example of this we can look at another interviewee, a man in his 70s, who had been living in Swansea for over 40 years and in the same house for the past 25 years, with his wife, a native of the area. They had three adult children, two of whom lived nearby, whom they saw regularly about once a fortnight to once a month. This interviewee spoke positively about the area, 'it's a good spot to live, quite frankly. The people are very friendly.... You know? We know the neighbours and they're very, very friendly indeed. But, and people passing by are friendly as well.' However, although he appeared to have access to an effective and supportive family network, when asked what makes somebody family, he initially said that he could not understand the question, then went on to define family as strictly limited to his children: 'Well, I mean, they're either your children or they're not, you know. It's as simple as that.' Neither did he place any significance on extended family ties.

> The family's, how can I put it? The older generation, they were all cousins. I, but their children didn't have anything in common with us.... Right? So, although I met them, or some of them, I've only met the odd few and some of those I've only met at funerals, you know? But we've nothing in common.... (Male, 78, Treforgan)

Nor did he regard friends and neighbours as close saying, 'I've always avoided close personal friendships, literally have avoided.' Furthermore, when asked about the importance of his family to him, he rejected any idea of a significant supportive role, even within his tightly circumscribed definition of family, saying they were,

> Not all that important, quite frankly. I mean, they'd manage without me if they had to and I dare say, I'd manage without them. I managed without them for eight years nearly. I, I, I mean, I'm grateful for all the help I get, don't misunderstand me but if I need something done, I can afford to have someone do it without imposing on them. I'm grateful when they offer to help and I'm grateful when they do help but it, it isn't essential, you know. (Male, 78, Treforgan)

Thus this man, who, to an observer, had quite significant resources for an extensive personal network, clearly did not perceive himself as in any way closely linked to either family or friends. It is noteworthy that he felt able to reject any such mutual dependency because his personal economic circumstances meant he was financially independent and able to pay for help when needed. Others have noted that this is more common among middle-class families and is associated with loose-knit networks (Gillies and Edwards, 2006).

Family and family-like relationships

People such as those above who did not appear to be embedded in networks made up of extended family and/or close friends and neighbours were a very small fraction of the interviewees in our ethnographic areas. Most people gave evidence of being embedded in such networks from which they received both material assistance and other kinds of personal support. As already noted, it was possible to link the existence or otherwise of such networks neither to interviewees' status as partnered or unpartnered nor to whether or not they had children, although women's networks tended to contain more people than did men's. Our ethnographic data, however, reveal a wide variety of extended family ties and other family-like relationships among our respondents, and we now turn to a closer examination of the varying forms that these social networks assume.

These networks are often understood as constituting social capital, and clearly 'the family is a critical, if taken-for-granted, institution in which aspects of social capital are rooted' (Warr, 2006, 501). It is often assumed that social capital enables people to 'get on'; however, the social capital that inheres in local social networks in conditions of socioeconomic deprivation, while enabling people to survive, may not enable them to get on. This has led some to suggest that such networks should be understood as providing social support rather than social capital (Warr, 2006). Furthermore, social capital tends to be regarded as beneficial but this ignores the ways in which close-knit networks may reinforce social divisions and operate as a means of exclusion and closure (Bourdieu, 1986; Portes, 1998; Li et al, 2003; Crow, 2004; Warr, 2006). We thus consider the significance to our interviewees of their social networks and ask whether these networks have enabled them to 'get ahead' or whether their primary function is to give support for 'getting along' day-to-day. In the analysis that follows we draw on the network diagrams completed by our interviewees.

Despite the differences in the density of social networks characterising our four ethnographic areas, we have examples from all four areas of interviewees who were embedded in quite extensive kinship networks, and the availability of such networks was found to have influenced their decisions, for example, about where to live. One woman in her fifties and married, with no children, said that she and her husband had returned to Swansea to be close to her family, after about a decade living elsewhere in Britain.

My parents are, touch wood, are both still alive, my mother is in her eighties and my father is coming up to 80. I have a sister, and they, we all live in the vicinity, in the area. Really that's probably one reason why I wanted to come back, so, we are a very close-knit family, and I found it very strange living in a place where there is no family. I'd grown up with my cousins, and my grandmother was very important to me, and we were a very close-knit family, and I missed the family. (Female, 50s, Fairview)

This woman said she had been very close to both her grandmothers, and that the families of their children 'would all congregate in the grandmothers' homes'; this had established close contact among the cousins which, due to the longevity of both grandmothers, continued into their adult lives, although she admitted that the death of the last grandmother 10 years previously had signalled a change in this pattern of regular contact. She also felt that having close family nearby had 'spoilt me, because I don't need to go out to make friends quite so much'. Nevertheless, in completing the network diagram, she included not only members of her extended family, for example her cousin's daughters, whom she referred to as nieces, but also several friends: 'I've got two ladies who work here [in her shop] as well, and they are almost like family really, but I see them mostly in the shop. But I am very, I am quite close to them.'

It was clear, nevertheless, from other interviewees, that simply having a large extended given family, even living in close proximity to them, did not mean that interviewees necessarily included family members in their personal networks or even that they thought of all kin as family. Thus, a divorced woman, living with her partner and their two children, had difficulty in responding to our question about who she regarded as family, 'because I don't feel that I've ever had a proper family. I've had a father, grandparents and, and people around you, you know? Like extended family, I don't feel as if I've had that.' She added that she did not have a good relationship with her mother and was not bothered at all by the fact that she never saw her father, although she did feel close to her brother. For this respondent friends were more important than family. 'I've been lucky that I've had mega friends. I've got, you know? I've got, I've got good neighbours who I class as friends.' She then expanded on this to develop her understanding of family-like relations among friends: 'I think basically it's people, people who are there for you. People that you can turn to and people who you love. I think that's ... my definition of family then.' (Female, 37, Treforgan)

Her friends were therefore like family for her and were defined in terms of 'being there' which, as we saw in Chapter 5, was a common way of defining someone as family.

For these two women, friends had become like family or almost like family. For others, however, family was strictly limited to those they took to be related either by blood or by marriage, and this was reflected in whom they included in their network diagram. Thus, one woman, who was divorced and who had her daughter, her daughter's partner and her three grandchildren living with her, had quite a strict interpretation of whom she could count as family and was very definite that friends did not fit into this category.

> [*But what makes you feel they're family?*] [Laughter] That's a very strange question.... It is a very strange, because, they're family, because they're related to you, aren't they? [*Fair enough. That's great.*] Because if it asks you about your family, you wouldn't name your friends as your family, would you? [*You might. [Pause] If you had very close friends, you might. Consider them as part of the family, I don't know?*] No, I wouldn't.... I know what you mean but when you ask me specifically to name my family ... I would make, only name people who are actually related to me, myself. (Female, 57, Treforgan)

However, this interviewee was atypical. The majority of our interviewees included in their network diagrams some kin but excluded others, many included friends, and some included their pets (for further discussion see Charles and Davies, 2008; Spencer and Pahl, 2006). The criteria they used to make their selections were variable; thus one woman included all her siblings, her husband's siblings and their partners, but drew the line at her husband's mother's partner because the partnership had resulted from divorce.

> It's a very difficult one because I, I can't really say that her partner is my family. He's not my family. He's a lovely chap and he obviously makes [husband's] mum very, very happy but he's not family.... I think it's just I've been brought up with Mum, Dad, brother and myself and no divorces and, so when all this sort of, when I came into all this, I found it very difficult. (Female, 33, Treforgan)

Another woman, in her 50s, said that her family included her immediate family of 'husband, three children, daughter-in-law, *mam-gu* [grandmother] and the wider family of cousins and relatives' and then added,

> And friends as well, very close friends I would count as family because sometimes, especially in our lives, we lost parents fairly quickly and you felt that things were, you know? [*Yes.*] Without friends, we wouldn't have been able to cope. (Female, 57, Treforgan)

This woman's close friends were women she had grown up with and their relationship had continued all their lives. This kind of experience was not uncommon, particularly among interviewees in Treforgan, the area with the greatest population stability, and it was reported by both men and women. Another interviewee from the area, a man in his 50s, said there was a group of boyhood friends, whom he had known since they were 7 or 8 years old, who were 'very close friends I look after as family. I look after them all' (Male, 50, Treforgan).

A final example of the varied nature of our interviewees' personal networks is a man in his 40s, married, with no children, living in Fairview. His inner circle included his wife and several boyhood friends ('I'm probably closer to them than some people are to their brothers'), who were dispersed across Europe but with whom he maintained contact. He included in the other circles his nieces and nephews, some of his wife's cousins, his father-in-law and his father-in-law's partner, and his wife's siblings, but was careful to point out that 'the mother-in-law isn't here'. In addition, he drew the interviewer's attention to another member of his network, the family dog, 'Very important part of the family. [*Yes. You are not the first one.*] German dogs, Schaeferhunds' (Male, 41, Fairview).

From this consideration of the ethnographic data, we would argue that the boundaries between relationships that are 'given', in terms of consanguineal and/or affinal links, and those that are 'chosen' ties of friendship do not determine the relative position of family and friends in people's personal networks (cf Pahl and Spencer, 2004a; Finch and Mason, 1993). Most of our interviewees considered some 'blood relatives' to be family and others not and they usually selected some in-laws as family and rejected others. In addition, the majority of our interviewees, even those with numerous close extended family members available to them, also included some friends in their definitions of family and in their network diagrams – friends who were so close that they were 'like family'. The reasons given for these various selections were not usually framed in terms of normative rules defining relational categories but instead were based on individual experiences, relationships and histories. And the theme that emerged most strongly from all these narratives was that of support that had been, or could be expected to be, given and received (see also Becker and Charles, 2006). This comes across in the comments of a woman who was in her thirties, living with her partner and their two children.

> What makes somebody family? Well family are blood relations isn't it, but I would consider, if you are looking at it in a different type of way, I would consider [names her two best friends] to be closer that way than my own family are, they are more of a, you know, I think I can ask them for more than I could ask from my own mother, most of the time, without being criticised or judged for anything you know. (Female, 35, Pen-cwm)

As we have already seen, families provided many different kinds of support for their members, and interviewees talked about those friends whom they regarded as family providing similar types of support. Thus a woman in her 30s said of her childhood friend,

> Now I could ring her and ask her for anything and she is the type of person, well I've done it actually, I phoned her and said, 'Will you pay for a holiday on your Visa for me and I'll give you the money back?' Because you couldn't book a holiday over the internet with cash, and I didn't have a Visa at the time. (Female, 35, Pen-cwm)

And a woman in her 70s, whose husband had died the previous year, spoke of the support she received from her church group.

> I regard them, those members of the church, as family.... [*Yes.*] And we're all there for each other. A very, very caring group and, you know? We greet each other on a Sunday morning with hugs. We don't shake hands, we hug. [*Yes.*] And it is, it is very meaningful. (Female, 74, Treforgan)

With the exception of the financial support that particularly middle-class parents can and do provide for their children, and which is clearly instrumental for their 'getting ahead', most of the support that is exchanged within these networks of family and close friends is of the sort that allows people to 'get along'. This is not to underestimate its importance in enabling people to lead satisfactory lives: most of our interviewees regarded their personal networks, and the support they provided, as essential and central to their personal well-being. But it does suggest that these personal networks, which are primarily composed of strong, horizontal links that bond people of similar status, are not likely to be the source of significant bridging social capital. Social capital that can provide new opportunities and facilitate economic advance is more likely to be accessible via weaker links that give access to wider social networks linking people whose circumstances differ (cf Warr, 2006, 502; Crow, 2004). Such links are more frequently associated with the looser-knit social networks of the middle classes (Gillies and Edwards, 2006).

Communities and social change

The social networks that we have discussed so far are largely made up of kin or friends who are 'like family' and, particularly in our working-class areas, are close knit. These local social relations form the basis of community and are what attaches people to place (cf Strangleman, 2001). The original study examined community through a detailed empirical exploration of the nature and significance of extended family ties in Swansea's distinctive residential settlements. Famously, it began with an eloquent description by a key informant, Mr Hughes, of the changes in patterns of extended family contacts over his lifetime that, it was argued, represented a shift from close-knit to loose-knit networks and a weakening of community cohesion (Rosser and Harris, 1965, 4–18). What has actually occurred over the past four decades is, however, more complicated than an extrapolation from the experiences of Mr Hughes and his family suggests and, in what follows, we explore the ways in which community continues to be experienced and understood by our interviewees.

The 2002 survey contained several questions from the original study designed to reveal various indicators of community, both attitudinal and behavioural. Respondents were asked their opinion of their neighbours, as well as to compare the present helpfulness of relatives with the past and to express an opinion about who should have primary responsibility for the care of older people. In addition, we asked about membership in community organisations, as well as looking at religious affiliations. We did find some significant changes when we compared the results of the two surveys. Our main finding with respect to religious indicators was that these were no longer particularly relevant (see Chapter 4). On the other hand, as we shall see, our ethnographic data revealed the continuing importance of religious organisations at the local level for providing a framework for many people's personal networks and as a form of social capital. And when we look at membership in other local organisations, we find that there has not been a major decline: in fact 28% of the respondents to the 2002 survey said they were members of a 'social club or other organisation' in their area, as compared to 23% in 1960; and 82% of these said they had attended a meeting within the past month, as compared to 66% in 1960. In the 2002 survey we also looked at gender and class differences in membership in local organisations and found that, in line with other studies (Li et al, 2003), men were more likely than women to belong to such organisations (34.5% as compared to 23.6%). A less expected finding was that middle- and working-class respondents were equally likely (30%) to belong to local organisations. The types of organisations had not changed dramatically since 1960, but the distribution of membership showed some variation, with sports clubs showing the biggest increase (up 9.9%), church or chapel guilds the biggest decrease (down 2.6%). Other changes of note were evening classes (up 2.6%) and local branch of a political party (down 1.7%). Turning to the attitudinal questions, the biggest change was shown in response to the question 'Do you think relatives do as much for each other as they used to in the past?', which showed a decline in those saying 'yes' from 39.5% to 28.2%. There was some decline in the percentage who thought that relatives should be mainly responsible for caring for elderly persons: from 72.4% to 66.3%. However, the percentage who said they found their neighbours 'very easy to get on with' had increased slightly (up nearly 2% to 77.6%) and the percentage of our respondents saying they 'don't notice their neighbours very much' had declined from 17.4% to 13.2%.

Clearly, neither attitudinal nor behavioural indicators from the 2002 survey support a presumption of community decline in the sense of involvement in associational life. This contrasts with Putnam's thesis that social capital is in decline, and also with trends in Britain that show a decline in working-class involvement in associations and steady, if fluid, engagement among the middle classes (Li et al, 2003). In what follows we explore two aspects of community: local social relations, including kinship networks, and the organisations and associations in which people were involved.

Communities in decline?

Many of our older interviewees, particularly those living in long-established, working-class areas which had undergone considerable change over their lifetime, echoed Mr Hughes's view that 'It's a different atmosphere altogether now, I tell you' (Rosser and Harris, 1965, 16). Many came from large families and several recounted their childhoods as having been spent sharing a home with one or another set of parents, grandparents, aunts, uncles and cousins. Several had lived with the wife's parents in the early years of their marriage before being able to move into a house of their own, as near as possible to their parents and siblings. These were the young married couples identified by Rosser and Harris who were living 'through and through' in 1960. They described close-knit communities where everyone knew everyone else's business but where everyone felt safe and where doors were never locked. Despite the fact that many of them had their adult children living close by (in the same or adjoining streets) and were involved in looking after their grandchildren, like Mr Hughes, they felt that things were not what they used to be.

Such change, as well as being linked to family change, was also understood as arising from industrial and economic developments, population movement and women's increased employment. Thus, in Treforgan, people spoke about the decline of the industrial base in the Swansea Valley, as in the following exchange with a single man in his 40s who was living with his father:

> *Father:* Treforgan was quite a hive of activity years ago, wasn't it? … With the tinplate works, you know? And this type of thing. Steelworks … [*But a lot of changes since the '60s, isn't there?*] Oh yes, tremendous …
>
> *Son:* It's like, you know? The [valley] was always full of steelworks and tinplate works. My grandfather worked …
>
> *Father:* Yes, for years.
>
> *Son:* That's gone. It's been transformed.
>
> *Father:* Completely changed. [*Yes.*]
>
> *Son:* And a lot of people have sort of moved away and a lot of people have stayed as well, I suppose. It's, it's not as, like the other areas you look at, the more transient. (Male, 42, Treforgan)

As the last comment indicates, this interviewee still regarded Treforgan as experiencing less population movement than other parts of Swansea; this reflects its high levels of geographical stability.

In Fairview people also spoke about how the community had changed, becoming both more prosperous economically and less close. One woman in her eighties told us about the support she had received as a child when she won a scholarship to secondary school. Her parents had not been able to afford the essential school uniform so the local primary school staff had taken a collection for them. 'It was a small community. And they were all proud of the children from their school who went.' She remembered the village which was the centre of the community as being comparatively homogeneous and providing the setting for 'a very happy childhood'. This woman had married and had brought up her son in a house near her mother's and described how he and his friends, even after moving away, continued to return to be married and to christen their children in the local church. She reflected on the changes.

> It has been a close community, it's, now it's more scattered because of all the building. They are all people who have come in. It's not so small, it's not so, as I say … Fairview has changed a lot. (Female, 80, Fairview)

These accounts emphasise the past, when families lived close and were more extensive and when people had more time to spend with each other. Such stories are commonly reported in community studies and care has to be taken in interpreting them (Crow and Allan, 1994). Indeed the similarity of the sentiments expressed by Mr Hughes in the original study and by interviewees in the restudy warns us that each generation tends to see a decline in family and community (that is, 'tradition') which cannot unproblematically be taken as reflecting processes of social change. In this context it is important to bear in mind the fact that families look different from a child's perspective and memories are, of course, precisely this. Although, from an adult perspective, there has been an increase in the proportion of women who do not have children and a fall in family size, an Australian study showed that the majority (61%) of children have mothers with three or more children (McDonald, 1995, 45). Moreover, the majority of children grow up with both biological parents and, because of high remarriage rates, even if their parents divorce they are likely to live with 'a step parent in new nuclear-family households' (Uhlmann, 2006, 30). Thus, in Britain, 65% of dependent children live with two parents – although not necessarily their biological parents (Hantrais, 2004, 60). There is therefore a discrepancy between a child's and an adult's perspective on families and this 'may account for the pervasive sense among many that the drop in family size between their parents' generation and theirs is more significant than it, in fact, is' (Uhlmann, 2006, 31). It might also go some way towards explaining the nostalgia for large, extended families expressed by many adults.

As a counterpoint to these perceptions of decline in community and neighbourliness, we found examples of quite dense locally based networks and many interviewees who experienced their locality (whether a village, part of a street, a housing estate or an established residential area covering several streets and including pubs and shops) as community. The basis of their assertions of community varied, but they tended to be either located in networks of kin (including, as seen above, friends who are like family) or experienced as membership in local organisations. We look at each of these in turn.

Communities and kinship

Community, especially for our older interviewees, was often based on close-knit kinship networks in an area which was clearly demarcated and where everyone knew everyone else. These families go back in time. Thus, as in other studies (e.g. Strathern, 1981; Edwards, 2000) there are references to 'old families' who have lived in the area over several generations. Our survey data, together with interviewees' accounts, testify to the fact that such networks are still widespread in the working-class areas and among the minority ethnic population of Swansea, despite the decline in frequency of face-to-face contacts between members of kinship networks since 1960. In Pen-cwm, for instance, a woman, whose mother lived just up the road and whose four siblings and their families lived nearby, developed an idea of community in which everybody was related to everyone else:

> This is what I mean, this is a close-knitted estate, you got family members that married other family members on the estate.... They are all related, the estate up here, I wouldn't move out of here for nobody, they'd have to pull my house down first. (Female, 41, Pen-cwm)

These extended family ties were particularly prevalent and important between women – mothers and daughters, sisters and sisters-in-law, as well as close female friends.

Such close networks of family and friends, mainly dependent on women's agency, were quite common in two of the other case study areas, Parkfields and Treforgan, where a significant proportion of the population was working class. One man, married with three adult children, described the area as 'a lot more stable' than the housing estate where they had previously lived and gave as an example an annual neighbourhood New Year's Eve party, usually including both neighbours and extended family: 'I can remember one New Year's Eve, I think it was our turn to put it on and we hadn't lived here long and we had about 15, 20 people in here at one time' (Male, 59, Treforgan). We also found similar networks of family and friends among our minority ethnic interviewees. For example, one of the women said,

> [B]ecause we are from ethnic backgrounds we have connection to Asians, Chinese, the Indians, Philippine and the rest of the community. We've got a lot of connections. But at the end of the day we seem to know everybody. By staying in the same place. (Female, 52, Parkfields)

She emphasises the importance of staying in a particular place for building up such close-knit networks, and she is right that geographical stability and close-knit networks are associated.

As well as providing support and a sense of belonging, however, close-knit networks could be experienced as controlling, thus revealing the downside of 'traditional' communities. One of our minority ethnic interviewees, who lived in her parents' house with her siblings and her husband and child, said she would prefer to live in her own house but felt unable to move out in case it brought shame on her family: 'I would have been gone by now, but my family is very important to me. And I find, with the community, they speak behind your back and say things, so I don't want my family to be talked about' (Female, 28, Parkfields). Bengali men also spoke about the control they exerted over their own behaviour in order to ensure that they were not gossiped about within the community and that the good reputation of their families was preserved. There are thus similarities in the way community is lived between the majority ethnic, working-class population and the minority ethnic, particularly Bangladeshi, population which we would suggest arise from the close-knit networks in which both these communities are based. This was particularly evident in Parkfields.

In Fairview, among our middle-class interviewees, kinship networks were looser than those found in working-class areas. This meant that they neither operated as social groups exerting control over their members nor were individuals involved in the multiplicity of roles that are typical of the close-knit networks characterising face-to-face communities rooted in place (Frankenberg, 1966). These differences were apparent in the frequent comment by our interviewees that community in Fairview did not involve 'living in each other's pockets'. And, as we saw in Chapter 7, Fairview and Parkfields have a more geographically mobile population than the other two areas. Some of those who had moved to these areas from other parts of Britain felt that in Wales the sense of community was stronger than elsewhere (see Charles and Davies, 2005; Davies, Charles and Harris, 2006).

Communities and local organisations

The other way in which people talked about belonging to a community was in terms of membership of local organisations and, as well as similarities, there were significant differences between our four ethnographic areas. Thus, in Fairview and Treforgan, the areas where a higher proportion of the population was middle class, we found the greatest range of local organisations. These included churches and chapels, community centres, sports and social clubs, mixed and male-voice choirs, local history societies, and special-interest voluntary organisations of all kinds. Among the most important organisations in both areas were local sports clubs, particularly the rugby clubs. In contrast, in Pen-cwm the range of organisations was limited to community centres (which had been established by outsiders), a church and a tenants' association. Some of these organisations were linked to different ethnic and class-based groups and played an important part in constituting a collective identity and sense of community. This was particularly true of religious organisations and, despite the decline in religiosity between the two studies (Charles, Davies and Harris, 2003), many of our interviewees participated in organised religion in one form or another. They spoke about the way this involvement created a sense of belonging. A woman in Parkfields, for instance, specifically linked community to her activities in the church, 'This is where the community is important. You know, if you feel you want to be involved with the church, it's not for everyone, but we are because we like being with people and we've got a common ethos' (Female, 43, Parkfields). And a man living in Treforgan emphasised that the relationships established through the church were similar to kinship ties:

> Since a youngster, I've been a member of a church. Not the same one, but ... [*A church?*] Yes. And I like to think

of that as another family. It's, you know, it's a family that we've got there, of people that we feel we have relationships with. We support each other in times of trouble. (Male, 68, Treforgan)

Many of those who spoke about their involvement with religious organisations likened it to being part of a family.

Schools can also be seen as community-based organisations and, in Parkfields, one of the primary schools had pupils from a range of different ethnic backgrounds and prided itself on its cultural inclusiveness. This extended to the efforts of parent-governors to persuade (successfully) minority ethnic parents to become school governors and enabled children to participate in each other's religious festivals.

In Pen-cwm many of our interviewees were involved with one of two community centres as volunteers, as part-time workers and as participants in their various programmes. They were mostly women which reflected the fact that many of the programmes were aimed at training for women and the centres also provided play groups for young children. However, men were more likely to be found in the few full-time jobs or administrative positions associated with these centres. Many of those who were leaders in the community centres lived in the community as a matter of principle. One couple, both of whom worked as volunteers in a church-run community centre, told us the only reason they had moved to Pen-cwm was because 'the church moved into the community and we thought, okay, if we want to work in the community we ought to live in the community' (Male, 25, Pen-cwm). Another local organisation in this area was the tenants' association. The chairperson of this organisation was involved in networks outside Pen-cwm which included members of the local council, those in charge of various community regeneration programmes and the National Assembly for Wales. For him this organisation acted as a form of 'bridging' social capital, although we do not have evidence to suggest that it operated in this way for its local members. Similarly the community centres, while providing training for some local residents with the possibility of enabling them to get better jobs as a result, can mainly be understood as a means of increasing solidarity and social cohesion within the local area.

As this discussion shows, there were differences between women and men in their engagement in local organisations. Women's role was important, particularly for their day-to-day running, but it was men who took on the leadership positions. Thus the parent–teacher associations in the primary schools were made up largely of women and it was they who organised the Christmas fairs and other fund-raising activities. The religious institutions also relied on a voluntary workforce of women and here it was generally older women who were involved. An exception to this was provided by the mosque, where almost all activities were run by men, and the sports clubs, which were primarily run by and for men. These latter, however, had women's committees and the associated social clubs included women as well as men. Their youth teams were an effective means of promoting links between age groups for men within the area, and their social clubs, besides being places for informal social contact, were often venues for other community activities, such as local fairs. Thus, although women play a very important role in the maintenance of community in the form of local organisations, there is generally a gender division of labour which means that men take on the more prominent leadership positions. In addition, men are more evident at this level of community while women are more involved in the maintenance and reproduction of kinship and friendship networks. This division of labour was noted by Frankenberg in his reflections on *Village on the Border* and is typical of community-based organisations (Frankenberg, 1976). Indeed, in England and Wales more men than women are active in associations, with women tending to be more involved at the level of informal social networks, including kin-based networks (Li et al, 2003).

The various local organisations can be seen as associated with different types of social capital, which depend partly on the areas in which they are located and partly on their relationship to the different populations making up the area. Moreover, there were processes of exclusion as well as inclusion taking place. Thus, religious institutions tended to separate those of different faiths, while educational and other institutions such as community centres brought them together; the former can be seen in terms of bonding social capital and the latter in terms of bridging social capital. Furthermore, religious organisations, sports clubs and most special interest groups are commonly connected to broader organisations with regional or national officers and programmes, and these connections can enable people to engage with wider networks. This sort of linking seemed to be more effective in organisations with a mainly middle-class membership.

Newcomers and community closure

There are therefore two aspects to the way interviewees talk about community: one relating to informal social networks and the other to their engagement in civic activities in the form of churches, schools, clubs and so on. Both these aspects of community are intertwined in our interviewees' accounts and it is through them that communities are defined in relation to others. This involves issues of belonging and identity, which often overlap with class, ethnicity and cultural difference, and which may be used either to include or to exclude. These processes of inclusion and exclusion, as well as providing the basis for organisations, were commented on by interviewees who had moved into our case study areas. Several incomers told us that they had worried about not being accepted as part of the community because of not being Welsh but that they had found everyone to be really friendly. One man, from England, who had married a woman from Treforgan and moved there in his early twenties, said: 'I've never known friendship until I, until I come to live down Wales or since I started coming down to Wales because people here are so friendly. If you go into a pub, within 10 minutes, somebody's talking to you' (Male, 68, Treforgan). Despite this friendliness it often took a considerable length of time before incomers felt that they belonged. One woman said, 'I like Fairview, yeah. I mean after being here 30 years out of my 54 I'm considered a local. At long last' (Female, 53, Fairview). Some people, however, spoke about the negative effect of people moving into and out of their localities. One Fairview woman in her eighties felt that the community had to some degree been compromised by its growth in recent years: 'I can go to Fairview now and sometimes not see a Fairview person. What I would call a Fairview person. Do you understand? They, you often see them, they meet you, "Oh, it was nice to meet you", you know. Old Fairview' (Female, 80, Fairview).

Some of those who lived in Parkfields, the area with the largest minority ethnic population and which is an area of transition, a stepping stone for those moving from East to West Swansea, also pointed to the influx of outsiders which, in their view, symbolised change and a loss of community. This process was analysed in terms of the old working-class population wanting to move out to 'better themselves' which meant that houses became available for outsiders to move into. In this area these 'outsiders' were mainly defined as minority ethnic families and students and, significantly, our older respondents often blamed the minority ethnic population for the alleged decline of community. Others, however, positively valued the cultural mix of their locality. A woman who had lived in the same neighbourhood all her life commented about new people moving in: 'Sometimes you do feel it's a transient area. But everybody seems to blend in and that's a good thing. I believe there's a good level of tolerance for all in this community. And you see that through the school' (Female, 43,

Parkfields). She saw openness and a willingness to embrace people with different cultural traditions as a hallmark of her community. And some felt that incomers were preserving cultural traditions that had been lost in other parts of Swansea. One of our interviewees, when asked about the way in which his neighbourhood had changed, replied that there were 'far less children'. He elaborated:

> And particularly what I consider British children. More Asian children. Not saying they've got it all wrong either because they are very family orientated.... It's nice to see them going to the mosque and whatever, when you see the grandfather, the father, the eldest son, the middle son and the youngest son ... and they certainly have the appearance of a closer knit family community than generally can be said for, now this sounds awful, than the council estate communities. (Male, 59, Parkfields)

Thus, incomers could be accepted as part of the community by some and even seen as upholding its lost cultural traditions while being blamed for its decline by others.

Many of the incomers to Pen-cwm had almost a sense of mission about the area as community, with a tendency to be defensive about its reputation for social problems. One of the men, who was from a more affluent part of Swansea, admitted,

> I have been surprised since I moved here that it's not as rough and as scruffy and dirty as people make out. We've got most of our neighbours, except for one or two, but most of our neighbours are very, very nice people and they've always got time to talk over the garden fence. (Male, 25, Pen-cwm)

And another, whose wife had grown up in the area, was passionate about Pen-cwm as a community:

> We like living in this area, obviously, and we don't like it when people gives this area a bad name, because the only people who gives it a bad name are people who don't live here. All right you get a few families who cause a bit of trouble, but overall, it's one of the nicest and safest places to live. (Male, 55, Pen-cwm)

The fourth case study area, Treforgan, given its somewhat greater stability of population, as well as what was perceived as a more Welsh cultural milieu, with a recent history of being Welsh speaking and the continued presence of substantial numbers of Welsh speakers, might be expected to present the greatest degree of closure to incomers. However, most interviewees who had moved there from outside reported various ways of becoming part of the community, from joining a local organisation to trying to learn Welsh. As one of our interviewees told us:

> I feel as if I belong here. I've not quite come to the stage yet where I've lived in Wales longer than in England. I'm getting close though. Now my wife has lived longer in Wales than she has in England because she's those few years younger than me. But I'm getting close to the stage now where I would have lived longer, next year I will have been longer in Wales than in England. But apart from length of time, I feel I belong here. And I've felt like that for a long time.... I don't think I'd go back to England to live now. I'll end my days in the graveyard up the road here. (Male, 68, Treforgan)

Discussion

There is clearly a strong sense of community expressed by our interviewees which is rooted in local social relations based around friends and family as well as in local organisations. There are, however, differences between our areas, both in the connectedness of local social networks and in the vibrancy of associational life. Indeed there is some indication that there is more associational activity where local social networks are looser and the population is more middle class than in those areas, like Pen-cwm, where social networks are very dense and the population is largely working class. This suggests that different forms of social capital are inversely related and bonding social capital, as well as helping people to 'get by', may operate in an exclusionary way, creating boundaries between social groups and networks rather than creating 'bridges' between them. On the other hand, as an essential aspect of mutual support in conditions of socioeconomic deprivation, bonding social capital has immeasurable value and it is largely women's networks which hold families and communities together (Campbell, 1993). Of course, social capital can only be effective as a means of 'getting on' if it is associated with other forms of capital and this is much more likely to be the case in middle-class than working-class networks. It therefore may be access to economic and cultural capital within middle-class networks rather than differences in the 'type' of social capital which can explain their greater effectiveness as a means of 'getting on' (see also Gillies and Edwards, 2006; Warr, 2006).

Our evidence also shows that there is a real sense in which family and friends are 'chosen' insofar as, when completing their network diagrams, people chose who to include and exclude on bases other than their being kin. Indeed, what makes people 'like family' is that they provide support and can be relied upon in times of crisis (cf. Pahl and Spencer, 2004a). Despite individual variation in the construction of personal networks, however, there is an underlying pattern in the way people define family, which relates to degrees of affinity and consanguinity (Becker and Charles, 2006). The fact that this does not automatically translate into who is included in the network diagrams underlines the importance of practices, such as the provision of support, in defining who is close and who is not. Other research suggests that it is among the geographically mobile, professional and intermediate service class that friends predominate in personal networks and that this relates to looser social networks, less social control and living away from kin (Pahl and Spencer, 2004b; Allan, 2005). For others, however, family members are a central element of personal networks and our findings support this (Pahl and Pevalin, 2005).

Finally, our evidence shows that the increased variety of living arrangements which characterises 21st-century Swansea is not associated with people being disembedded from local social networks. On the contrary, hardly any of our interviewees were isolated either from friends or from kin in the sense of not being able to include people in their network diagrams and, for most, a large proportion of their network diagrams consisted of kin and friends who were locally based. Having said that, however, there were a few who were very isolated; they were more likely to be men than women. There were also gender differences in the number of people included in network diagrams. This, we suggest, reflects the continuing importance of women as kin-keepers, with all that this implies for the generation of social capital.

Notes

[1] As we noted in Chapter 2, there have been significant changes in the supply of housing between 1960 and 2002 and the availability and type of housing is clearly significant in affecting household composition. Thus, in 1960 many young married couples had to live for a while with the parents of one of the partners, usually the wife, and this was

reflected in the number of extended-family households in 1960s Swansea. In 2002, however, these households had virtually disappeared. This relates to the fact that there was no longer a shortage of housing in the sense of the council having a long waiting list of households wanting accommodation. Neither was there an absolute shortage of housing, although its distribution was clearly affected by rising house prices and people buying to let. This changed availability of housing meant that it was possible for people to live on their own should they so wish and may partly explain the rise in single-person households among those of working age (Wasoff et al, 2005). Similarly, the lack of housing suitable for large, extended families partly explains the changing living arrangements of our Bangladeshi interviewees, some of whom were unable to find accommodation which was suitable for occupation by joint families.

[2] The notion of 'personal communities' has been advanced as a way of understanding the mix of friends and family that is important to people. This term recognises that people's friends and family may not actually constitute *social networks* because they may neither know nor interact with each other (Pahl and Spencer, 2004a). We, however, refer to those included by interviewees in their network diagrams as personal networks.

NINE

What is the future for the family?

In this final chapter we interrogate the notion – common to grand theory and government statements, to academic analysis of family change and policy research – that we are living in a period of transition. We show that although there are significant changes in household composition and in the proportion of the population that chooses to partner and parent, there are important continuities in the practices by means of which we 'do' family and that, given the overall rate of social change, family lives exhibit a quite surprising degree of continuity with the past. This is particularly unexpected given Rosser and Harris's predictions that increasing occupational and geographical differentiation would lead to a decrease in extended family cohesion and that the de-domestication of women would mean that the effectiveness of the extended family, 'as a mechanism of support in need', would depend on 'the willingness of women to accept the burdens involved' (Rosser and Harris, 1965, 290). The main finding of their study was that a modified extended family had emerged, which was

> more widely dispersed, more loosely-knit in contact, with the women involved less sharply segregated in role and less compulsively 'domesticated', and with much lower levels of familial solidarity and a greater internal heterogeneity than was formerly the case in the traditional 'Bethnal Green' pattern. It is a form of family structure in which expectations about roles and attitudes are radically altered – and, in particular, in which physical and social mobility are accepted. It is the form of extended family which is adjusted to the needs of the mobile society. (Rosser and Harris, 1965, 301)

Our findings are surprisingly similar and show, above all, that extended family networks are resilient and are reproduced across time and space through family practices. Moreover, friends become 'like family' when they engage in similar practices, providing support and coming together for the major rituals of family life surrounding birth, death and the different occasions that mark progress through the life course. Contra those who argue that 'the family' has changed dramatically, we suggest that, while the extended family has been further modified in the years since 1960, the elementary family has not fragmented under pressure of time–space distanciation, nor been undermined by processes of individualisation, and is still crucially supported by a penumbra of wider kin.

We begin this chapter by looking at changes in the welfare state and family policies between 1960 and 2002, exploring how they relate to and are affected by the ways in which families have changed over the same period. Together with the socioeconomic and cultural changes outlined in Chapter 2, policy development is part of the context within which changes and continuities in family lives have to be understood. We focus particularly on the shift from supporting a male-breadwinner form of family, which was the bedrock of social policy when the original study was carried out, to supporting an adult earner form of family and the family policies that have been developed since 1997 by New Labour. We then discuss our main findings, drawing out their implications for policy and, in particular, for debates about social capital and social exclusion and their relation to class, gender and ethnicity. Next we explore the theoretical and conceptual implications of our findings and of the way in which the baseline study and the restudy conceptualise social change. We suggest that there is much in common between the Durkheimian conceptions of social change and social solidarity underpinning the baseline study and the assumptions about social cohesion that provide the basis for many social policy developments. This gives the restudy a certain topicality and, because it is using the same language, enables us to show that many of the assumptions governing policy are problematic. Theoretically, we are able to demonstrate that predictions of family collapse are based on similar assumptions to the original study but that they are not borne out by our findings.

Finally, we turn to a discussion about the future, something which is always difficult in social research but which is important, given public debate about the changes that are besetting families and family life and the assumptions about the future direction of change that were built into the baseline study. We suggest that, rather than increasing differentiation leading to the ultimate disappearance of the extended family, there are different futures which are likely to coexist and that these will vary with class, place and cultural identity. These differences are reflected in the variety of forms taken by partnering and parenting rather than in the resilience of the social networks within which families exist.

The policy context

Family forms and unpaid care work

The welfare state in 1960 was underpinned by a male-breadwinner model of the family which assumed that men were engaged in full-time paid work while married women carried out unpaid care work within the home and relied on their husbands for financial support. This form of family had been made explicit in Beveridge's proposals for the reform of social insurance and allied services in 1942 and meant that unpaid care work was supported by the state 'indirectly via the male taxpayer or benefit recipient' (Land, 2002, 14; Lewis, 2007). The gendering of market work and care work was therefore institutionalised in the form of the male-breadwinner family. This form of family had its golden age in the 1950s when a large proportion of the adult population lived in heterosexual partnerships with the man as the main provider and the woman as the home maker (Seccombe, 1993). However, even then significant proportions of married women were in paid employment and, by 1951, 25% 'of married women were economically active, double the proportion Beveridge had assumed in his report' (Land, 1994, 104). It was in this context that the original study was carried out and its assumptions about a male head of household and female dependent reflected both policy prescriptions and widespread conformity to the male-breadwinner family.

State support for unpaid care work carried out by women in the home amounted to women's domestication, something that Rosser and Harris commented on in the 1960 study. They pointed out that, the greater women's domestication, 'the stronger the cohesion of the extended family and the more effective its function of support for the individuals or elementary families who "belong"' (Rosser and Harris, 1965, 290). They also pointed out that social change in the period leading up to the time of their study had produced 'a profound social revolution in the status and attitudes and interests of women' (Rosser and Harris, 1965, 290) and that this would have an impact on the extended family because of its effect on women's domestication. Following Bott (1957), they posited a relation between the 'degree of domesticity of women, the nature of the marital relationship, and the shape of the external kinship network', with women's de-domestication leading to a loosening of the networks of which elementary families were part.

This de-domestication can also be understood as a process of individualisation involving women's increasing participation in the labour market and a reduction in their dependency upon men within marriage. This process had been developing since at least the 19th century and women's ability to operate as individuals rather than as the legal and financial dependents of men was one of the aims of both first- and second-wave feminism (Sevenhuijsen, 1998). Thus the opposition of first-wave feminism to such measures as the married women's property act in 19th-century Britain, and its subsequent repeal, was part of this process, as were second-wave feminism's campaigns for an end to assumptions of women's financial dependence on men in marriage and cohabiting relationships within the Social Security system in the early 1970s. Such independence is increasingly enshrined in law, although it is not consistently applied across different legislative spheres (Lewis, 2001a, 174). Individualisation, however, has a masculine face and, despite these changes, has progressed further for men than for women, with men being more likely to be able to achieve economic self sufficiency (Mackinnon, 2006; Lewis, 2007).

Assumptions about women's individualisation underpin the policies of New Labour (Lewis, 2007). Indeed it is almost as if New Labour has read the individualisation thesis as an accurate representation of what is happening to families and individuals and is developing policies on this basis. This is ironic, as Beck's apocalyptic vision of the future is partly designed as an Awful Warning (Lovell, 1987) of what might happen should processes of individualisation be taken to their logical conclusion; the end result would be a society where nobody cared (Beck and Beck-Gernsheim, 2002). Policy makers also assume that women are fully individualised in the sense that they are able to support themselves financially in the same way as men (Lewis, 2007). Given the gender segregation of employment, the high proportion of women who work part-time hours and their generally lower levels of pay as compared to men, this assumption is not justified. Furthermore, the fact that women continue to take responsibility for unpaid care work reproduces their disadvantaged position in the labour market.

Women's continuing responsibility for care work also suggests that the decline of the male-breadwinner family may not have gone as far as is assumed (Crompton, 1999; Glucksmann, 2000; Charles and James, 2005). Indeed, in Britain and in the EU the most common family form is that of one and a half earners, with men working longer hours than women (Lewis, 2007). This is a modified male-breadwinner family form and indicates that the male-provider and female-carer roles are still prevalent (Pfau-Effinger, 1999). Social policy, however, assumes an adult-worker model family which, if it does not yet exist, will be brought into being through the operation of social and employment policy (Lewis, 2007). This implies that all adults are citizen-workers, that all adults are able to support themselves through employment or access to benefits and that they are all therefore fully individualised. Apart from the fact that this model does not reflect social reality, it also assumes that it is possible and desirable to 'de-familialise' and 'commodify' care (Lister, 2003; Lewis and Giullari, 2005), thereby ensuring that women as well as men are freed from unpaid care work and can participate fully in the labour market. Clearly, freedom from the labour of caring is viewed as a good thing, thus ignoring both the fact that there are limits to the commodification and de-familialisation of care (Lewis, 2007) and that most families do not want to 'cease caring altogether' (Land and Himmelweit, 2007: v). Our research shows how important extended family networks are as a source of support and how much people rely on kin for childcare to enable them to go out to work. The informal care provided by kin is also crucial in enabling older people to continue to live in their own homes. Such care is often provided by grandparents (for children), by women and men for their parents (when needed) and by older people in the locality for neighbours and friends. Moreover, informal care is used to a greater extent than formal care, particularly by working-class families, and research shows that it is the preferred form of care (LaValle et al, 2000).

Considerable attention has been paid to the issue of care and how the need for care is to be met if all those who are engaged in informal care are to be fully incorporated into the labour market. The problem is precisely that set out by Beck, that if all adults are pursuing full-time careers, little time will be left for the essential care work that keeps society going. New Labour is tackling this through its National Childcare Strategy and the introduction of measures to facilitate a balance between work and family; these include the ability to request flexible working and improved maternity and paternity leave entitlements (Land and Himmelweit, 2007; Lewis and Campbell, 2007). Its aim, in line with EU policy, is to increase employment rates among women and older people. This is seen as essential in order both to enlarge the tax base so as to enable European societies to support their ageing populations and to improve economic competitiveness (Hantrais, 2004). However, Britain has a long-hours culture, which means that participation in full-time employment leaves little time for care work or for maintaining the informal networks which are a vital source of care even when formal care is available (Land, 2002; Dex, 2003; Land and Himmelweit, 2007). Furthermore, in Britain there is no sign that this long-hours culture is regarded as a problem, quite the opposite in fact, as the opt-out from the EU Working Time

Directive indicates (Land, 2002). This opt-out is framed in terms of 'choice' and ensures that men's hours of work, in particular, are likely to remain excessively long. Long hours of work create problems for engaging in the reciprocity which is essential for the maintenance of active networks of kin. Our findings suggest that the resulting pressure on time does indeed lead to lower rates of contact with kin, something which is regretted by our interviewees and which is more noticeable in our middle-class areas. It therefore results in informal networks of care being put under strain (Land, 2002).

Social exclusion

The emphasis on increasing participation in employment is framed as a means of promoting social inclusion. The implications of this are that unpaid care work is not seen as a means of social inclusion and is not therefore a legitimate activity (Levitas, 2006). Our findings suggest, however, that exclusion from paid work cannot necessarily be equated with social exclusion, particularly for women who are involved in reciprocal networks of care with their female kin and friends. Men are not tied into connectedness with others through caring, nor are their social networks as extensive as those of women. This means that unemployment for them is more likely to be associated with social exclusion. It is because of this that we argue that social exclusion is gendered and seeing employment as the only legitimate means of social inclusion is based on men's experiences of paid work. Moreover, there is evidence that paid employment can involve exclusion from 'social relations and patterns of sociability' (Levitas, 2006, 123) – precisely those things that other areas of policy are seeking to nourish. This has led to a questioning both of the coherence of social exclusion as a concept and of the coherence of government policy towards families. Ruth Levitas, for instance, argues that social exclusion is an incoherent concept which is almost always used in conjunction with poverty; its only possible advantage being that it 'draws attention to the social aspects and consequences of poverty' (Levitas, 2006, 154). Its incoherence derives from the fact that measures of social inclusion work against each other, as with participation in paid work and inclusion in 'social relations and patterns of sociability' and, furthermore, paid work may not encourage social integration because of low pay and long hours, which cannot lift people out of poverty (Levitas, 1996).

Apart from the National Childcare Strategy, which has been adopted with very little change in Wales (Ball, 2006), and measures to facilitate a work–family life balance, New Labour's family policy consists of measures to enable parents better to 'invest' in their children and to encourage social cohesion, particularly in areas where it has allegedly broken down. Although New Labour does not argue for a return to the 'traditional' family, it is clear that it regards marriage as the best environment in which to bring up children and commits itself to doing 'what it can to strengthen marriage' (Barlow et al, 2002, 117). This preference for heterosexual marriage can also be found in Giddens's manifesto for third way policies which is significant, given his key role as adviser to the former Labour Prime Minister, Tony Blair, and his explanations of the transformations taking place in families and intimate life (Giddens, 1992, 1998). As Sevenhuijsen points out, this privileging of a certain form of family as the best form of parenting implicitly denigrates parenting by lone parents or by gay men and lesbians (Sevenhuijsen, 2000). The discourse is therefore at odds with policy developments such as the fact that you need be neither in a couple relationship nor heterosexual to be able to adopt a child. It is also at odds with the government's own statements, such as 'By the 1980s, families were in a transition from a society in which there was a single overriding norm of what a family should be like to a society in which a plurality of norms were recognised as legitimate' (Cabinet Office, 2007, 15). Notwithstanding the conceptual confusion evident here, it is clear that there is a recognition that the move away from the normative family of the post-war years means that it is difficult for the state to legislate for one form of family over and above any other. Instead its focus is on the child and, specifically, parent–child relations, which are seen as a legitimate sphere for intervention. No matter what happens to relationships between parents, parental responsibilities for children are binding and policies have been developed to ensure that this is so.

These take the form of measures to 'support' families and the nature of these measures suggests not only that policy is operating with a deficit model of parenting but also that it aims to inculcate middle-class parenting skills into working-class parents (Gewirtz, 2001). Thus, parents, particularly those living in a 'culture of low achievement', are to be persuaded and coerced into participating in paid employment and parenting in particular ways (Barlow et al, 2002; Gillies, 2005). The culture of low achievement is a thinly disguised way of talking about a culture of poverty and the idea that poverty and social exclusion are transmitted intergenerationally. This ignores research into the cycle of deprivation in the 1970s which showed that there was little evidence to support the idea that poverty was transmitted through a distinct culture of poverty and its associated attitudes and values (Gillies, 2005). Indeed those whom we interviewed in Pen-cwm showed little evidence of living in a culture apart from mainstream culture and were extremely concerned about the difficulties of bringing up children in an area where it was especially easy for boys to be led astray by their peers. And counter to the idea of a culture of poverty, our interviewees echoed the concerns of government about decreasing respect and the loss of core moral values. It was regretted that children had no respect, were allowed to get away with anything and were given far too many 'things'. They also lamented the fact that children were no longer able to go about in public in safety on their own and that the streets were unavailable for them to play in as they had been in their young day. They did not necessarily think that parents were to blame for these changes. One of our female interviewees, a retired teacher, said:

> It's different now, quite different.... society has altered so much, you wonder where children can get their standards from these days don't you. There is so much television, there is so much time on the television focused on violence and the undesirable elements in society, that young people and children now seem to think that's the norm.... You know when young girls become parents before they've left their teens, what sort of standards are they going to pass on to their offspring? And where is the security for those children? (Female, 70s, Fairview)

Another woman, who had worked as a cleaner and learning support assistant in a primary school, mirrored these views, relating them to the prohibition on physical punishment and what she saw as the difficulty of disciplining children.

> And of course you notice though, when my children were little, the respect the children had for the teaching staff which they haven't got now. It's, it's awful I think, they know now you can't have a smack, you can't do this, you can't do, you know, that to me. And once they get to juniors they get so rude the children do, and we just didn't have that when we were in school. You respected your teacher, you know what I mean, and I would never swear in front of my parents or anything, my son does, my son does, my daughter has tried but she doesn't any more. (Female, 53, Pen-cwm)

Others commented on the way parents indulge children which, of course, is one of the effects of consumer capitalism.

> Oh I don't know, kids are cheekier. They want more I suppose. Yes I suppose uhm, it's our fault really because we try to give them what they want, and more, more, more you know sort of thing. Easy come easy go.... Like my mother and father said, we were just happy to have food at Christmas, not thousands and thousands of pounds worth of things you know. So, but that's changed definitely, they can't just have a pair of trainers, they've got to have the ones that got the name on them, they are fifty-odd pounds, so oh definitely things have changed. (Female, 36, Pen-cwm)

These changes were sometimes blamed on parents' lack of concern although, if our interviewees were anything to go by, they all wished to bring their children up 'properly'. One of them told us:

> I think my parents were stricter with us than we are with ours, ours have got a lot more freedom than we ever had, ever. But I don't know whether that's a good or a bad thing, because I mean as I said both my children are fairly well adjusted, so I suppose a bit of leeway here and there makes no difference. (Female, 45, Pen-cwm)

These concerns were similar to those expressed by interviewees living in other parts of Swansea and do not support the idea of a separate culture of poverty which can be invoked to explain 'low achievement'. The worry about what would happen to boy children was, however, more apparent in Pen-cwm than in our other areas. Boys' involvement in delinquent and criminal activities is linked by policy makers to family breakdown and poor parenting skills and part of the solution is seen to lie with fathers' greater involvement with their children (Giddens, 1998; Gillies, 2005). How this is to be achieved at the same time as fathers are engaged in working some of the longest hours in Europe, however, is not clear. Furthermore, it was certainly the case that delinquent and criminal activity was higher in Pen-cwm than in our other areas and that those working in the community centres were attempting to integrate boys into organised activities. The establishment of such centres in communities can be seen as an investment in social capital.

Social investment and social capital

Besides attempts to combat social exclusion through integration in paid employment, an important way of building social cohesion and enabling people to 'get on' is through investment in human and social capital at the level of both family and community. Thus, the 1994 Commission on Social Justice proclaimed that investment in 'skills, research, technology, childcare and community development' was central to sustainable growth (Lister, 2003, 429). The state can therefore be seen as a social-investment state and, 'as investment in "human" and social capital becomes a primary function of the social investment state, the child and the community have become its emblems' (Lister, 2003, 437; Dobrowolsky and Jenson, 2005). This is reflected in New Labour's strategy for 'neighbourhood renewal animated with the "vision that, within 10 to 20 years, no one should be seriously disadvantaged by where they live"' (Social Exclusion Unit, 2001 cited in Lister, 2003, 430). The National Assembly for Wales has similarly privileged an ideal of community, both in its vision of 'inclusivity' as characterising the devolved Wales and in many of its policy initiatives, such as its Communities First programme. Again this is aimed at identifying excluded communities experiencing high levels of poverty and other measures of exclusion and providing, through economic development and support for families, a means of social integration and civic renewal (see Charles and Davies, 2005). This commitment to families and communities reflects the communitarianism of New Labour as well as the resonance of ideas of community in Wales and also involves an engagement with the 'third sector'. Thus, the involvement of civil society organisations (that is, NGOs) is seen as key to 'investment' in social capital and, more cynically perhaps, as a way in which communities can be revitalised without major government expenditure (Molyneux, 2002).

Underpinning these policy prescriptions is the acceptance of the argument that social capital is in decline. However, far from social capital being undermined, our findings show that the social networks which constitute it are widespread in Swansea, in both working-class and middle-class areas. There are differences between the areas insofar as the social capital in working-class areas takes the form of close-knit networks while the networks characterising middle-class areas are looser and there is more engagement in associational activities. It is clear, however, that the social capital that takes the form of close-knit networks is judged differently from that which takes the form of loose-knit networks. Thus the bonding social capital characterising working-class areas is seen as inward looking and conservative while bridging social capital is outward looking and progressive (Putnam, 2000); bridging social capital is also instrumental and associated with class mobility. It is these middle-class forms of social capital that are approved of by government and the working class is being disciplined in order that it generate the 'right sort' of social capital (Gewirtz, 2001). This is reminiscent not of the 1960s but of Victorian Britain, when lady health visitors were instructed to teach mothering skills to working-class women, and harks back to the tradition of instructing the working class in how to behave which has a long history within the Labour Party. This conceptualisation of different types of social capital, and their unstated link to gender and class, ties in with notions of a culture of low achievement. What is left unsaid, though, is that these differences are underpinned by a lack of resources which government policy turns attention away from by focusing on individual solutions. The problem is defined as a lack of parenting skills, the solution is to invest in human and social capital by providing 'support' in the form of training and education. This draws attention away from the structural inequalities and associated lack of resources which lead to poverty and social exclusion and individualises both the problem and the solution.

Contradictions in policy

What this overview of policy change between 1960 and 2002 shows is that there has been a very real shift in the assumptions underpinning both employment and family policy which reflects the social changes characterising the intervening period. Moreover, there are two conflicting threads to policy development which partly relate to the difference between employment policy and social policy and which have marked economic and social policies since the inception of the post-war welfare state (Wilson, 1977). Thus, on the one hand, families are no longer assumed to conform to a male-breadwinner model, in its stead is the adult-worker model of families. Policies based on this model take very little cognisance of the importance of extended networks of kin and friends on which families rely for care and other forms of support. Indeed they threaten to undermine them by emphasising paid employment as the only means of social inclusion and encouraging and forcing all sections of the population, even those who are actively engaged in providing informal care, into the paid workforce. This is likely to have the effect, and is already doing so in some of our ethnographic areas, of reducing the time that members of extended families have to visit and care for each other. In so doing it will contribute to the decline in social capital that is also a focus of government policy and something that it ostensibly wishes to reverse. Underpinning employment policy is the idea that all adults are now fully individualised, an argument epitomised in the individualisation thesis. On the other hand, family policy has been heavily influenced by communitarian thinking and theories of social capital. This results in a contradiction between these two areas of policy, one emphasising the autonomous individual, the other emphasising the importance of the social in the form of the family and community. Policy concern with social capital derives from the communitarian influence, as does support for the 'traditional' family which takes the form of supporting marriage and parenting. This tension is also to be found in Giddens's discussion of third way politics (Giddens, 1998), in contrast with Beck, who takes the individualisation thesis to its logical conclusion of a society where no one cares.

Thus, the current policy context is contradictory for families. On the one hand it is assumed that all adults will participate in the labour market on equal terms and that the adult-worker model of the family has superseded the male-breadwinner model; this will ensure social inclusion and, more importantly, enlarge the tax base of society. On the other hand, it is assumed that parents (gender unspecified) will be engaged in active parenting and that everyone will be involved in civil society, generating the social capital that is necessary to ensure social cohesion, stability and a strengthening of the shared moral values which form the basis of a stable society.

This discussion shows that theoretical debates about the family and social change are influential in terms of policy development. Moreover, policy, like much of the theory on which it is based, pays scant attention to the realities of family lives. In contrast to the sorry tale of family and community decline which policy is attempting to address, our findings tell a different story – one which is far less dramatic but no less interesting than those told by grand theories of social change.

The findings of the restudy

The most striking finding of our study is that there is considerable continuity in family practices between 1960 and 2002. Thus, those who partner and parent in 2002 do so in very similar ways to those who partnered and parented in 1960; families are embedded in networks of kin and provide their members with substantial support over the life course; mothers and their adult daughters are at the heart of kinship networks and it is women who do the kin work. And in important ways our findings echo those of the original study. Rosser and Harris concluded that very few families were entirely isolated from kin but that there was considerable variety both in the type of contact they had with each other and in the importance attached to relationships, so have we. They deduced from this that the extended family is a 'variable, amorphous, vague social grouping' which 'is not so much decomposed by current social change, but ... is rather modified to produce a looser, more adaptable structure' (Rosser and Harris, 1965, 288), so have we. They found that mothers and their adult daughters saw each other more frequently than other categories of kin and that women's networks were at the heart of extended family networks, so have we. The main difference between the two studies is that the frequency of contact between kin, particularly siblings, has fallen, although not nearly as much as might have been expected. This means that the links between members of potential extended family groupings are star shaped rather than like a net and that the kin-connectedness of society has been weakened.

Although increasing geographical and occupational differentiation do not seem to have had the effects predicted by Rosser and Harris, insofar as they have not led to a loss of cohesion and intergenerational solidarity in extended family networks (with the possible exception of a reduction in solidarity between siblings), women's de-domestication has. Thus, full-time employment has a significant effect on frequency of contact between kin and, we would suggest, is what explains gender differences in patterns of contact. And following Rosser and Harris, we agree that this poses a threat to the ability of networks of kin and friends to provide support and care for their members and may indeed lead to an attenuation of kinship groups. This shortage of time for contact with kin and for engaging in the generalised reciprocity which ensures that kinship networks endure was remarked on in our interviews and has significant policy implications, as we have already discussed.

Data from our ethnographic studies show that close-knit networks of kin and friends are still very much in evidence in Swansea, especially in working-class neighbourhoods and among the minority ethnic population, and that there is a cultural association of close-knit kinship networks both with the 'traditional' working class and with being Welsh (Davies, Charles and Harris, 2006). As Elizabeth Bott (1957) long ago observed, close-knit networks flourish where there is geographical stability and, despite the increased geographical mobility between 1960s Swansea and the Swansea of today, levels of geographical stability remain high and people are still engaged in multiple roles. We suggest that this is associated with the fact that a relatively high proportion of Swansea's population is working class (even in the 21st century almost half of our respondents classified themselves as working class) and that, even in our most middle-class neighbourhood, kinship ties, though looser, still tend to be locally based. Moreover, families operate as transmitters of cultural identity through the practices in which they engage, and extended family networks are symbolic of particular cultural identities. However, there is evidence that people engage reflexively with tradition in constructing their identities. This is shown by the ways in which our Bangladeshi interviewees selected some aspects of tradition to support their arguments for greater individual freedom and the ways in which our more middle-class and highly educated interviewees talked about class. Thus, tradition is recreated and often transformed through family practices. We also found class-specific processes of individualisation evident in the higher valuing of independence and the pursuit of individual life goals separate from the family among some of our middle-class interviewees. This form of individualisation is, we suggest, class and possibly culturally specific and can be related to a particular middle-class habitus (see also Savage, 2000).

The breadth of our study and the inclusion of respondents and interviewees from different cultural groups and social classes means that we can see how different patterns of family formation and family practices diverge and come together. Thus, there is a sense in which kin are chosen; people maintain contact with some and not with others on the basis of the support that they exchange and their frequency of contact. This also applies to friends and it is through engaging in family practices that friends become like family. In this sense all families can be seen as families of choice. But it is also apparent that those who have denser kinship networks and higher rates of contact with kin, who are also those who are less geographically mobile, are likely to include more family than friends in their social networks.

It has been remarked that those who study community and conclude that it is in decline are asking the wrong questions and that, rather than focusing on place as the basis of community, they should be exploring people's social networks (Pahl and Spencer, 2004b). Rosser and Harris did precisely this, investigating patterns of contact between members of extended families from the point of view of individual social actors and asking about respondents' contact with different categories of kin. In replicating this we have found only a slight decline in frequency of contact, suggesting that kin-based personal networks have not changed significantly. This shows that, despite a reduction in the kin-connectedness of society, individuals and families are still embedded in social networks, many of which include friends who are 'like family'.

Perhaps our most important finding is that family solidarity is maintained despite the changing and fluid patterns of sexual partnerships. This insight is only possible because we have taken the perspective of extended families rather than focusing on family households and have constructed patterns of residence and contact from the point of view of individual social actors. We have found considerable intergenerational solidarity which becomes stronger on the birth of children, and we have found that family practices, particularly the provision of support, are essential to the reproduction of family networks.

These findings are surprising, given the enormous changes there have been over the same period in household composition and patterns of family formation and the significant decrease in the proportion of the population that is partnering and parenting. It is such change, we suggest, that has led to the cry that the family is in terminal decline and, with it, the moral values essential for the maintenance of a stable society. What our findings show, however, is that in the midst of all this change, there is considerable continuity in family practices and that it is through these practices that families continue to provide their members with support and a sense of belonging. This happens not only when members of extended family groupings live in the same place but also when they are dispersed geographically, often over considerable distances. Extended family networks therefore endure through space and over time and are reinforced through the exchange of support, visits, and rituals which are engaged in together.

Implications for theory

These findings suggest that those who develop what have been termed data-free theories of social change would do well to take into account the empirical data generated by studies which are located in place. Such studies throw light on the way social processes affect daily life and can also illuminate grand-theoretical claims about the nature of social change (Crow, 2002c). Thus, claims about the decline of social capital (Putnam, 2000) and the disembedding of families from local social relations are, at the very least, premature (Charles and Davies, 2005). And Giddens's claim that social relations are 'lifted out' of 'local contexts' and rearticulated 'across indefinite tracts of time–space' (Giddens, 1991, 18) seem hardly to be applicable to family life in Swansea at the beginning of the 21st century. No more does his claim that place only has meaning in terms of 'distant influences drawn upon in the local arena' and that the 'local community' has disappeared (Giddens, 1994, 101). Contra Giddens, we would suggest that a society in which all social relations and institutions were 'lifted out' of their local contexts is unimaginable. There will, however, be variation in the degree to which different social institutions need to be 'embedded' in matrices of social interaction to function effectively. Our evidence suggests that most families in Swansea are very much embedded in the local context and that place has meaning precisely because of the local social relations, of which kinship networks are an important part, which constitute it.

How, then, are we to understand social change? Rosser and Harris related the occupational and cultural heterogeneity that they observed within kinship networks to increasing occupational and geographical mobility and the emergence of what they termed the 'mobile society'. We have argued that these trends have continued into the 21st century. Thus, what has occurred since 1960 may be conceptualised as an increasing differentiation of the social structure deriving from economic differentiation at the level of both occupations and industries, one of the most important aspects of which has been the enormous growth in employment opportunities for women, leading to higher rates of female labour market participation. At the same time, changes in the industrial structure have led to a decline in men's labour market participation. The population is still occupationally mobile but the mobility is of a quite different kind from that experienced by the 1960 respondents. This is because it is not the result of educationally induced increased rates of mobility between positions in a relatively stable structure but results from the rapid differentiation of the structure itself. At the cultural level these changes have been paralleled by the *de-institutionalisation* of the expectations and practices constituting the family with the result that issues that were once decided by normative rules are now left to individuals to negotiate (Finch, 1989).

The term 'de-institutionalisation' does not of course refer to a type of society but rather to a process of change whereby components of a pre-existing social structure are transformed. It occurs not merely because an institution's 'charter' (to use Malinowski's useful term) loses its legitimacy but when the range of social situations governed by the rules based on the charter become so various that the rules no longer apply. The decline of the normative structure is preceded by the decline in the utility of the rules predicated upon it. Progressive structural differentiation is therefore the precursor of de-institutionalisation; both entail an increase in the range of choices faced by individuals, so that, by virtue of the choices they make, people become increasingly *individuated*. Families are made up of people who are increasingly individuated and, as a result, family life is made up of the unscripted choices negotiated by family members between one another (Beck, 1992). As a result, de-institutionalisation, combined with the increasing internal differentiation of family groups, means that families as well as people are now increasingly individuated in the sense of being distinct from each other.

This does not mean that we are in a situation of anomic individualism, however, which is often how Beck's individualisation is interpreted, but of moral individualism. This comes across from the qualitative data which show that, although there is a considerable variety of family forms, people are guided in their actions by a morality which is far from individualistic. They take into account how their actions will affect those they are close to, and also what expectations there are about how those who are close to each other should behave (cf Williams, 2004; Duncan and Irwin, 2004; Smart and Shipman, 2004).

Alongside these processes of de-institutionalisation, families continue to be reproduced through family practices and our findings show that engaging in mutual support which is governed by expectations of generalised reciprocity ensures the reproduction of social networks which constitute extended families. Moreover, the fact that nuclear-family households have declined as a proportion of all households does not mean that we have moved away from a nuclear-family system. As Harris commented in 1994, to claim that a society has a nuclear-family system, 'tells us nothing about the distribution of household composition'. Indeed, 'at the structural level, the system of family formation in these islands has been nuclear for at least five centuries', which indicates that 'the young couple is not under the jural, political, religious or economic authority of the natal groups of either partner and that whatever relationships may be empirically found to exist between the couple and such groups are the result of negotiation between formally autonomous parties and not the result of adherence to cultural prescriptions.' Furthermore, 'at the cultural level, family behaviour has been informed by individualistic values, so that however strong the ties between family members may have been, their strength is the result of personal affection or loyalty to individuals arising out of family living rather than the result of affection or loyalty to a kin group. It is precisely the universal presence of these particular cultural and structural features which makes possible the diversity, which in turn makes empirical generalisation so difficult' (Harris, 1994, 45). In other words, changes in household composition do not mean that the nuclear-family system is breaking down. Neither does the fact that the family is undergoing a process of de-institutionalisation mean that the idea of the family has lost its symbolic and discursive power (Somerville, 2000).

The original study was, as we have already noted, framed by Durkheimian theoretical assumptions about the nature of social solidarity and cohesion and how these would be undermined by economic and cultural differentiation. Ironically, these are the assumptions which underpin much family policy and lead to claims that social capital is in decline. Social and employment policy, at regional, national and EU level, is couched in terms of social inclusion, social cohesion and social solidarity, although nowhere in any New Labour document is the phrase 'social solidarity' used (Land and Himmelweit, 2007). Underpinning these discourses is a Durkheimian conceptualisation of society which sees social stability as dependent upon social cohesion and shared norms and values. These shared assumptions make our findings more telling. This is because, even within a Durkheimian framework which predicts that increasing differentiation will lead to a decline in social cohesion, our findings show this not to be the case. Because our research took the form of a restudy we have asked the same questions as Rosser and Harris did in the baseline study. We have therefore explored the effects of increasing differentiation on family solidarity, investigating differentiation within extended family networks in terms of occupation, geographical mobility and culture, and charting patterns of residence and contact. We found increased occupational and geographical differentiation between 1960 and 2002 and, in occupational terms, differentiation now exists within the elementary as well as extended family, something which was not the case in 1960 as most married women were not in paid employment. However, we found that extended family networks still operate as an important source of support and identity to their members. This suggests that Durkheim's assumptions about social solidarity and the effects of differentiation need to be modified and we have done this by focusing on family practices. This has allowed us to explain why it is that families continue to adapt and provide support and a source of identity to their members even in a highly differentiated and mobile society which is characterised by high rates of 'family breakdown'. It is these practices which reproduce family and kinship relations. The importance of family practices in reproducing extended networks of kin which, to a greater or lesser extent, also include friends, suggests that Bourdieu is more helpful in allowing us to understand processes of change and continuity than are Beck or Giddens. It is not the institutional form that holds people together but the social practices in which they engage and through which they are fundamentally connected to each other.

What is the future for the family?

The original study was careful not to make predictions about families and social change, although Rosser and Harris pointed to the likely effects of increasing occupational and geographical differentiation and women's de-domestication on extended family networks. They suggested that both developments could lead to a decrease in extended-family cohesion and a loosening of the extended social networks in which families are located. Insofar as there has been a reduction in the kin-connectedness of society between the two studies, they were right. And it is certainly the case that higher rates of women's employment are to be found in our middle-class areas, where families are more likely to have experienced geographical mobility and, as a result, have an external environment characterised by loose-knit networks. But these changes do not appear to have seriously undermined the ability of extended families to provide a source of support and social identity to their members. Thus, although the changes they predicted have come to pass, they have not had the expected outcomes. We suggest that, rather than increased occupational and geographical differentiation undermining the social solidarity of extended families, it is the pressure of time arising from increasing labour market activity of women and men which is likely to have this effect. This is because it will impinge on the ability of social actors to engage in those practices which reproduce extended families and hold them together. It would be unwise, however, to predict that this will actually happen, as there are many possible resolutions of the current contradiction between increasing participation in paid work and the continuing need for participation in care work, one being that hours of work are reduced for all, thereby enabling men as well as women to combine paid work with caring for themselves and others.

On a more general level we suggest that what we have termed de-institutionalisation means that there are few accepted and received ways of 'doing' family and that socially acceptable alternatives coexist. The future of the family is likely to be characterised by variations in patterns of family formation and household composition and, in this sense, we can say that there are diverse futures for the family and personal life. One future is that family life goes on much as it did in the 1960s, with high rates of contact between family members living in different households, low rates of geographical mobility and women being at the centre of kinship networks. This future includes reconstituted families with the increase in the number of potential kin in different generations that they imply. Another is that there is much greater diversity in living arrangements, with many more people choosing not to have children or not to partner, and that there is more gender equality between couples, resulting from younger women's tendency to have higher-status occupations than their partners. Finally, there are kinship networks that link kin (and often include friends) even though they live considerable distances from each other and that are not necessarily weakened by geographical distance. These networks condition the socially acceptable alternatives that are available to their members. All these futures coexist, although their incidence is affected by class and culture. This diversity of family lives and the networks within which they are embedded needs to be taken into account by both social theorists and social policy makers. Like Therborn, we think that the future of families will be marked by complexity, 'a contingency of sexual relations, partnerships and family forms', but with 'a modal pattern of long-term, institutionalised heterosexual coupling' (Therborn, 2004, 314). Indeed Therborn interprets family change over the last century in terms not of individualisation but of the gradual weakening of patriarchy and the end to the '20th century industrial standardisation' of the socio-sexual order (Therborn, 2004, 313). What has happened since 1960 is that the western European family has returned to its 'modern historical complexity, including non-marriage as well as marriage, variable age at marriage, informal cohabitation and extra-marital births' (314). And it is this which distinguishes contemporary de-institutionalisation.

The advantages of a restudy are not that it allows one to predict the future by drawing a line from 1960 to 2002 and projecting it onward, for example, to 2042, but that it allows us to see 1960 and 2002 in historical perspective. What had appeared to be the cast-iron social institutions of the Edwardian period gave way to the more relaxed institutions of the sixties. 'De-institutionalisation', had the term been invented, could well have been applied to the era whose theme song was 'anything goes'. 'Anything goes' can be translated as 'everything is permitted'. *Who* is permitted is the *individual*. But who does the permitting is not specified. The sociologist, coming to the aid of the song writer, would point out that there are two candidates for 'permitter': individuals, other people, acting independently of each other, who can positively or negatively sanction an individual's actions (public opinion); and 'society', that is, regularities in the actions of individuals deriving from shared, normative expectations about the actions of others. Clusters of such expectations have classically been described as 'social *institutions*'.

What Edwardians experienced between the wars may be defined as a reduction in the level of *social control* of the individual which arose *both* from a shift in social attitudes *and* institutional change. When these types of change go together it is easy to refer to both without distinguishing them by loose terms such as 'the permissive society'. This term is defective as a description of the type of society coming into being in the 1960s because what was happening was not an increase in permissiveness but a reduction in the scope of what can be forbidden. The value of the term de-institutionalisation in characterising the nature of social change in the late twentieth century is that it makes it possible to avoid the use of the excessively general term 'social control' by specifying that what is decreasing is that particular form of social control provided by the existence of social institutions which no longer prescribe or proscribe the behaviour of individuals to the extent that they have done in the past.

Methodological problems in comparisons of class over time

In the original Swansea study respondents' occupations were classified according to the classification system used in the decennial census, Registrar General's Social Class. This was designed to produce six 'social classes' which are similar to the SEGs/occupational groups in Table 2.3. Thus, classes I & II correspond to the uppermost of the three classes in that table, classes IIIM, IV and V (skilled manual and manual supervisory, semi-skilled and unskilled) correspond to 'Manual', and IIIN (defined as Non manual but not in I or II) corresponds to 'other non-manual'. For purposes of comparison we had to follow this procedure when coding occupation in the 2002 survey. But we then ran up against the problem that, in the original study, married women were not classified. This was because it was assumed that the occupation of the head of household determined the social honour and life chances of its members and therefore the classification of the household. Obviously, under contemporary cultural and labour market conditions it was inappropriate to use the Registrar General's male-based system of classification, but to abandon it would have made comparison between the 1960 and the present surveys problematic. In the 2002 survey women's occupations were therefore coded twice; one coding (called 'male-based') assigned a woman's male partner's occupation to her even where she already had an occupation of her own (as would have been done in 1960); the other coding simply coded the woman's occupation without reference to her male partner's occupation.

We then had further problems in comparing our survey data both with the 2001 Census and with the original study. We could not compare the Registrar General's Social Class distribution of the 2002 survey with the 2001 Census because this variable had been abandoned by ONS. We could not straightforwardly compare it with the 1961 Census because that classified males only. We could not compare it with the full 1960 survey male-based distribution because Rosser and Harris (1965) does not contain full data. What it does contain, however, is a collapsed version of their RGSC 1960 data to form three occupational categories by combining classes I & II and IIIM-V, leaving IIIN on its own. Rosser and Harris called these three categories Managerial,

Artisanal and Clerical respectively (1965, 102). By confining ourselves to these three Rosser and Harris categories, we are able to compare the distribution of the two survey samples and this is done in Table Ai.1.

The two columns in the middle of this table represent the androcentric view of the changes in the last 40 years: a redistribution of men between the bottom and top classes in favour of the latter. However, if we look at the non-male-based classification, the table reflects the changes in the occupational structure between 1960 and 2002. There has been a shift from the pyramidical structure of the first half of the 20th century to a structure in which the 'people in between' form almost as large a percentage of the workforce as do the traditional two classes. It is a *post*-industrial structure in the sense that it represents a major departure from the occupational structure of the 100 years before 1960 (as Rosser and Harris's quaint nomenclature suggests) but is only intelligible as a variation on it: an increase by the 21st century in the numbers of the 'people in between', 40% of whom are women.

The authors of the original study were also concerned with the 'people in between' (Harris, 1962; Rosser and Harris, 1965, 93–9 *passim*), although not on account of their gender, in three senses. The first refers to the 'other non-manuals' many of whom, in spite of their non-manual *status*, have income levels and life chances below those of members of the upper strata of the manual group; those who, in George Orwell's vivid phrase, 'forget their incomes and remember their accents' (Orwell, 1962, 199; cited in Rosser and Harris, 1965, 94). The second refers to those whose self-ascribed class is at odds with their occupational status. The third refers to those who are mobile over two generations as a result of the even then (1960) already fast-changing

Table Ai.1: 1960 and 2002 surveys, Registrar General's Social Classes collapsed into three categories following Rosser and Harris (1965, 100-1) (%)

	Men only	Both sexes: male based		Both sexes not male based
Class	1960	1960*	2002	2002
Managerial	22	21	34	33
Clerical	10	15	18	28
Artisanal	68	64	48	39
Total	100	100	100	100

*Source: Rosser and Harris, 1965, 2 (upper table)

occupational structure. These include among their number some of those denoted by the first sense of 'in between' but also comprise those who remember their incomes and forget or (unlike Catherine Zeta Jones) succeed in changing their accents so that they are appropriate to their higher occupational position. They also included those who married into a different occupational group from that of their parents.

These concerns led to Rosser and Harris developing their own *social class* classification taking into account the occupational class membership of respondents over two generations *and* subjective social class. Given the massive changes in occupational structure over the period since 1960, the replication of the original study's social class classification was a matter of considerable complexity and was only attempted on a sub-sample of the survey's achieved sample. For the whole 2002 sample the Rosser and Harris tripartite *occupational* classification (managerial/clerical/artisanal) of the *respondent only* was used; in the baseline study the occupational classification of respondent's father had also been included. This was then modified by the introduction of self-assessed class, yielding four classes: A, which was managerial with a self-assessment as 'middle class'; AX, which included managerial with a 'working class' self-assessment along with those who were clerical and assessed themselves as 'middle class'; BX, which included clerical with a 'working-class' self-assessment and artisanal with a 'middle class' self-assessment; B, those who were artisanal and assessed themselves as 'working class'. This set of categories was termed 'Rosser and Harris Social Class *modified*'. This was compared with the 1960 sample and the results can be seen in Table Ai.2.

This shows that adding in self-assessed class vastly increases the in-between category in comparison with Table Ai.1 and also that the in-between category is now more numerous than it was in 1960. It is not altogether clear what is the significance of this, apart from the fact that it

Table Ai.2: Rosser and Harris's Social Class (modified) 2002 compared with Rosser and Harris's Social Class (original) 1962 (1965, 105) (%)

Class	1960		2002	
A (middle class)	11		23	
AX (lower middle class)	12	36	21	45
BX (upper working class)	24		24	
B (working class)	53		32	

would be expected, given the increased complexity of the occupational structure and the associated likelihood that respondents' backgrounds, in class terms, will be different from their current occupational status. That having been said, only the broadest conclusions concerning change in 'class' structure can be drawn from this comparison because of the difference in the construction of the two measures. However, the direction of those changes is in line with the changes in the occupational structure described in Chapter 2: a dramatic shrinkage of the bottom class, an enlargement of the upper class and an expansion of the people in between (AX+BX), to a point where they form the largest single group in the hierarchy, which includes nearly half of the population.

Moreover, the 2002 class X differs from the original class X. There was a satisfactory class gradient between Rosser and Harris's two X classes when tabulated against related dependent variables (1965, 107). The 2002 X classes did not consistently show such a gradient. However, the X class taken as a whole is genuinely a class in that it was found to be truly distinct from the classes above and below it. It is not, however, a class in terms of its internal coherence, since its members belong to it by virtue of different combinations of criteria.

Swansea boundary changes

The area termed 'Swansea' has changed twice since the original 1960 survey. At that time, Swansea was a county borough whose area comprised its urban core and environs. The 1974 Local Government Act expanded it to include the rural Gower Peninsula. Since then Swansea has become a city, and it was again expanded in 1997, when it became a county with the inclusion of the township of Pontardulais and its rural hinterland. The present local authority area therefore includes, as its current name ('City and County') suggests, an urban central place together with its hinterland. The expansion of the local authority area since 1960 reflects the increased interconnectedness of the original Swansea settlement with the surrounding area, which together have long constituted the node of the local labour market. The sequence of areas therefore reflects the changing economic conditions of action for the inhabitants of that part of those areas which corresponds to the area of the County Borough of Swansea in 1960 and who constitute the survey population for the purposes of the present study. At various points in the text of this book we refer to data on economic variables for each of these three areas.

The case of Registrar General's Social Class (RGSC) differs somewhat from the other economic variables since we are considering occupations as attributes of individuals rather than distributions of occupations as attributes of collectivities. We were committed to using RGSC because it was used by the original 1960 study and, given that, it was ideally desirable to compare the distribution of our respondents over RGSC categories with recent census data. There were a number of difficulties with this, chief of which were that the 1961 Census only provided social class data for males, current census data was not available for the 1960s Swansea area and the 2001 Census had abandoned the RGSC classification. However, Swansea City and County had published 1991 Census data down to ward level and this was used to construct the 1991 RGSC parameters of the population of the 1960 area.

Table Aii.1 gives full RG Social Class for males in the 1960 survey and compares it with full data for both sexes from the 1991 Census for the area corresponding to 1960s Swansea reconstructed from ward level data for 1991 published by the Swansea City and County (as it has recently become) and the full data for both sexes from the 2002 survey.

Table Aii.1: Full Registrar General Social Class data for 1960 and 2002 surveys and Census data for 1991 for the area corresponding to the County Borough of Swansea as at 1960

	Swansea County Borough 1960 survey, males only	Swansea County Borough equivalent 1991 Census, both sexes	Swansea County Borough equivalent 2002, both sexes
I	4.6	3.9	5
II	17.2	24.5	28
IIIN	10.1	22.1	28
IIIM	43.9	20.1	17
IV	11.1	15.5	15
V	13.1	7.5	7
Other	–	6.2	–

Bibliography

Ackers, L. and Stalford, H. (2004) *A community for children? Children, citizenship and internal migration in the EU*, Ashgate: Aldershot.

Adam, B. (1996) 'Detraditionalization and the certainty of uncertain futures', in P. Heelas, S. Lash and P. Morris (eds) *Detraditionalization*, Oxford: Blackwell, pp 134–8.

Adkins, L. (2002) *Revisions: Gender and sexuality in late modernity*, Buckingham: Open University Press.

Adkins, L. (2004) 'Gender and the post-structural social', in B.L. Marshall and Anne Witz (eds) *Engendering the social: Feminist encounters with sociological theory*, Buckingham: Open University Press, pp 139–54.

Adkins, L. (2005) 'Social capital: the anatomy of a troubled concept', *Feminist Theory*, vol 6, no 2, pp 195–211.

Allan, G. (2005) 'Boundaries of friendship', in L. McKie and S. Cunningham-Burley (eds) *Families in society: Boundaries and relationships*, Bristol: The Policy Press, 227–40.

Allan, G. and Crow, G. (2001) *Families, households and society*, Basingstoke: Palgrave.

Atkinson, A.B. (2000) 'Distribution of income and wealth', in A.H. Halsey and J. Webb (eds) (2000) *Twentieth-century British social trends*, Basingstoke: Macmillan, 348–81.

Baldassar, L., Baldock, C.V. and Wilding, R. (2007) *Families caring across borders: Migration, ageing and transnational caregiving*, Basingstoke: Palgrave Macmillan.

Ball, W. (2006) 'Making a difference, promoting gender equality? Transforming childcare policies for mothers, fathers and children in Wales', unpublished PhD thesis, University of Wales Swansea.

Barlow, A., Duncan, S. and James, G. (2002) 'New Labour, the rationality mistake and family policy in Britain', in A. Carling, S. Duncan and R. Edwards (eds) *Analysing families: Morality and rationality in policy and practice*, London and New York: Routledge, 110–28.

Beck, U. (1992) *Risk society*, London: Sage.

Beck, U. and Beck-Gernsheim, E. (2002) *Individualization*, London: Sage.

Beck-Gernsheim, E. (1998) 'On the way to a post-familial family: from a community of need to elective affinities', *Theory, Culture and Society*, vol 15, nos 3–4, pp 53–70.

Becker, B. and Charles, N. (2006) 'Layered meanings: the construction of the family in the interview', *Work, Family and Community*, vol 9, no 2, pp 101–22.

Bell, C. (1968) *Middle class families*, London: Routledge and Kegan Paul.

Bell, C. (1977) 'Reflections on the Banbury re-study', in C. Bell and H. Newby (eds) *Doing sociological research*, London: George Allen and Unwin, pp 47–62.

Bjornberg, U. (2001) 'Working and caring for children: family policies and balancing work and family in Sweden', in A. Carling, S. Duncan and R. Edwards (eds) *Analysing families: Morality and rationality in policy and practice*, London and New York: Routledge, 93–100.

Bott, E. (1957) *Family and social network*, London: Routledge and Kegan Paul.

Bourdieu, P. (1986) 'The forms of capital', in P. Bourdieu (ed) *Handbook of theory and research for the sociology of education*, New York: Greenwood Press.

Bourdieu, P. (1996) 'On the family as a realized category', *Theory, Culture and Society*, vol 12, no 3, pp 19–26.

Bourdieu, P. (1998) *Practical reason*, Cambridge: Polity Press.

Bradley, H., Fenton, S., Devadason, R., West, J. and Guy, W. (2005) 'Young adults' experiences in the "new economy"', in P. Stewart (ed) *The future of employment relations*, London: Palgrave.

Brannen, J. (2003) 'Towards a typology of intergenerational relations: continuities and change in families', *Sociological Research Online*, vol 8, no 2, http://0-www.socresonline.org.uk.pugwash.lib.warwick.ac.uk:80/8/2/brannen.html.

Bryson, L. and Winter, I. (1999) *Social change, suburban lives: An Australian new town 1960s to 1990s*, St Leonards, NSW: Allen and Unwin/Australian Institute of Family Studies.

Cabinet Office (2007) *Building on Progress: Families*, HM Government Policy Review, www.cabinetoffice.gov.uk/policy_review/.

Campbell, B. (1993) *Goliath: Britain's dangerous places*, London: Methuen.

Chambers, P. (2005) *Religion, secularization and social change in Wales*, Cardiff: University of Wales Press.

Charles, N. and Davies, C. (2005) 'Studying the particular, illuminating the general: community studies and community in Wales', *Sociological Review*, vol 53, no 4, pp 672–90.

Charles, N. and Davies, C. (2008) 'My family and other animals: pets as kin', Paper presented to the annual conference of the British Sociological Association, University of Warwick, 28–30 March.

Charles, N. and Harris, C. (2007) 'Continuity and change in work–life balance choices', *British Journal of Sociology*, vol 58, no 2, pp 277–95.

Charles, N. and James, E. (2005) '"He earns the bread and butter and I earn the cream": job insecurity and the male breadwinner family', *Work, Employment and Society*, vol 19, no 3, pp 481–502.

Charles, N. and Kerr, M. (1988) *Women, food and families*, Manchester: Manchester University Press.

Charles, N., Davies, C. and Harris, C.C. (2003) 'Family formation and kin relationships: 40 years of social change', paper presented to the BSA annual conference, York (available at www.swan.ac.uk/sssid/Research/R&H/Working%20Papers.htm).

Charles, N., Davies, C. and Harris, C.C. (2008) 'The family and social change revisited', in R. Edwards (ed) *Researching families and communities*, London and New York: Routledge, 114–32.

City & County of Swansea (2001) *Still paying the price? A poverty profile of Swansea 2001*, Swansea: City & County of Swansea.

Coleman, J.S. (1988) 'Social capital in the creation of human capital', *American Journal of Sociology*, vol 94, pp S95-S120.

Crompton, R. (1999) (ed.) *Restructuring gender relations and employment*, Oxford: Oxford University Press.

Crow, G. (2002a) 'Families, moralities, rationalities and social change', in A. Carling, S. Duncan and R. Edwards (eds) *Analysing families: Morality and rationality in policy and practice*, London and New York: Routledge, 285–96.

Crow, G. (2002b) *Social solidarities: Theories, identities and social change*, Open University Press: Buckingham.

Crow, G. (2002c) 'Community studies: fifty years of theorisation', *Sociological Research Online*, vol 7, no 3, www.socresonline.org.uk/7/3/crow.html.

Crow, G. (2004) 'Social networks and social exclusion: an overview of the debate', in C. Phillipson, G. Allan and D. Morgan (eds) *Social networks and social exclusion: Sociological and policy perspectives*, Aldershot: Ashgate, 7–19.

Crow, G. (2008) 'Thinking about families and communities over time', in R. Edwards (ed.) *Researching families and communities*, London and New York: Routledge.

Crow, G. and Allan, G. (1994) *Community life: An introduction to local social relations*, London: Harvester Wheatsheaf.

Crozier, G. and Davies, J. (2006) 'Family matters: a discussion of the Bangladeshi and Pakistani extended family and community in supporting the children's education', *The Sociological Review*, vol 54, no 4, pp 678–95.

Dale, A., Shaheen, N., Fieldhouse, E. and Kaira, V. (2002) 'The labour market prospects for Pakistani and Bangladeshi women', *Work, Employment and Society*, vol 16, no 1, pp 5–25.

Davies, C.A. and Charles, N. (2002) 'The piano in the parlour: methodological issues in the conduct of a restudy', *Sociological Research Online*, vol 7, no 2, www.socresonline.org.uk/7/2/davies.html.

Davies, C.A., Charles, N. and Harris, C.C. (2006) 'Welsh identity and language in Swansea, 1960–2002', *Contemporary Wales*, vol 18, pp 28–53.

Davies, J. (1993) *The family: Is it just another life-style choice?*, London: Institute for Economic Affairs.

Daycare Trust (2007) *Listening to lone parents about child care*, www.daycaretrust.org.uk.

Deacon, A. and Williams, F. (2004) 'Introduction. Themed section on care, values and the future of welfare', *Social Policy and Society*, vol 3, no 4, pp 385–90.

Dench, J., Gavron, K. and Young, M. (2006) *The new East End: Kinship, race and conflict*, London: Profile Books.

Dex, S. (2003) *Families and work in the twenty-first century*, York: Joseph Rowntree Foundation.

di Leonardo, M. (1987) 'The female world of cards and holidays: women, families and the work of kinship', *Signs*, vol 12, no 3, pp 440–53.

Dobrowolsky, A. and Jenson, J. (2005) 'Social investment perspectives and practices: a decade in British politics', in M. Powell, L. Bauld and K. Clarke, (eds) *Social policy review*, Bristol: The Policy Press, 203–30.

Doyal, L. (1981) *The political economy of health*, London: Pluto Press.

Duncan, S. and Edwards, R. (1999) *Lone mothers, paid work and gendered moral rationalities*, Basingstoke: Macmillan.

Duncan, S. and Irwin, S. (2004) 'The social patterning of values and rationalities: mothers' choices in combining caring and employment', *Social Policy and Society*, vol 3, no 4, pp 391–99.

Duncan, S. and Smith, D.P. (2002) 'Geographies of family formations: spatial differences and gender cultures in Britain', *Transactions of the Institute of British Geographers*, vol 27, pp 471–93.

Duncan, S. and Smith, D.P. (2006) *Individualisation versus the geography of 'new' families*, Families and Social Capital ESRC Research Group, London: London South Bank University.

Duncan, S., Edwards, R., Reynolds, T. and Alldred, P. (2003) 'Motherhood, paid work and partnering: values and theories', *Work, employment and society*, vol 17, no 2, pp 309–30.

Dunne, G. (1997) *Lesbian lifestyles*, Basingstoke: Palgrave.

Durkheim, E. (1984) *The division of labour in society (1893)*, Basingstoke: Macmillan.

Edwards, J. (2000) *Born and bred*, Oxford: Oxford University Press.

Edwards, R. (2004) 'Present and absent in troubling ways: families and social capital debates', *The Sociological Review*, vol 52, no 1, pp 1–21.

Elias, N. (1996) *The Germans*, Cambridge: Polity Press (English edition of *Studien uber die Deutschen*, Suhrkamp Verlag, 1989).

Fielding, T. (1995) 'Migration and middle-class formation in England and Wales', in T. Butcher and M. Savage (eds) *Social change and the middle class*, London: UCL Press.

Finch, J. (1989) *Family obligations and social change*, Cambridge: Polity Press.

Finch, J. and Mason, J. (1993) *Negotiating family responsibilities*, London and New York: Tavistock/Routledge.

Frankenberg, R. (1966) *Communities in Britain: Social life in town and country*, Harmondsworth: Penguin Books.

Frankenberg, R. (1976) 'In the production of their lives, men (?) … sex and gender in British community studies', in D. Leonard Barker and S. Allen (eds) *Sexual divisions and society: Process and change*, London: Tavistock Publications.

Franklin, J. (2007) *Social capital: between harmony and dissonance*, Families and Social Capital ESRC Research Group, London: London South Bank University.

Furstenberg, F.F. (2006) 'Banking on families: how families generate and distribute social capital', in R. Edwards, J. Franklin and J. Holland (eds) *Assessing social capital: Concept, policy and practice*, Newcastle: Cambridge Scholars Press, 95–110.

Gallie, D. (2000) 'The labour force', in A.H. Halsey and J. Webb, (eds) *Twentieth-century British social trends*, Basingstoke: Macmillan.

Gardner, K. (2002) 'Death of a migrant: transnational death rituals and gender among British Sylhetis', *Global Networks*, vol 2, no 3, pp 191–204.

Gerson, K. (1998) 'Moral dilemmas, moral strategies, and the transformation of gender: lessons from two generations of work and family change', *Gender and Society*, vol 16, no 1, pp 8–28.

Gewirtz, S. (2001) 'Cloning the Blairs: New Labour's programme for the re-socialization of working-class parents', *Journal of Education Policy*, vol 16, no 4, pp 365–78.

Giddens, A. (1990) *The consequences of modernity*, Cambridge: Polity Press.

Giddens, A. (1991) *Modernity and self identity: Self and society in the late modern age*, Cambridge: Polity Press.

Giddens, A. (1992) *The transformation of intimacy: Sexuality, love and eroticism in modern societies*, Cambridge: Polity Press.

Giddens, A. (1994) 'Living in a post-traditional society', in U. Beck, A. Giddens and S. Lash (eds) *Reflexive modernization: Politics, tradition and aesthetics in the modern social order*, Cambridge: Polity Press.

Giddens, A. (1998) *The third way: The renewal of social democracy*, Cambridge: Polity Press.

Gillies, V. (2005) 'Meeting parents' needs? Discourses of "support" and "inclusion" in family policy', *Critical Social Policy*, vol 25, no 1, pp 70–90.

Gillies, V. and Edwards, R. (2006) 'A qualitative analysis of parenting and social capital: comparing the work of Coleman and Bourdieu', *Qualitative Sociology Review*, vol 11, no 2, pp 42–60.

Glucksmann, M. (2000) *Cottons and casuals: The gendered organisation of labour in time and space*, Durham: Sociologypress.

Goffman, E. (1969) *The presentation of the self in everyday life*, London: Allen Lane.

Gray, A. (2005) 'The changing availability of grandparents as carers and its impolications for childcare policy in the UK', *Journal of Social Policy*, vol 34, no 4, pp 557–77.

Gross, N. (2005) 'The detraditionalization of intimacy reconsidered', *Sociological Theory*, vol 23, no 3, pp 286–311.

Halpern, D. (2005) *Social capital*, Cambridge: Polity Press.

Hansen, K.V. (2005) *Not-so-nuclear families: Class, gender, and networks of care*, New Brunswick, NJ, and London: Rutgers University Press.

Hantrais, L. (2004) *Family policy matters: Responding to family change in Europe*, Bristol: The Policy Press.

Harris, C.C. (1962) 'The people in between', *New Society*, November.

Harris, C.C. (1979) *Fundamental concepts in the sociological enterprise*, London: Croom Helm.

Harris, C.C. (1987) *Redundancy and recession*, Oxford: Blackwell.

Harris, C.C. (1994) 'The family in post-war Britain', in J. Obelkevich and P. Catterall (eds) *Understanding post-war British society*, London: Routledge.

Heelas, P. (1996) 'On things not being worse, and the ethic of humanity', in P. Heelas, S. Lash and P. Morris (eds) *Detraditionalization*, Oxford: Blackwell 200–22.

Hochschild, A.R. (1997) *The time bind: When work becomes home and home becomes work*, New York: Henry Holt and Company/Metropolitan Books.

Holmes, M. (2004) 'The precariousness of choice in the new sentimental order: a response to Bawin-Legros', *Current Sociology*, vol 52, no 2, pp 251–7.

Hughes, C. and Blaxter, L. (2007) 'Feminist appropriations of Bourdieu: the case of social capital', in T. Lovell (ed) *(Mis)recognition, social inequality and social justice: Nancy Fraser and Pierre Bourdieu*, London, Routledge, 103–25.

Inglehart, R. (1990) *Culture shift in advanced society*, Princeton, NJ: Princeton University Press.

Inglehart, R. and Norris, P. (2003) *Rising tide: Gender equality and cultural change around the world*, Cambridge: Cambridge University Press.

Jamieson, L. (1998) *Intimacy: Personal relationships in modern societies*, Cambridge: Polity Press.

Johnson, J., Rolph, S. and Smith, R. (2007) 'Revisiting "the last refuge": present day methodological challenges', in M. Bernard and T. Scharf (eds) *Critical perspectives on ageing societies*, Bristol: The Policy Press, 89–103.

Jones, S. (2003) 'Supporting the team, sustaining the community: gender and rugby in a former mining village', in C.A. Davies and S. Jones (eds) *Welsh communities: New ethnographic perspectives*, Cardiff: University of Wales Press.

Khanum, S.M. (2001) 'The household patterns of a "Bangladeshi village" in England', *Journal of Ethnic and Migration Studies*, vol 27, no 2, pp 489–504.

Kiely, R., McCrone, D. and Bechhofer, F. (2006) 'Reading between the lines: national identity and attitudes to the media in Scotland', *Nations and Nationalism*, vol 12, no 3, pp 473–92.

Kovalainen, A. (2004) 'Rethinking the revival of social capital and trust in social theory: possibilities for feminist analysis', in B.L. Marshall and A. Witz (eds) *Engendering the social: Feminist encounters with sociological theory*, Buckingham: Open University Press, 155–70.

Land, H. (1994) 'The demise of the male breadwinner – in practice but not in theory: a challenge for social security systems', in S. Baldwin and J. Falkingham (eds) *Social security and social change: New challenges to the Beveridge model*, London: Harvester Wheatsheaf, 100–15.

Land, H. (2002) 'Spheres of care in the UK: separate and unequal', *Critical Social Policy*, vol 22, no 1, pp 13–32.

Land, H. and Himmelweit, S. (2007) *Supporting parents and carers*, Manchester: Equal Opportunities Commission.

LaValle, I., Finch, S., Nove, A. and Lewin, C. (2000) *Parents' demand for child care*, Research Brief 176, London: Department for Education and Employment.

Lempert, L.B. and deVault, M.L. (2000) 'Guest editors' introduction: special issue on emergent and reconfigured forms of family life', *Gender and Society*, vol 14, pp 6–10.

Leonard, D. (1980) *Sex and generation: A study of courtship and weddings*, London: Tavistock.

Levitas, R. (1996) 'The concept of social exclusion and the new Durkheimian hegemony', *Critical Social Policy*, vol 16, pp 5–20.

Levitas, R. (2006) 'The concept and measurement of social exclusion', in C. Pantazis, D. Gordon and R. Levitas (eds) *Poverty and social exclusion in Britain: The millennium survey*, Bristol: The Policy Press, 123–60.

Lewis, J. (1992) *Women in Britain since 1945*, Oxford: Blackwell.

Lewis, J. (2001a) 'Debates and issues regarding marriage and cohabitation in the British and American literature', *International Journal of Law, Policy and the Family*, vol 15, pp 159–84.

Lewis, J. (2001b) *The end of marriage? Individualism and intimate relations*, Cheltenham: Edward Elgar.

Lewis, J. (2002) 'Individualisation, assumptions about the existence of an adult worker model and the shift towards contractualism', in A. Carling, S. Duncan and R. Edwards (eds) *Analysing families: Morality and rationality in policy and practice*, London and New York: Routledge, 51–6.

Lewis, J. (2007) 'Gender, ageing and the "new social settlement": the importance of developing a holistic approach to care policies', *Current Sociology*, vol 55, no 2, pp 271–86.

Lewis, J. and Campbell, M. (2007) 'UK work/family balance policies and gender equality, 1997–2005', *Social Politics*, vol 14, no 1, pp 4–30.

Lewis, J. and Giullari, S. (2005) 'The adult worker model family, gender equality and care: the search for new policy principles and the possibilities and problems of a capabilities approach', *Economy and Society*, vol 34, no 1, pp 76–104.

Li, Y., Savage, M. and Pickles, A. (2003) 'Social capital and social exclusion in England and Wales (1972–1999)', *British Journal of Sociology*, vol 54, no 4, pp 497–526.

Lister, R. (2003) 'Investing in the citizen-workers of the future: transformation in citizenship and the state under New Labour', *Social Policy and Administration*, vol 37, no 5, pp 427–43.

Lovell, T. (1987) *Consuming fiction*, London: New Left Books.

Mackinnon, A. (2006) 'Fantasizing the family: women, families and the quest for an individual self', *Women's History Review*, vol 15, no 4, pp 663–75.

Mand, K. (2006) *Social capital and transnational South Asian families: Rituals, care and provision*, Families and Social Capital Research Group, London: London South Bank University.

Marshall, G., Newby, H., Rose, D. and Vogler, C. (1988) *Social class in modern Britain*, London: Hutchinson.

Marwick, A. (1998) *The sixties: Cultural revolution in Britain, France, Italy, and the United States, c.1958–c.1974*, Oxford: Oxford University Press.

Mason, D. (2000) *Race and ethnicity in modern Britain*, 2nd edn, Oxford: Oxford University Press.

Mason, J. (1999) 'Living away from relatives: kinship and geographical reasoning', in S. McRae (ed) *Changing Britain: Families and households in the 1990s*, Oxford: Oxford University Press, 156–75.

Mason, J. (2004) 'Managing kinship over long distances: the significance of "the visit"', *Social Policy and Society*, vol 3, no 4, pp 421–29.

McCrone, D. (2002) 'Who do you say you are? Making sense of national identities in modern Britain', *Ethnicities*, vol 2, no 3, pp 301–20.

McCrone, D., Stewart, R., Kiely, R. and Bechhofer, F. (1998) 'Who are we? Problematising national identity', *The Sociological Review*, vol 46, no 4, pp 629-52.

McDonald, P. (1995) *Families in Australia: A socio-demographic perspective*, Melbourne: Australian Institute of Family Studies.

McDowell, L., Ray, K., Perrons, D., Fagan, C. and Ward, K. (2005) 'Women's paid work and moral economies of care', *Social and Cultural Geography*, vol 6, no 2, pp 219–35.

McGlone, F., Park, A. and Roberts, C. (1999) 'Kinship and friendship: attitudes and behaviour in Britain, 1986–1995', in S. McRae (ed) *Changing Britain: Families and households in the 1990s*, Oxford: Oxford University Press, 1141–55.

McNay, L. (1999) 'Gender, habitus and the field: Pierre Bourdieu and the limits of reflexivity', *Theory, Culture and Society*, vol 16, no 1, pp 95–117.

McRae, S. (1999) 'Introduction: family and household change in Britain', in S. McRae (ed) *Changing Britain: Families and households in the 1990s*, Oxford: Oxford University Press, 1–33.

Modood, T., Berthoud, R., Lakey, J., Nazroo, J., Smith, P., Virdee, S. and Beishon, S. (1997) *Ethnic minorities in Britain: Diversity and disadvantages*, London: Policy Studies Institute.

Molyneux, M. (2002) 'Gender and the silences of social capital: lessons from Latin America', *Development and Change*, vol 33, no 2, pp 167–88.

Morgan, D. (1996) *Family connections*, Cambridge: Polity Press.

Mumford, K. and Power, A. (2003) *East Enders: Family and community in East London*, Bristol: The Policy Press.

Nolan, J. and Scott, J. (2006) 'Gender and kinship in contemporary Britain' in B. Lindlay, M. Richards, F. Ebetehaj and M. Lamb (eds) *Kinship matters: Relationships and law in a changing society*, Oxford: Hart.

ONS (Office of National Statistics) (2001a) *Population trends*, London: The Stationery Office.

ONS (2001b) *Social trends*, vol 31, London: The Stationery Office.

ONS (2002a) *Population trends*, Summer, London: The Stationery Office.

ONS (2002b) *Census 2001: Key statistics for local authorities: Wales*, London: The Stationery Office.

ONS (2002c) *Social trends*, vol 32, London: The Stationery Office.

Orwell, G. (1962) *The road to Wigan Pier*, Harmondsworth: Penguin.

Pahl, R. (1970) *Pattern's of urban life*, London: Longmans.

Pahl, R. (1984) *Divisions of Labour*, Oxford: Basil Blackwell.

Pahl, R. and Pevalin, D.J. (2005) 'Between family and friends: a longitudinal study of friendship choice', *The British Journal of Sociology*, vol 56, no 3, pp 433–50.

Pahl, R. and Spencer, E. (2004a) 'Personal communities: not simply families of "fate" or "choice"', *Current Sociology*, vol 52, no 2, pp 199–221.

Pahl, R. and Spencer, E. (2004b) 'Capturing personal communities', in C. Phillipson, G. Allan and D. Morgan (eds) *Social networks and social exclusion: Sociological and policy perspectives*, Aldershot: Ashgate, 72–96.

Parry, J. (2003) 'The changing meaning of work: restructuring in the former coalmining communities of the South Wales valleys', *Work, Employment and Society*, vol 17, no 2, pp 227–46.

Pescosolido, B. and Rubin, B. (2000) 'The web of group affiliations revisited: social life, postmodernism, and sociology', *American Sociological Review*, vol 65, pp 52–76.

Pfau-Effinger, B. (1999) 'The modernization of the family and motherhood in Western Europe', in R. Compton (ed) *Restructuring gender relations and employment*, Oxford: Oxford University Press.

Pfau-Effinger, B. and Geissler, B. (2002) 'Cultural change and family policies in East and West Germany', in A. Carling, S. Duncan and R. Edwards (eds) *Analysing families: Morality and rationality in policy and practice*, London and New York: Routledge, 77–83.

Phillipson, C., Ahmed, N. and Latimer, J. (2003) *Women in transition: A study of the experiences of Bangladeshi women living in Tower Hamlets*, Bristol: The Policy Press.

Phillipson, C., Bernard, M., Phillips, J. and Ogg, J. (1998) 'The family and community life of older people: household composition and social networks in three urban areas', *Ageing and Society*, vol 18, no 3, pp 259–89.

Phillipson, C., Bernard, M., Phillips, J. and Ogg, J. (2000) *The family and community life of older people: Social networks and social support in three urban areas*, London: Routledge.

Phizacklea, A. and Wolkowitz, C. (1995) *Homeworking women: Gender, racism and class at work*, Sage: London.

Portes, A. (1998) 'Social capital: its origins and application in modern sociology', *Annual Review of Sociology*, vol 24, no 1, pp 1–24.

Putnam, R. (1995) 'Bowling alone: America's declining social capital', *Journal of Democracy*, vol 6, no 1, pp 65-78.

Putnam, R. (2000) *Bowling alone: The collapse and revival of American community*, New York: Simon and Schuster.

Reay, D. (1998) 'Rethinking social class: qualitative perspectives on class and gender', *Sociology*, vol 32, no 2, pp 259–75.

Ribbens McCarthy, J., Edwards, R. and Gillies, V. (2003) *Making families: Moral tales of parenting and step-parenting*, Durham: Sociologypress.

Rose, N. (1996) 'Authority and the genealogy of subjectivity', in P. Heelas, S. Lash and P. Morris (eds) *Detraditionalization*, Oxford: Blackwell, 294–327.

Roseneil, S. (2005) 'Living and loving beyond the boundaries of the heteronorm: personal relationships in the 21st century', in L. McKie and S. Cunningham-Burley (eds) *Families in society: Boundaries and relationships*, Bristol: The Policy Press, pp 241–58.

Roseneil, S. and Budgeon, S. (2004) 'Cultures of intimacy and care beyond "the family": personal life and social change in the early 21st century', *Current Sociology*, vol 52, no 2, pp 135–59.

Rosser, C. and Harris, C.C. (1965) *The family and social change*, London: Routledge and Kegan Paul.

Sahlins, M. (1972) *Stone age economics*, New York: Aldine de Gruyter (reprinted 2002).

Savage, M. (2000) *Class analysis and social transformation*, Buckingham/Philadelphia: Open University.

Savage, M., Bagnall, G. and Longhurst, B. (2001) 'Ordinary, ambivalent and defensive: class identities in the Northwest of England', *Sociology*, vol 35, no 4, pp 875–92.

Seccombe, W. (1993) *Weathering the storm: Working-class families from the industrial revolution to the fertility decline*, London/New York: Verso.

Sevenhuijsen, S. (1998) *Citizenship and the ethics of care*, London/New York: Routledge.

Sevenhuijsen, S. (2000) 'Caring in the third way: the relation between obligation, responsibility and care in Third Way discourse', *Critical Social Policy*, vol 20, no 1, pp 5–37.

Shaw, A. (2000) *Kinship and continuity: Pakistani families in Britain*, Amsterdam: Harwood Academic Publishers.

Sheldon, S. (1948) *The social medicine of old age*, Oxford: Oxford University Press.

Sherwin, S. (coordinator) (1998) *The politics of women's health: Exploring agency and autonomy*, Philadelphia: Temple University Press.

Smart, C. (2005) 'Textures of family life: further thoughts on change and commitment', *Journal of Social Policy*, vol 34, no 4, pp 541–56.

Smart, C. (2007) *Personal life: New directions in sociological thinking*, Cambridge: Polity Press.

Smart, C. and Neale, B. (1999) *Family fragments*, Cambridge: Polity Press.

Smart, C. and Shipman, B. (2004) 'Visions in monochrome: families, marriage and the individualization thesis', *The British Journal of Sociology*, vol 55, no 4, 491–509.

Social Exclusion Unit (2001) *A new commitment to neighbourhood renewal*, London: Cabinet Office.

Somerville, J. (2000) *Feminism and the family*, Basingstoke: Macmillan.

Song, M. (1999) *Helping out: Children's labour in ethnic businesses*, Philadelphia: Temple University Press.

Spencer, E. and Pahl, R. (2006) *Rethinking friendship: Hidden solidarities today*, Princeton/Oxford: Princeton University Press.

Stack, C. and Burton, L.M. (1993) 'Kinscripts', *Journal of Comparative Family Studies*, vol 24, no 2, pp 157–70.

Strangleman, T. (2001) 'Networks, place and identities in post-industrial mining communities', *International Journal of Urban and Regional Research*, vol 25, no 2, pp 253–67.

Strathern, M. (1981) *Kinship at the core*, Cambridge: Cambridge University Press.

Strathern, M. (1992) *After nature: English kinship in the late twentieth century*, Cambridge: Cambridge University Press.

SWEP (South Wales Evening Post) (2003) 29 October.

Therborn, G. (2004) *Between sex and power: Family in the world 1900–2000*, London/New York: Routledge.

Thompson, J.B. (1996) 'Tradition and self in a mediated world', in P. Heelas, S. Lash and P. Morris (eds) *Detraditionalization*, Oxford: Blackwell, pp 89–108.

Townsend, P. (1957) *The family life of old people*, London: Routledge and Kegan Paul.

Townsend, P. (1962) *The last refuge*, London: Routledge and Kegan Paul.

Uhlmann, A.J. (2006) *Family, gender and kinship in Australia*, Aldershot: Ashgate.

Warr, D.J. (2006) 'Gender, class, and the art and craft of social capital', *The Sociological Quarterly*, vol 47, pp 497–520.

Wasoff, F. and Jamieson, L. with Smith, A. (2005) 'Solo living, individual and family boundaries: findings from secondary analysis', in L. McKie and S. Cunningham-Burley (eds) *Families in society: Boundaries and relationships*, Bristol: The Policy Press, 207–25.

Weeks, J., Heaphy, B. and Donovan, C. (2001) *Same sex intimacies: Families of choice and other life experiments*, London: Routledge.

Wheelock, J. and Jones, K. (2002) '"Grandparents are the next best thing": informal childcare for working parents in urban Britain', *Journal of Social Policy*, vol 31, no 3, pp 441–63.

Williams, F. (2004) *Rethinking families*, London: Calouste Gulbenkian Foundation.

Wilson, E. (1977) *Women and the welfare state*, London: Tavistock.

www.statswales.wales.gov.uk, accessed 1/4/08.

Yeandle, S. (1999) 'Women, men, and non-standard employment: breadwinning and caregiving in Germany, Italy, and the UK', in R. Crompton (ed) *Restructuring gender relations and employment*, Oxford: Oxford University Press, 80-104.

Young, M. and Willmott, P. (1957) *Family and kinship in East London*, London: Routledge and Kegan Paul.

Zontini, E. and Reynolds, T. (2007) 'Ethnicity, families and social capital: caring relationships across Italian and Caribbean transnational families', *International Review of Sociology*, vol 17, no 2, pp 257–77.

Index

lack of data on married women 235
and residential proximity to parents
61, 67, 71, 72, 79
and social capital 11-12
and social exclusion 218
and support 118-19, 133-4, 136-7,
167-8
see also gendered division of labour;
men; women
gender culture and moral values 14
gendered division of labour
and caring 118-19, 156-8, 215-18
and community work 205-6
domestic division of labour 118-19,
156-7
and employment 116-18
matriarchal families 101
and social capital theory 11, 21, 115
geographical location
and cultural identity 81-3, 112-13
distance and support 163, 167-9,
172-3, 176
and ethnographic research in
Swansea 43-51
grandparents and childcare 145-6
and individualisation thesis 16
mobility *see* geographical mobility
residence patterns 53, 59-63, 103,
225
significance of place 16, 183-5,
227-8
geographical mobility 59-60, 61, 63,
67, 68-9, 79, 230
and class 75, 163, 164-6, 170-3, 175,
204
and support 120, 124
see also 'mobile society'
Giddens, Anthony 3, 4-5, 12, 39,
227-8
and 'third way' policies 219, 224
Gillies, V. 11
grandparents 68, 153
grandmothers and childcare 58,
142-9

H

habitus 6-7, 18-21
Harris, C.C. xiii-xiv, 8, 114*n*, 229
The family and social change see
Rosser
heterogeneity and kinship groups
cultural heterogeneity 110-14
and occupation 53, 77-8, 79, 228,
230

heterosexual-couple households
without children 189
higher education
financial support 124
and geographical mobility 170-1
household as distinct from 'family' 20
household composition
changing patterns 54-8, 187, 188-
92, 229-30
and demographic change 27
ethnographic research areas 44, 45,
46, 47, 48, 82
in future 231-2
and lifecourse stages 187
types of household 188-9
and individualisation thesis 15-16,
224
see also extended-family households;
intergenerational households;
single-person households
household size xii, 188, 201-2
housing 35-7, 44, 45, 46
and household composition 210-
11*n*
setting up home and support 123-4
sharing parents' home 55, 56*tab*,
71-2, 104-6, 143-4, 146, 203
see also residence patterns
human capital and investment 222-3

I

identity
construction and *habitus* 6-7
see also cultural identity
ill-health and caring 154-6
immediate family *see* 'close' family
'in-betweeners' category 236-8
independence
and caring for parents 152-3, 172-3
and closeness to family 192
and geographical mobility 171, 172,
173-5
of women 216
individualisation thesis 1, 2, 3-9, 53
and class 15, 226
and gender 3-4, 7-8, 22, 215-16
and moral values 12, 13, 21
and New Labour policies 216, 224
research on 14-16, 18
and support 128, 131-2, 136
individualism
anomic individualism 12, 13, 229
and de-institutionalisation of family
228-30, 232-3

Working Together for Children series

Published in association with The Open University

Connecting with children
Developing working relationships
Edited by **Pam Foley** and **Stephen Leverett**

"Working with children and their families is a serious and often complex undertaking for professionals. This book encourages students and practitioners to reflect, within both practical and theoretical perspectives, on the key issues of developing effective communication and participation with children in processes that may significantly affect their lives."
Maurice Crozier, educational psychologist

This accessible textbook illustrates how good communication and positive and participative relationships can be developed with children across the range of universal and specialist children's services.

PB £19.99 **ISBN** 978 1 84742 058 9 312 pages February 2008

To order copies of this publication or any other Policy Press titles please visit **www.policypress.org.uk**

Connecting with children
developing working relationships
Edited by Pam Foley and Stephen Leverett

About the series
This innovative series brings together an interdisciplinary team of authors to provide an accessible collection of ideas, debates, discussion, and reflections on childhood, practice and services for children.

The books have been designed and written as illustrative teaching texts, giving voice to children's and practitioner's own accounts as well as providing research, policy analysis and examples of good practice.

Working Together for Children series

Published in association with The Open University

The Open University

Promoting children's wellbeing
Policy and practice
Edited by **Janet Collins** and **Pam Foley**

"We owe it to ourselves and our children to take this book, study it, debate, argue with it, but above all learn from it. This book allows us to consider the whole child and challenges us to communicate in a meaningful way so that the wellbeing of the child is secured. If you think that caring for a child is 'child's play', you may be nearer than you think to understanding and respecting the child's world." **Glo Potter, foster carer**

This attractive and accessible textbook analyses and examines the policies, services and practice skills needed for collaborative, effective and equitable work with children.

PB £19.99 **ISBN** 978 1 84742 059 6 268 pages April 2008

To order copies of this publication or any other Policy Press titles please visit
www.policypress.org.uk

Promoting children's wellbeing
policy and practice

Edited by Janet Collins and Pam Foley

About the series
This innovative series brings together an interdisciplinary team of authors to provide an accessible collection of ideas, debates, discussion, and reflections on childhood, practice and services for children.

The books have been designed and written as illustrative teaching texts, giving voice to children's and practitioner's own accounts as well as providing research, policy analysis and examples of good practice.

Working Together for Children series

Published in association with The Open University The Open University

Changing children's services
Working and learning together
Edited by **Pam Foley** and **Andy Rixon**

"Multi-agency working is one of the biggest challenges facing Children's Services today. This book not only explain the issues effectively, drawing upon a variety of theoretical, professional and research perspectives, but also gives clear pointers as to how practice in working together can be improved."
Professor Denny Hevey, The University of Northampton

This attractive textbook critically examines the potential for closer 'working together', its effectiveness and its impact on children, parents and children's services as a whole.

PB £19.99 **ISBN** 978 1 84742 060 2 298 pages July 2008

To order copies of this publication or any other Policy Press titles please visit
www.policypress.org.uk

Changing children's services
working and learning together
Edited by Pam Foley and Andy Rixon

About the series
This innovative series brings together an interdisciplinary team of authors to provide an accessible collection of ideas, debates, discussion, and reflections on childhood, practice and services for children.

The books have been designed and written as illustrative teaching texts, giving voice to children's and practitioner's own accounts as well as providing research, policy analysis and examples of good practice.

Making sense of 'Every Child Matters'

Multi-professional practice guidance

Edited by **Richard Barker**

"This book provides child practitioners in public, private and voluntary settings with a valuable text to guide their practice. It is an essential text for students studying for child and young people's care qualifications and undergraduate studies, while post-graduate students will find it an excellent reference resource." *Brenda Roberts, Academic Lead Children and Young People, Edgehill University*

This much-needed book examines the implications of the 'Every Child Matters' (ECM) agenda for working with children. It analyses the key issues from the perspective of the different professions that make up the 'new children's workforce' and explores inter-professional considerations.

Features:
- describes and analyses the Every Child Matters programme in relation to the wider social context for children, with a consideration of inter-professional issues;
- chapters give an overview of the recent history, current position, and main trends of the specific professions;
- includes practice issues and case examples from health, education, social work, playwork, children's centres and early years;
- updated to take into account recent changes including the creation of the new Department of Children, Schools and Families;
- considers the opportunities and challenges presented by the current agenda, including the possible implications for future multi-disciplinary working.

Offering a clear guide to the implications of 'Every Child Matters' upon practice, this book will be widely welcomed by tutors and practitioners alike, enabling readers to make sense of the legislation and national guidance, and to better understand the new agendas for children's services.

PB £19.99 ● ISBN 978 1 84742 011 4 ● 224 pages tbc ● July 2008

To order copies of this publication or any other Policy Press titles please visit **www.policypress.org.uk**